THE WAY OF CH'AN

THE
WAY *of* CH'AN

*Essential Texts of the
Original Tradition*

EDITED AND TRANSLATED BY

DAVID HINTON

SHAMBHALA

SHAMBHALA PUBLICATIONS, INC.
2129 13th Street
Boulder, Colorado 80302
www.shambhala.com

Cover art: Cloudy Mountains, Fang Congyi (Chinese, ca. 1301–after 1378),
Ex coll.: C. C. Wang Family, Purchase, Gift of J. Pierpont Morgan,
by exchange, 1973
Cover design: Daniel Urban-Brown and Kate Huber-Parker
Interior design: Steve Dyer

9 8 7 6 5 4 3 2 1

FIRST EDITION
Printed in the United States of America

Shambhala Publications makes every effort
to print on acid-free, recycled paper.
Shambhala Publications is distributed worldwide by
Penguin Random House, Inc., and its subsidiaries.

Library of Congress Cataloging-in-Publication Data
Names: Hinton, David, 1954- translator.
Title: The way of Ch'an: essential texts of the original tradition /
edited and translated by David Hinton.
Description: First edition. | Boulder, Colorado: Shambhala Publications,
Inc., [2023] | Includes bibliographical references.
Identifiers: LCCN 2022041939 | ISBN 9781611809237 (trade paperback;
acid-free paper)
Subjects: LCSH: Zen Buddhism—China. | Zen Buddhism—
China—History. | China—Civilization—Zen influences.
Classification: LCC BQ9262.9.C5 W39 2023 |
DDC 294.3/9270951—dc23/eng/20221027
LC record available at https://lccn.loc.gov/2022041939

CONTENTS

V Realized Ch'an: T'ang Dynasty Masters (7th–10th centuries C.E.)

THE WAY OF CH'AN

INTRODUCTION

THE CHINESE IDEOGRAM FOR *BUDDHA* IS 佛, WHICH contains two pictographic elements. The element on the left (亻) means "a person," and is a stylized form of 人, side-view of a person walking. The element on the right portrays a loom, with its warp-threads and weft-threads weaving together: 弗. This loom was a central concept in early Chinese philosophy, where it was a mythological description for an origin-place that weaves out the fabric of reality, a "loom-of-origins." Chuang Tzu, the seminal Taoist writer (p. 38), describes it like this: "The ten thousand things all emerge from a loom-of-origins, and they all vanish back into it." Here is Ch'an in a nutshell: Buddha, the awakened one, as a person integral to the loom-of-origins, integral to the source of all existence and its ongoing process of change and transformation. And Ch'an practice is all about cultivating that integration, that dwelling or belonging, which is itself the awakening of Buddha.

This anthology traces the historical development of Ch'an, its cultivation of awakening as 亻 integral to 弗. The entire Ch'an project revolves around the cosmological/ontological source. As we will see, this source is not some kind of metaphysical pool of pregnant emptiness from which things emerge. Understood with empirical clarity, it is instead simply the Cosmos itself recognized as a single generative tissue that is female in nature and is constantly reconfiguring itself: the ten thousand things in perpetual transformation. Ch'an's central project is the reintegration of

I

consciousness with that source-tissue, a reintegration that represents a return to our deepest roots in the Paleolithic with its reverence for the generative female nature of reality. This reintegration is also our deepest form of love, a kindred love at primordial levels for the loom's ten thousand things in their vast transformations. But however ancient, Ch'an's insight remains open to us in our everyday contemporary experience: Ch'an as both primal and postmodern.

This collection presents the essential source material for original Ch'an. Although Ch'an insight and awakening is famously Bodhidharma's "a separate transmission outside all teaching," the nature of that wordless insight and awakening is determined by the conceptual world within which it operates. This may seem contradictory. But even empty-mind (consciousness emptied of all contents), which would appear to be by definition most radically outside of words and teaching, is defined by its conceptual context. Christian mystics cultivated that same state of consciousness, but they understood it entirely differently based on religious ideology. They imagined that state was a direct experience of God's overwhelming grace or love, or that it was even nothing less than union with God. In today's secular context, it's experienced as a kind of nirvana-tranquility (Zen and other Buddhist practices) or perhaps nothing more than simple stress-reduction. Even though the state of consciousness itself is the same, Ch'an explores deeper through clear observation of empirical facts. And the conceptual framework resulting from that exploration defined the assumptions through which people understood Ch'an experience in ancient China. Importantly, it turns out to be much different than is commonly understood in modern Zen, and we need to understand it as preparation for Ch'an's direct and wordless insight.

That framework is summarized in the Key Terms appendix at the end of this book (p. 321), which can be read straight through as an introductory essay. And a companion book describes it in extensive detail: *China Root: Taoism, Ch'an, and Original Zen*. In this, *China Root* serves as the full conceptual introduction to this collection, which in turn presents representative selections from the original texts that illustrate *China Root*'s argument—that is, the texts in which Ch'an's conceptual world was articulated. As such, this collection traces the historical development of Ch'an's foundational concepts from their origins in China's native Taoist philosophy (12th–6th centuries B.C.E.) through the reformulation of Taoism under the influence of imported Indian Buddhism to form Ch'an (2nd–5th centuries C.E.), and then follows the development of that framework within Ch'an itself (6th–13th centuries). If the texts articulating these concepts sometimes seem difficult, it's good to remember that the authors/teachers were struggling to speak at the limit of their understanding, and they inevitably often fall short. We should never assume that their explanations are perfect; that if we don't understand, it is our fault.

This is a revisionary history of Ch'an in a number of ways, a project of recovery. It traces the development of Ch'an's deepest philosophical levels, the conceptual assumptions that make awakening possible and are largely lost in modern Zen practice and literature (as *China Root* demonstrates). This history reveals Ch'an to be essentially a refinement and extension of Taoism—again, as *China Root* demonstrates. (Tao, the central concept of Taoism, translates as "Way," hence the title of this book: *The Way of Ch'an*.) When Dhyana Buddhism arrived from India (first century C.E.), it acted as a catalyst that transformed Taoism into Ch'an. It wasn't that Ch'an adopted new truths and insights that it found in Dhyana Buddhism, but that it recognized new and exotic manifestations of Taoist insight in some key Buddhist sutras—largely by misunderstanding and mistranslating them through the Taoist lens. But perhaps the most important influence was a clearly defined form of meditation practice.

In the alchemy that created Ch'an, the catalyst largely disappeared. In fact, Ch'an is radically anti-Buddhist at its core—a realization first proposed in English by the great literary figure and Ch'an scholar Hu Shih (1891–1962).[1] Although traditional Buddhist elements certainly frequented Ch'an teaching and texts, they functioned primarily to further merely institutional Ch'an, or as a means of engaging students who had been schooled in that tradition. And at a philosophical level, once essential Buddhist concepts were translated into Chinese, they lost their original meanings in Indian Buddhism and became Taoist concepts—so translating them now in their original Buddhist sense is inaccurate.

Conventional Indian Buddhism functioned largely as a religion, but Ch'an had no patience for that: it is instead a tradition of philosophers working out a lived philosophy based on the empirical and directly observable facts that define consciousness and Cosmos. The core levels of their philosophic system, the levels that define and enable awakening, operated outside of institutional structures—teaching and authority, tradition and certainty—even if the people involved lived in some kind of Ch'an institution. Insight and enlightenment positively require a detached relation to teaching and authority and the self-assurance that accompanies powerful institutional structures. Emblematic of this in Ch'an's legendary history is the famous split between northern and southern Ch'an in the seventh century: the Sixth Patriarch was a peasant who fled south and taught in small ramshackle monasteries, whereas Spirit-Lightning Flourish (Shen Hsiu) was an aristocrat who went north and taught at wealthy state-sanctioned and urbane monasteries in capital cities. It was the Sixth Patriarch's tradition that became Ch'an, and many teachers in that lineage, including major figures like Purport Dark-Engima (Lin Chi; p. 208) and Visitation-Land (Chao Chou; p. 220), taught at small out-of-the-way centers. That "core Ch'an" involved dismantling all conceptual structures, and Buddhism was its primary target. This spirit allowed a particular interest in Dhyana Buddhism, which focused less on religious doctrine than on meditation, with its almost scientific observation of the contents of consciousness. In fact, *dhyana* means "meditation," and "Ch'an" was originally a transliteration of the Sanskrit *dhyana*.

. . .

As it turns out, accurate translation is central to rediscovering Ch'an's original nature, its defining constellation of ideas and practices. The selections in this book emphasize the most influential texts in the tradition's development, but also the most known and influential in modern American Zen. This latter allows comparison with earlier translations, which reveals how thoroughly mistranslation has misrepresented Ch'an and its conceptual world. Here, this book functions as an extension of *China Root*'s appendix, "Lost in Translation."

There are several reasons for this wholesale mistranslation and the resulting misunderstandings. First, translators have understood the essence of Ch'an/Zen to be a kind of impenetrable perplexity. This has justified endless poor translation, for translators have not insisted on understanding and translating passages with clarity. But Ch'an texts, sentence by sentence, generally make clear sense. Even if conceptually they are often enigmatic and philosophically complex, they are linguistically clear in their statements.

Second, translators were simply unaware of specific philosophical terms and concepts, and in general they didn't understand the whole native Chinese philosophical/cultural context—so they systematically failed to translate the foundational cosmological/ontological framework (most notably, the concepts defined in the Key Terms appendix on pp. 321–35. Instead, they either left those terms untranslated or they translated them into Western terms of metaphysical abstraction that impose Western structures of understanding and have no real meaning, such as "Truth," "Principle," "Absolute," "Ultimate/True Reality."

Finally, translators have assumed Ch'an to be a form of Buddhism and interpreted everything through the lens of conventional Buddhist religious thought, which was quite abstract and metaphysical in nature—both qualities antithetical to Ch'an. One important example is how Buddhist texts from India—and several were important to Ch'an—are read in the Ch'an context as if they are still the original texts. But when they were translated into Chinese, the fundamental philosophical concepts were (mis-)translated into Taoist concepts. That is, translators and scholars (mis-)understood the Sanskrit texts as exotic formulations of their native Taoist understanding. This isn't surprising; it was China's first encounter with a large intellectual system outside of its own, and scholars assumed their philosophical system was the only way to understand existence. So, for China's artist-intellectuals (including the Ch'an community), these texts were functionally native Chinese texts operating in the Taoist framework. And if we are trying to understand Ch'an, that is how we must understand them—and translate them.

As *China Root* shows, Ch'an is a refinement of native Taoist thought and practice: empirical philosophy, not religion. Taoism's conceptual framework is the philosophical heartbeat of the Ch'an tradition, but also of all Chinese culture—for artist-intellectuals were shaped by it from its Taoist beginnings through to mature Ch'an and beyond, even up to today. Ch'an is often seen as a quasi-religious institution separate from the general (secular) culture, but that misrepresents Ch'an's true nature. We sometimes find the superficial trappings of the conventional

Buddhism that came from India—but anytime Ch'an touches ground philosophically or experientially, it is in terms of Taoist concepts. This Ch'an is integral to the full expanse of Chinese culture: virtually all artist-intellectuals practiced Ch'an in some sense, and the culture they created can only be understood in that context. To say it again: Ch'an is, in fact, resolutely anti-Buddhist. Even the understanding of Buddha as 佛 (person + loom) is radically different from the conventional Indian understanding of Buddha as a quasi-deified master of nirvana-tranquility. Indeed, as we will see, Buddha is finally absorbed into the Taoist framework and becomes synonymous with Tao itself, that generative tissue of existence.

All of this becomes a much larger problem because classical Chinese grammar leaves a great deal unstated and open to interpretation. If you don't approach it with native philosophical assumptions, you will necessarily make broad interpretive errors. Compounding this, earlier Zen translators generally had very little sense of translation as a literary art, or of the original texts as literary masterpieces. Instead, they approached Ch'an texts as simple religious doctrine to be translated in flat utilitarian prose, often even employing loose paraphrase that replaces the original with a translator's flawed understanding. It is worth noting here that China's philosophical masterworks from the beginning were always very literary in nature: full of storytelling, interesting characters, satire, humor, poetry, etc. And Ch'an texts carried on this tradition.

The very origin of Ch'an's legendary history, Mahakasyapa's smile (p. 292), is a perfect example. Ch'an's legendary history traces its direct lineage of wordless transmission back to Mahakasyapa simply smiling when Buddha holds up a flower. This smile is generally described as "faint" or "subtle," implying a kind of knowing tranquility. But the Chinese word is 微 (*wei*), which invests the common meaning of "faint, subtle, sparse" with a philosophical meaning: to be just emerging into existence from the generative source. Hence, it isn't simply that the smile revealed a tranquility of silent knowing (the assumption that follows from conventional Buddhist teaching); it's that Mahakasyapa's smile emerges spontaneously from the generative source. It is action at origins: Mahakasyapa in his Buddha-nature as a person (亻) integral to that loom-of-origins (弗): 佛.

Ch'an isn't so very difficult: you just need to understand a constellation of concepts and spend enough practice time (meditation) to see how those concepts work. But it can seem impossibly difficult for us because the conceptual framework that defines Ch'an practice has been misconstrued in English, making Ch'an as a whole into a seemingly inaccessible system of paradox and abstraction. That changes once the concepts are understood clearly. Then, rather than the seemingly impenetrable and abstract "Zen perplexity" that we generally encounter and that was essential to the popularization of Zen when it was introduced into America during the fifties and sixties, we find empirically based depths and earthy mystery that are accessible and readily practiced in daily life.

. . .

This book traces a lineage of teachers and ideas—an unavoidably simplistic line, only a few highlights, and yet plenty enough for a full understanding of Ch'an's wordless teaching. Rather than a plethora of teachers in small selections that all sound alike, this anthology contains relatively few teachers in selections large enough to give a sense of individuality and singular vision, as self-reliant individuality is crucial to Ch'an. The masculine nature of this lineage is historically devastating, of course, excluding women as it did. Ancient Chinese society was virulently misogynistic, women largely excluded from intellectual and cultural life. When women did produce cultural work, it was (with the rarest of exceptions) not preserved. But philosophically, Taoist/Ch'an practice is centered around the female principle at a cosmological level: the Cosmos as a single generative source-tissue. And importantly for both women and men in our independent-minded contemporary culture—it is finally a lineage without lineage, a lineage of teachers and ideas that insists on no teachers or ideas. For Ch'an insists on the obvious: cultivating empty-mind and seeing one's original-nature can only be an immediate and personal experience. It has nothing to do with teachers or teachings, as in the famous Ch'an/Zen claim that it is "a separate transmission outside all teaching" (see below).

Hence, another of Ch'an's central insistences: you are yourself always already Buddha, the awakened one—another radical departure from the conventional Indian understanding of Buddha. And so, there is no subservience to a hierarchy of (male) teachers: you are yourself your only real teacher. This self-reliance is there at the beginning, in Bodhidharma (p. 123), Ch'an's first patriarch, who is credited with a poem that is the definitive distillation of Ch'an's essential nature:

> A separate transmission outside all teaching
> and nowhere founded in eloquent scriptures,
>
> it's simple: pointing directly at mind. There,
> seeing original-nature, you become Buddha.

But again, all of this is only true within the body of assumptions that defines Ch'an's conceptual framework: what remains when you dispense with the teachings and eloquent scriptures.

We are each, in our own original-nature, Buddha (a concept stripped in Ch'an of all religious significance). Hence, we are each always already awakened. The discipline of Ch'an practice is designed to make us see that—indeed, simply "seeing original-nature" (見性: *chien-hsing*; Japanese: *kensho*) is itself the term meaning "enlightenment" in Ch'an terminology. In meditation's attention to thoughts emerging from an empty source, in its dwelling as integral to that empty-mind source, we see that tranquil emptiness (center of conventional Indian Buddhist practice) is actually full of dynamic and generative energy. That is, we "see" our "original-nature" is nothing other than that loom-of-origins.

Fundamental to that "seeing" is getting free of the limited spirit-center self, that illusory structure that radically separates us from the Cosmos and its ten thousand things. As thoughts are the medium of our self-identity, watching them unfurl in meditation reveals that we are quite separate from the limited identity-center self. That alone is the liberation of Buddha. And indeed, the common meaning of 弗 (loom) is "not," which produces an alternative and complementary meaning for 佛 (Buddha): person + not. This kind of philosophical wordplay is important in the Ch'an literature, and here it distills the Ch'an understanding that only without self can we dwell as integral to the loom-of-origins and its weave of existence, that only without our limited identity-center self can we inhabit our largest self as that loom (弗) itself. And in this primordial love and kinship, we are each ourselves nothing less than Buddha: 佛.

READER'S NOTE

THE KEY TERMS APPENDIX (P. 321) MENTIONED ABOVE explains the key concepts in the Taoist/Ch'an conceptual framework. These concepts are absolutely essential to understanding the texts that follow, but because they occur with such frequency, they are not foot-noted. Again, this glossary of key concepts can be read straight through as an essay outlining Ch'an's conceptual world. The terms are:

Absence
Absence-action
Actualization
Awakening/Enlightenment
Ch'i
Ch'i-weave mind
Dark-enigma
Dragon
Emptiness
Empty-mind
Existence-tissue
Eye/Sight
Heaven
Idleness
Inner-pattern

Loom-of-origins
Mind
Mirror
No-mind
Occurrence-appearing-of-itself
Origin-dark quiet
Origin-tissue
Potency
Presence
Shadowed-emergence
Source-ancestral
Unborn (Absence-born)
Wandering boundless and free
Way (Tao)

The Glossary of Buddhist Terms (p. 337) explains a number of recurring Buddhist terms, their meanings, and how those meanings were redefined as Taoist concepts when the Sanskrit terms entered the Chinese language and philosophical context. These frequently occurring terms are also not footnoted in the texts that follow. The terms are:

Bodhi
Buddha
Buddha Existence-Tissue Arrival
Dharma
Kalpa
Karma
Prajna
Samadhi
Samsara
Sunyata

There is a troubling and widespread trend among American scholars to dismiss Ch'an and most Ch'an figures in this book as mere literary fabrications, the records of their lives and teachings created long after their deaths to further institutional interests. But even if they came later, those records were no doubt based on reliable material now vanished: oral histories, student notes, hand-copied texts. These methods of transmission were typical for ancient Chinese sage-teachers and poets. And yes, those records are clearly crafted as literature that intends to create a direct literary/spiritual experience, and this no doubt entailed rewriting and embellishment and exaggeration. In any case, however, the existing textual tradition is, as a matter of strict fact, quite simply what Ch'an is. Ch'an teachers are therefore, by definition, who they are in these texts. It is their teachings that open the whole world of understanding and insight and practice that defines Ch'an. And so, this book generally takes the tradition at face value and assumes major figures are who they are in the existing textual tradition.

PART I

Taoist Origins

(ca. Paleolithic–4th century B.C.E.)

THE ADVENTURE OF CH'AN BEGINS AMONG GYNOCENTRIC hunter-gatherer cultures of the Paleolithic, where the empirical Cosmos was recognized as female in its fundamental nature, as a magisterial and perpetually generative organism in constant transformation. Paleolithic people assumed that the human was wholly integral to that process, which was itself the "sacred." There was no isolate identity-center, no sense of an individual self that was fundamentally different than or separate from earth and its ten thousand things. Spiritual practices celebrated that generative Cosmos as a Great Mother who continuously gives birth to all creation, and who also takes life and regenerates it in an unending process of life, death, and rebirth. And those practices also functioned to renew or revitalize our belonging to that wondrous Cosmos.

As the Neolithic replaced the Paleolithic, people settled in agricultural villages, which created a human realm separate from "nature." With the advent of writing came the illusion of a changeless subjective realm separate from the objective. This resulted in a rupture of that Paleolithic wholeness: it was a deracination of human consciousness, which became a kind of spirit-center radically other than "nature." This is the spirit-center so familiar to us in the Judeo-Christian West, where self is assumed to be a transcendental "soul" that is made of an entirely different substance from the earth we actually inhabit: spirit rather than matter. Taoism and Ch'an Buddhism defined spiritual practice throughout the Chinese cultural tradition, and it was essentially the same as in the Paleolithic: to cultivate consciousness integral to the vast and wondrous tissue of reality; to cultivate a sense of wholeness and belonging, a sense of home and kinship. This was simultaneously a practice of self-realization—for as we will see, in that reintegration we find the full dimensions of what we really are. It is no surprise, then, that the two seminal books of Chinese spiritual philosophy, the *I Ching* and the *Tao Te Ching*, seem to be largely constructed from fragments handed down from the Paleolithic in an oral wisdom-tradition. It is a joy to imagine that the earliest of China's sages, those responsible for the core regions of Taoist/Ch'an thought, were in fact women from the culture's proto-Chinese Paleolithic roots.

易經

I Ching (ca. 12th century B.C.E.)

I CHING MEANS "THE CLASSIC OF CHANGE." THE BOOK is normally dated to circa 1200 B.C.E., but its focus on the concept of change links it immediately to that Paleolithic description of reality as a generative tissue in constant transformation. And as we have seen, its core philosophical utterances appear to reflect an oral wisdom-tradition originating in the Paleolithic. In ancient Chinese cosmology, the two fundamental principles that generate the process of change were *yin* (female, dark, cold, earth) and *yang* (male, light, heat, sky). These two principles are represented in the lines of the *I Ching*'s hexagrams: solid lines being *yang*, and broken lines *yin*. Each chapter of the *I Ching* is built around a hexagram containing six lines. The book contains sixty-four hexagrams, every possible combination of *yin* and *yang*, and therefore every possible configuration in the process of change.

The architecture of the *I Ching* is remarkably complex considering its antiquity: hexagrams and layer after layer of commentaries. In this, it established the precedent for commentary as a major philosophical form that we will see playing an important role in the Ch'an tradition. The entire text is a commentary on the hexagrams, and commentaries on those commentaries. According to legend, these various layers of the *I Ching* were written by the first emperor, a man who was half human and half dragon, by other legendary rulers, and even by Confucius himself. But again, its philosophical sources seem clearly in the Paleolithic.

The *I Ching* was traditionally read in two interrelated ways: as a divination text and as a philosophical text. These two dimensions of the text both function like those spiritual practices in the Paleolithic: to reintegrate the human into the Cosmos. The intent of the *I Ching* is to return us to the source, to identify the inner-pattern governing the unfolding of things, and to use it to integrate oneself into the unfolding of Presence (the ten thousand things) from the generative source, Absence. As we will see, this remained the bedrock purpose of Taoist/Ch'an understanding and practice. And the *I Ching*'s philosophical approach to that reintegration is, in embryonic form, no different than the Ch'an tradition that eventually evolved from these roots. Hence, the *I Ching* is nothing less than Ch'an's primeval source.

As a divination text, the *I Ching* doesn't simply give answers to questions about the future. Instead, the hexagrams locate us in the process of change through their different combinations of *yin* and *yang*. Once it locates us in the process of change, it explains the forces at play, which allows us to contemplate which course of action might be best suited to those forces and will therefore result in the best outcome. Hence, we find a prefiguration of Ch'an's insistence not on answers from some authority, but self-cultivation. Further, *I Ching* divination practice operates on the primal assumption that we are an integral part of the Cosmos, of the ceaseless unfolding of change. And using it is a practice of reintegrating ourselves into the ontological tissue, the intent of Ch'an practice to come.

The *I Ching*'s second dimension, the philosophical, is the content of the book—its poetic and mysterious description of reality. As such, it presents in embryonic form the conceptual world that came to shape Taoist and eventually Ch'an thought and practice. In addition, here begins the understanding that reintegrating with the generative Cosmos entails exploring beyond our workaday experience of consciousness. This involves cultivating silence, as the *I Ching* says directly:

> When there's talk, there's no sincerity, no accuracy. *Revere words, and you soon wither impoverished away.*

And it involves in primeval form a number of other strategies that came to define Taoist and then Ch'an strategies for seeing through the conventional structures of thought and identity: paradoxical utterances, mysterious ideas, fragmentary forms that frustrate normal linear understanding. All of these strategies were designed to tease the mind outside our workaday assumptions and the limitations of identity. For there begins the possibility of knowing oneself as integral to the existence-tissue Cosmos.

I

Heaven

All origins penetrating everywhere, heaven[1] is inexhaustible
in bringing forth wild bounty.

PRESENTATION

How vast and wondrous the heaven of origins!
The ten thousand things all begin from it. It governs the sky—the
movement of clouds, the coming of rain. It gives all the various
things their distinct forms. How vast its illumination
of endings and beginnings!

When the potent places of these six lines are realized
in their proper seasons, the seasons mount the six sun-dragons
and soar through the sky.

The Way of heaven is all change and transformation at
the hinge of things, where the unfurling nature of each thing
itself is perfected. It nurtures vast harmony in wholeness,
and remains inexhaustible in bringing forth wild bounty.
When its dragon-head rears up among the innumerable things,
it unites the ten thousand kingdoms in wholeness and peace.

Earth

All origins penetrating everywhere, earth is inexhaustible
as a mare horse in bringing forth wild bounty. And so it is that
when the noble-minded set out in the lead toward a destination,
they soon fall into confusion; but when they follow, they find
the bounty of that wondrous host. Finding friends on southwest
plains, losing friends in northeast mountains—the noble-minded
remain inexhaustible and serene, and so come to good fortune.

PRESENTATION

How perfect and wondrous the earth of origins! The ten
thousand things are all born from it. Yielding and devoted as a
river, it supports the sky. It carries things along in its generosity,
joins them boundlessly in its heart-sight clarity, opens them away
all vast radiance in its embrace. And it unites all the various
things in wholeness penetrating everywhere.

A mare horse is like the land, for it roams the land boundlessly.

All tender assent, yielding and devoted as a river, earth is
inexhaustible in bringing forth wild bounty. *And so it is that when
the noble-minded set out in the lead toward a destination, they soon
fall into confusion* and lose the Way. But when they follow yielding
and devoted as a river, they master constancy. *Finding friends on
southwest plains*, they move with kindred spirits. *Losing friends in
northeast mountains*, they know blessings whole and through to
completion. Inexhaustible and serene in their good fortune,
they live boundless as the land.

Return

All return penetrating everywhere, things emerge and die back without any anxious longing. Friends come without going astray. They turn back, returning to travel their own Way, and after seven days come, returning again. Setting out toward a destination brings forth wild bounty indeed.

PRESENTATION

All return penetrating everywhere, everything steely as a mountain in cloud turns back, moves with the dragon's inciting force, yielding and devoted as a river. This is to *emerge and die back without any anxious longing.*

Friends come without going astray. They turn back, returning to travel their own Way, and after seven days come, returning again. This is the movement of heaven.

Setting out toward a destination brings forth wild bounty indeed. In this, everything steely as a mountain in cloud persists.

In return itself, you can see the very heart-mind of all heaven-and-earth.

Exhaustion

In exhaustion penetrating everywhere, a great sage is inexhaustible, bringing forth good fortune and never going astray. When there's talk, there's no sincerity, no accuracy.

PRESENTATION

In exhaustion, the noble-minded are hemmed in and steely as a mountain in cloud. They master opening and delight amid danger. In exhaustion, they never lose those depths that penetrate everywhere. Isn't that what makes them noble-minded?

A great sage is inexhaustible, bringing forth good fortune, for he is centered as a steely mountain in cloud.

When there's talk, there's no sincerity, no accuracy. Revere words, and you soon wither impoverished away.

☰ (hexagram)

Stillness

Stillness in your back. Expect nothing from your life.
Wander the courtyard where you see no one. How could
you go ever astray?

PRESENTATION

Stillness is the same as abiding.

In the season for abiding, abide. In the season for moving, move.

If you take action in the proper season and cultivate quiet
in the proper season, your Way is radiant with the illumination
of sun and moon and the dragon's inciting force.

Stillness in abiding means abiding in whatever you are.

Lofty and lowly stand in opposition; they share nothing. This is
why you never go astray when you *expect nothing from your life*,
when you *wander the courtyard where you see no one*.

老子

Lao Tzu (ca. 6th century B.C.E.)

LAO TZU IS A LEGENDARY SAGE (HIS NAME SIMPLY MEANS "Old Master") who reputedly wrote the seminal *Tao Te Ching* (道德經). The book is in fact an assemblage of fragments deriving from an oral wisdom-tradition apparently stretching back to the Paleolithic, though there probably was a sage philosopher (maybe several over decades) who worked with that ancient material to conjure a philosophical vision that feels utterly contemporary in its poetry of evocative fragmentation. Here, the generative fabric of reality that was the Paleolithic "sacred" appears in recurring references to it as female: "mother," "mother of all beneath heaven," "nurturing mother," "valley spirit," "dark female-enigma." But its dark mystery is everywhere in the *Tao Te Ching*, for it is nothing other than Tao itself, the book's central concept. It appears in the title, which literally means "The Classic of Tao and Integrity (to Tao)," and is also the namesake of Taoism, the philosophical system for which the *Tao Te Ching* is the seminal text. The concept appears a number of times in the *I Ching*, but in the *Tao Te Ching* it takes center stage and is extensively described in poetic and evocative ways.

Tao originally meant "way," as in "pathway" or "roadway," a meaning it has kept. But Lao Tzu reconceived it as a generative cosmological process, an ontological "path*Way*" by which things come into existence, evolve through their lives, and then go out of existence, only to be transformed and reemerge in a new form. This Way endures as a central concept throughout the Ch'an tradition, the term itself a veritable fixture in all Ch'an texts. It is integral to the entire conceptual framework that defines Ch'an understanding and practice. And indeed, this framework, including nearly all its key terms and concepts (see Key Terms, p. 321), is first articulated here in the *Tao Te Ching*.

Lao Tzu established the reintegration of consciousness with Way's generative cosmological/ontological process as the goal of spiritual self-cultivation—an assumption that continues in Ch'an, defining the terms of understanding and practice. We find already here the quintessential Ch'an idea that Way is beyond words and understanding, that dwelling as integral to Way requires the cultivation of a mind empty of language and idea, empty finally even of self—a meditative practice that is poetically described in a number of ways that presage Ch'an practice to come, such as the concise "sitting still in Way's company." This is reflected in the book's structure, the dark mystery of its utterances deepened by its fragmentary form. And so, already here we find the native Chinese source of Ch'an's foundational ideas: the entire cosmological/ontological framework, emptiness, empty-mind, mirror-mind, meditation, non-dwelling, and deep understanding being only possible outside of words and concepts.

Tao Te Ching

I

A Way you can call Way isn't the perennial Way.
A name you can use to name isn't the perennial name:

the named is mother to the ten thousand things,
but the unnamed is origin to all heaven-and-earth.

In perennial Absence you see mystery,
and in perennial Presence you see appearance.
Though the two are one and the same,
once they arise, they differ in name.

One and the same they're called *dark-enigma*,
dark-enigma deep within dark-enigma,

gateway of all mystery.

2

All beneath heaven knows beauty is beauty
only because there's ugliness,
and knows good is good
only because there's evil.

Presence and Absence give birth to one another,
difficult and easy complete one another,
long and short measure one another,
high and low fill one another,
music and noise harmonize one another,
before and after follow one another:

that's why a sage abides in the realm of Absence-action,
living out that wordless teaching.
The ten thousand things arise without beginnings there,
abide without waiting there,
come to perfection without dwelling there.

Without dwelling there: that's the one way
you'll never lose it.

6

The valley spirit never dies.

It's called *dark female-enigma*,
and the gateway of dark female-enigma
is called *the root of heaven-and-earth*,

gossamer so unceasing it seems real.
Use it: it's effortless.

7

Heaven goes on forever.
Earth endures forever.

There's a reason heaven-and-earth goes on enduring forever:
their life isn't their own
so their life goes on forever.

Hence, in putting himself last
the sage puts himself first,
and in giving himself up
he preserves himself.

If you aren't free of yourself
how will you ever become yourself?

Can you let your spirit embrace primal-unity
without drifting away?

Can you focus *ch'i* into such softness
you're a newborn again?

Can you polish the dark-enigma mirror
to a clarity beyond stain?

Can you make loving the people and ruling the nation
Absence itself acting?

Can you be female
opening and closing heaven's gate?

Can you fathom earth's four distances with radiant wisdom
and know nothing?

Give birth and nurture.
Give birth without possessing
and foster without dominating:

this is called *dark-enigma Integrity.*

15

Ancient masters of Way
all subtle mystery and dark-enigma vision:
they were deep beyond knowing,

so deep beyond knowing
we can only describe their appearance:

perfectly cautious, as if crossing winter streams,
and perfectly watchful, as if neighbors threatened;
perfectly reserved, as if guests,
perfectly expansive, as if ice melting away,
and perfectly simple, as if uncarved wood;
perfectly empty, as if open valleys,
and perfectly shadowy, as if murky water.

Who's murky enough to settle slowly into pure clarity,
and who still enough to awaken slowly into life?

If you nurture this Way, you never crave fullness.
Never crave fullness
and you'll wear away into completion.

There was something all murky shadow,
born before heaven-and-earth:

O such utter silence, utter emptiness.

Isolate and changeless,
it moves everywhere without fail:

picture the mother of all beneath heaven.

I don't know its name.
I'll call it *Way*,
and if I must name it, name it *Vast*.

Vast means it's passing beyond,
passing beyond means it's gone far away,
and gone far away means it's come back.

Because Way is vast
heaven is vast,
earth is vast,
and the true emperor too is vast.
In this realm, there are four vast things,
and the true emperor is one of them.

Human abides by earth.
Earth abides by heaven.
Heaven abides by Way.
Way abides by occurrence-appearing-of-itself.

40

Return is the movement of Way,
and yielding the method of Way.

All beneath heaven, the ten thousand things: it's all born of Presence,
and Presence is born of Absence.

43

The weakest in all beneath heaven gallops through the strongest.

Absence is all idleness infusing Presence:
I know by this the value of Absence-action.

The teaching without words,
the value of Absence-action:
few indeed master such things.

52

There's a source all beneath heaven shares:
call it the mother of all beneath heaven.

Once you fathom the mother
you understand the child,
and once you understand the child
you abide in the mother,

self gone, free of danger.

. . .

56

Those who know don't talk,
and those who talk don't know.

Block the senses
and close the mind,
blunt edges,
loosen tangles,
soften glare,
mingle dust:

this is called *dark-enigma union*.

It can't be embraced
and can't be ignored,
can't be enhanced
and can't be harmed,
can't be treasured
and can't be despised,

for it's the treasure of all beneath heaven.

莊子

Chuang Tzu (ca. 4th century B.C.E.)

CHUANG TZU IS THE SECOND SEMINAL TAOIST SAGE. His insight survives in the eponymously titled *Chuang Tzu*, where he added new dimensions to the conceptual framework that Lao Tzu laid out in his *Tao Te Ching*. While Lao Tzu relied on a mysterious poetry of dark ambiguities and evocative silences, Chuang Tzu described the spiritual ecology of ancient China in a comprehensive way by plundering the full range of literary play: humor, parable, irony, caricature, myth, story, philosophical argument, poetry, fable, allegory, paradox, satire. Here we find the deep source for so much of Ch'an lore: strange and profound stories about zany sage-masters who teach through astonishing actions and enigmatic utterances.

There are a number of descriptions that evoke, *avant la lettre*, Ch'an meditation in remarkably lyrical ways. And Chuang Tzu's concept of "wandering boundless and free" (sections 1.10, 1.16, 6.11) is the seminal description of Ch'an enlightenment. It is emphasized in Kuo Hsiang's commentaries on the *Chuang Tzu* (p. 65) and echoes through the Ch'an tradition (see Key Terms, p. 321) as the very nature of wholesale enlightenment.

Beyond this, Chuang Tzu expands on Lao Tzu's insights, revealing even more clearly that there is virtually no fundamental dimension of Ch'an that can't be found in early Taoist teachings: empty-mind, mirror-mind, meditation, zany sages, illogic, acting with the selfless spontaneity of the Cosmos, the need to see through language and ideas, unborn belonging to the Great Transformation of things, etc. And again prefiguring Ch'an, it is all deployed as literature that creates an immediate experience in the reader, rather than simply imparting information or ideas. And in both Chuang Tzu and Ch'an, the intent of such literary experience is to dismantle our everyday assumptions and open us to the true nature of self and Cosmos.

NOTE

For translation comparison: bracketed numbers refer to chapter and section in the *Chuang Tzu*, for which see my *Chuang Tzu: The Inner Chapters* (also included in *The Four Chinese Classics*).

Chuang Tzu

Lieh Tzu² rode the wind and set out, boundless and clear, returning after only fifteen days. To be so blessed is rare—and yet however free that wind made him, he still depended on something. But if you mount the source of heaven-and-earth and the ten thousand things in their vast transformations, if you ride the six seasons of *ch'i* in their endless dispute—then you travel the inexhaustible, depending on nothing at all. Hence the saying: *The realized remain selfless. The sacred remain merit-less. The enlightened remain nameless.* [1.10]

. . . a village where there's nothing at all, a land where emptiness stretches away forever. Then you could be Absence itself drifting lazily beside it, wander boundless and free . . . [1.16]

If you follow the realized mind you've happened into, making it your teacher, how could you be without a teacher? You don't need to under-stand the realm of change: when mind turns to itself, you've found your teacher. Even a numbskull has mind for a teacher. Not to realize your-self in mind, and to insist on *yes this* and *no that*³—it's like leaving for Cross-Beyond when you've already arrived there. It's like believing that what isn't is. What isn't is—even that great sage-emperor Yü couldn't understand such things, so how could someone like me? [2.8]

Only one who has seen through things understands *moving freely as one and the same.* In this way, rather than relying on your own distinc-tions, you dwell in the ordinary. To be ordinary is to be self-reliant; to be self-reliant is to move freely; and to move freely is to arrive. That's almost it, because to arrive is to be complete. But to be complete without under-standing how—that is called *Way.* [2.12]

Now, I have something to say about these things. I don't know if it's similar to *this*, or if it's dissimilar. But similar and dissimilar are quite similar in the end, so it can't be much different from *that*. But be that as it may, let me try to say it:

Presence all beginning. Presence not yet beginning to be Presence all beginning. Presence not yet beginning to be a not-yet beginning to be Presence all beginning. Presence all Presence. Presence all Absence. Presence not yet beginning to be Presence all Absence. Presence not yet beginning to be Absence not yet beginning to be Presence all Absence. Then suddenly, Presence all Absence. And when it comes to Presence all Absence, I don't know yet what's Presence and what's Absence.

There now: I've spoken. But I still don't know whether it was Presence spoken or Absence spoken. [2.15]

"May I ask about the mind's fast?"

"Center your attention," began Confucius. "Stop listening with your ears and listen with your mind. Then stop listening with your mind and listen with your primal spirit. Hearing is limited to the ear. Mind is limited to tallying things up. But the primal spirit's empty: it's simply that which awaits things. Way is emptiness merged, and emptiness is the mind's fast."

"Before I begin my practice," said Sunset-Peak Return, "I am truly Sunset-Peak Return. But once I'm in the midst of my practice, I've never even begun to be Sunset-Peak Return. Can this be called *emptiness*?"

. . .

You've heard of using wings to fly, but have you heard of using no-wings to fly? You've heard of using knowing to know, but have you heard of using no-knowing to know?

"Gaze into that cloistered calm, that chamber of emptiness where light is born. To rest in stillness is great good fortune. If we don't rest there, we keep racing around even when we're sitting quietly. Follow sight and sound deep inside, and keep the knowing mind outside. [4.1]

"Just let your mind wander along in the drift of things. Trust yourself to what is beyond you—let it be the nurturing center. Then you've made it. In the midst of all this, is there really any response? Nothing can compare to simply living out the inevitable unfurling of your life. And there's nothing more difficult." [4.2]

. . . If a mirror is bright, dust never settles on it. If dust can settle on it, the mirror isn't bright. . . .⁴ [5.2]

"Can a person really have no nature?" asked Hui Tzu of Chuang Tzu.

"Yes," replied Chuang Tzu.

"But if you have no nature, how can you be called *human*?"

"Way gives you this shape and heaven gives you this form, so why can't you be called *human*?"

"But if you're called *human*, how can you have no nature?"

"*Yes this* and *no that*—that's what I call *human nature*," replied Chuang Tzu. "Not mangling yourself with *good* and *bad*—that's what I call *no nature*. Instead of struggling to improve on life, you simply abide in occurrence-appearing-of-itself." [5.6]

We're cast into this human form, and it's such happiness. This human form knows change, but the ten thousand in their vast transformations are utterly boundless. Who could calculate the joys they promise?

And so the sage wanders where nothing is hidden and everything is preserved. The sage calls dying young a blessing and living long a blessing, calls beginnings a blessing and endings a blessing. We might make such a person our teacher, but there's something the ten thousand things belong to, something all change depends upon—imagine making that your teacher! [6.6]

Way has its own nature and its own reliability: it's Absence-action; and so, has no form. It can be passed on, but never received and held. You can master it, but you can't see it. Its own source, its own root—it was there before heaven-and-earth, firm and constant from ancient times. [6.7]

Adept Mulberry-Gate, Adept Elder-Contrary, and Adept Strung-*Ch'in*[5] had become friends. One day they said: "Who can associate in non-association and cooperate in noncooperation? Who can ascend heaven, wander mists, and roam the boundless, forgetting their lives together for endless eternities?"

The three of them looked at each other and laughed. There was no disparity in their minds: they were friends.

Things went along quietly for a time. Then Adept Mulberry-Gate passed away. Before he was buried, Confucius heard about his death and sent Adept Kung to pay his respects at the funeral. When he arrived, Elder-Contrary was cooking up tunes, and Strung-*Ch'in* was thrumming a *ch'in*. Suddenly they broke into song together:

> *O Mulberry-Gate, how could you,*
> *O Mulberry-Gate, how could you:*
>
> *already back in your true form,*
> *you've left us here in the human!*

Adept Kung hurried in and demanded, "Singing to your dead friend's corpse—how can this be in accordance with Ritual?"

Looking at each other, the two friends laughed and said, "What does this guy know about Ritual?"

When he returned home, Adept Kung told Confucius what had happened, and then asked: "What kind of people are they? They're completely uncivil. They cultivate Absence and shuck off their physical form. They sing to their dead friend's corpse, not a trace of grief in their faces. There aren't words to describe them. What kind of people are they?"

"The kind that wander beyond this realm we know," replied Confucius. "And I'm the kind that wanders within it. Beyond and within—

they can never meet. So it was clumsy of me, sending you to mourn such a person.

"Companions in their realm to the Maker-of-Things, they're in human form for now, wandering the one *ch'i* that breathes through all heaven-and-earth. For them, life is a useless appendage, a swollen tumor, and death is like a boil breaking open or pus draining from a festering sore. So how would they choose between life and death, before and after?

"On loan from everything else, they'll soon be entrusted back to the one body. Forgetting liver and gallbladder, abandoning ears and eyes, they'll continue on again, tumbling and twirling through a blur of endings and beginnings. They roam at ease beyond the tawdry dust of this world, all Absence-action wandering boundless and free through the selfless unfolding of things." [6.11]

Sunset-Peak Return said, "I'm gaining ground."

"What do you mean?" asked Confucius.

"I sit quietly and forget."

Confucius shifted around uneasily. "What do you mean *sit quietly and forget*?" he asked his disciple.

"I let the body fall away and the intellect fade. I throw out form, abandon understanding—and then move freely, blending away into the Great Transformation. That's what I mean by *sit quietly and forget*." [6.14]

"Let your mind wander the pure and simple," replied No-Name. "Blend your *ch'i* into the boundless, follow occurrence-appearing-of-itself in things, and don't let selfhood get in the way. [7.3]

> Don't be a carcass of names
> or treasure-house of schemes,
>
> don't be a servant of pursuits
> or proprietor of fine wisdom.

Make the inexhaustible your body
and wander beyond origins.

Make everything heaven gave you treasure enough
and know you have nothing.

Live empty, perfectly empty.

Sage-masters always employ mind like a pure mirror:
welcome nothing, refuse nothing,

reflect everything, hold nothing.
And so they triumph over things with never a wound. [7.6]

PART II

Dark-Enigma Learning

(3rd–4th centuries C.E.)

Buddhism arrived in China during the first century c.e., and began to establish itself over the next few centuries. Meanwhile, independent of this new Buddhist influence, a native school of neo-Taoist philosophy arose: Dark-Enigma Learning. Dark-Enigma Learning focused on exploring the deep cosmological/ontological levels of Taoist thought. Hence, its name: *dark-enigma*, meaning the generative ontological tissue before it is named or conceptualized. This "before it is named" grows out of the realization that language only cages us inside thoughts and concepts, obscuring our direct experience of that ontological tissue, separating us from it—whether we call it *Way* (*Tao*) or *Absence*, *tzu-jan* or *dark-enigma*, or (as Ch'an terminology evolves) *dharma* or *Buddha*. We have already seen this problematic in Taoist thought, and it continues as a major consideration all the way through the Ch'an tradition.

In its exploration, Dark-Enigma Learning gave full definition to the conceptual world that would shape thinking among China's artist-intellectuals to follow. Those artist-intellectuals ran the government, and they considered a mastery of Dark-Enigma Learning insight essential not just for self-cultivation, but also for successful governing. This is an assumption that would continue through the tradition among artist-intellectuals, who nearly all practiced Ch'an in some sense. This class of artist-intellectuals also created the elite culture (philosophy,

49

poetry, painting, calligraphy), and it included the scholars and practitioners who would very soon begin to formulate Ch'an as an amalgam of Taoist Dark-Enigma Learning and newly arrived Dhyana Buddhism (part III, pp. 73–115).

Wang Pi and Kuo Hsiang were the two most influential figures in Dark-Enigma Learning, and their philosophical work took the form of commentaries on the seminal Taoist classics—*I Ching, Tao Te Ching, Chuang Tzu*—which came to be known as the "Dark-Enigma Three." Commentary meant more than simple explication, though—for it generally used the original text as a starting point for developing new ideas by exploring and expanding nascent ideas in the original. This was a major philosophical/literary form from the beginning—the *I Ching* is virtually all commentary, layer upon layer of commentary—and it continued through to a culmination in the sangha-case collections of the Sung Dynasty (part VI, pp. 257–308), which are structured as commentary on historic anecdotes and texts. Indeed, it was this native Chinese history of commentary as a major philosophical/literary form that made those sangha-case collections possible.

But there's much more. In the Chinese textual tradition, commentaries are printed as an integral part of the original text. There is typically a short passage of original text, then a passage of commentary, then the original text resumes. Wang Pi's and Kuo Hsiang's broad influence derives from this fact: all artist-intellectuals studied the "Dark-Enigma Three" assiduously, and in doing so they necessarily studied the commentaries assiduously. Indeed, they saw those classics through the lens of Wang Pi's and Kuo Hsiang's Dark-Enigma Learning. And so, Dark-Enigma cosmology/ontology became the body of assumptions through which those artist-intellectuals operated. And again, these are the people we will see in the following sections forging the terms of Ch'an insight and practice.

Dark-Enigma Learning is the source of Ch'an not as a religious project, but as a philosophical one. Indeed, Dark-Enigma Learning began in part to advocate and advance philosophical Taoism, as opposed to the many popular forms of religious Taoism that traded in superstition and magic, gods and the supernatural—an impulse that continues in Ch'an, with its dismantling of all religious dimensions of Buddhism. It was an attempt to return Chinese culture/spirituality to a strictly empirical framework (again, with the ultimate intent of cultivating more able government and more ordered society). Wang Pi and Kuo Hsiang were philosophers, and their philosophical Taoism was from the beginning meant to be a philosophy of personal transformation. It defined sagehood as living integral to Way's unfurling process. But Taoism and Dark-Enigma Learning said little about actual practices of self-cultivation that might bring about such transformation. It remained a body of profound ideas, the understanding of which was assumed to bring about that transformation.

When Buddhist scholars began infusing the Taoism of Dark-Enigma Learning with Buddhist practices (traced in part III and following), the possibility of transformation inherent in Taoism and Dark-Enigma Learning was dramatically augmented by those practices—primarily meditation, and later sangha-case practice (p. 257ff.). Still, it never functioned as Buddhism, but as an enhanced form of Taoism. Indeed, virtually all fundamental aspects of Ch'an awakening, already present in the original Taoist texts, are broadly developed in Dark-Enigma Learning. Focusing on the deep cosmological/ontological dimensions of consciousness and Cosmos, Dark-Enigma Learning opens the depths that allow Ch'an to invest immediate experience with such profundity. And from this came Ch'an at its most profound levels as a lived philosophical practice capable of bringing people to a liberation of deep insight and awakening.

王弼

Wang Pi (226–249)

OF THE DARK-ENIGMA THREE, WANG PI WROTE THE defining philosophical commentaries for the two primordial texts— *I Ching* and *Tao Te Ching*—and he emphasized their primordial dimensions. Wang Pi's approach transformed the *I Ching* from a divination text into a philosophical text. To do this, he applied the deep cosmological/ontological ideas from Taoism, thereby reinventing the *I Ching* as a Taoist text, which is how it was known from then on among artist-intellectuals. In his commentary on the *Tao Te Ching*, with its exhaustive exploration and expansion of Lao Tzu's most profound cosmological/ontological insights, Wang describes self-cultivation in ways that would come to define Ch'an practice. This involves both stillness and movement: stillness in the form of a meditative exploration of the weave of consciousness and Cosmos at the deepest levels; and movement in the form of Absence-action (*wu-wei*), meaning "to act as the generative tissue of Absence unfurling its possibilities, as integral to the unfolding of occurrence-appearing-of-itself (*tzu-jan*).

One example of this appears in Wang Pi's commentary to the *I Ching*, where he begins a passage addressing the nature of Absence and Presence with:

> Return means turning back to the source-tissue, and that source-tissue is the very mind of all heaven-and-earth itself.

Wherever movement ceases, stillness begins—but there's no opposition between movement and stillness. Wherever words end, silence begins—but there's no opposition between silence and words.

In speaking of "no opposition between movement and stillness," Wang Pi is describing the unity of Absence and Presence in the empirical Cosmos, in personal action, and in consciousness. In speaking of "no opposition between silence and words," he is describing the unity of Absence and Presence in the realm of consciousness. Here already, we have a description of mature Ch'an practice, as well as its insistence that we are always already enlightened and therefore have no need of practice. And it will be described again and again in various ways by the Ch'an masters to come. Purport Dark-Enigma, to take an example using the same terminology, said: "Movement and stillness are both the self-nature of Absence . . . a person of Way who depends on nothing makes use of both movement and stillness."

NOTE

For translation comparison: Bracketed numbers indicate the chapters to which Wang Pi's commentary is appended in the *Tao Te Ching* and *I Ching* (some of which can be found in the relevant chapters above). They can be thereby located in Richard John Lynn's *The Classic of the Way and Virtue* (1999) and *The Classic of Changes* (1994), which include full translations of Wang Pi's commentaries. For the "Outline Introduction to Lao Tzu," and the "Addendum" (*I Ching*), bracketed numbers refer to page numbers in Lynn's *The Classic of the Way and Virtue* and *I Ching*, respectively.

Commentary on the *Tao Te Ching*

OUTLINE INTRODUCTION TO LAO TZU

From the formless born, from the nameless emerging: that's how things come to birth and completion. Formless, nameless—such is the source-ancestral of the ten thousand things in their vast transformations. [30]

If you analyze and systematize Lao Tzu's sage eloquence, you lose its wordless teaching. If you categorize and critique it, you ravage its meaning. Why? Because he's always talking about the majestic source at origins—and in that, identifying the original-nature of occurrence-appearing-of-itself. He's always revealing the furthest depths of origin-dark quiet—and in that, resolving our bewilderment of doubt and delusion. [33]

Setting out on the current where things are not and nothing emerges, we declare it *Way*. Searching through the place where mystery is not and nothing arises, we call it *dark-enigma*. All mystery arises from dark-enigma; all things emerge from Way: hence, Lao Tzu's "Give birth and nurture." Moving without obstruction or hindrance, you fathom the original-nature of things: this too we call *Way*. "Give birth without possessing, / and foster without dominating": that is the Integrity of heart-sight clarity without any master, dark-enigma Integrity. Therefore, we call dark-enigma *deep and profound*; and we declare Way huge and vast.[1] [36]

I

Absence is the origin of Presence in its every particular. When it has no form and no name, Absence originates the ten thousand things in their vast transformations, gives birth to them. When it has form and name, it completes them, fosters and shelters them, nourishes them, nurses them as a mother. Lao Tzu says Way, having no form and no name, both originates the ten thousand things and completes them. And of their origination and completion, those things know nothing. Here lies the dark-enigma deep within dark-enigma.

In its furthest depths, shadowed-emergence is mystery. The ten thousand things originate in shadowed-emergence, and then come to completion. They originate in Absence, come to birth and life. It's there, in the empty-sky emptiness of perennial Absence, that you can see the deep-mystery origin of things.

The two [Absence and Presence] are origin and mother. They emerge from dark-enigma together—but once named, they're no longer the same. Speaking of beginnings, we say *origin*; speaking of endings, *mother*. But dark-enigma itself is shadowy blackness and silence all Absence where origin and mother emerge.

5

Heaven-and-earth institute nothing. They function through Absence-action occurrence-appearing-of-itself. And it's the inner-pattern of these ten thousand things that shapes their movements together.

6

The valley spirit is Absence at the valley's center—Absence without form or image, resistance or dissension. It abides low and unnoticed, keeps still and guards tranquility—and so, it never crumbles with age. It completes us, but we cannot see its form. It is the perfection of things themselves. And because it abides so low and unnoticed, we cannot name it. Therefore, we call it *dark female-enigma*.

7

If you're free of yourself, you are yourself Absence-action—yourself last, and so first; yourself given up, and so preserved. In this, as Lao Tzu says, you *become yourself.*

Dark-enigma is the furthest depths of things. Here, Lao Tzu is saying that if you can polish away twisty thoughts and deceptions, then you can fathom the dark-enigma mirror's furthest depths. Once you give up using things to transform your flaws into illumination, you live integral to dark-enigma whole. . . . And once the dark-enigma mirror is all clarity beyond stain, you're done with sagehood.

[*When we don't have selves,*] we are returned home to occurrence-appearing-of-itself.

In womb-dark, it's through inner-pattern that things come to light. In murkiness, it's through settling that things come to clarity. In stillness, it's through movement that things come to life. This is the occurrence-appearing-of-itself Way.

It is in emptiness and stillness that you can watch things return to their root. Presence in its every particular arises out of emptiness, moves out of stillness. And so, even though the ten thousand things move as a whole, they each end by returning home to emptiness and stillness. This is their furthest periphery and tranquil center.

When you return home to the root, you grow still. In this, you are called *stillness*. Once still, you've returned to the inevitable unfurling of things. In this, you can be called *the inevitable unfurling of things*. And once you return to the inevitable unfurling of things, you've realized the perennial unfurling of your own original-nature. In this, you can be called *perennial*.

Heart-sight clarity in accord with heaven, insight penetrating Way's potency deep and vast—master that, and you'll fathom the furthest depths of empty-sky Absence.

Exhaust the furthest depths of empty-sky Absence, and you realize Way's perennial nature. Then you fathom how inexhaustibly those depths open and open.

23

It is through formless Absence, through Absence-action, that Way completes and nurtures the ten thousand things in their vast transformations. Practice Absence-action, practice the wordless teaching that cannot be taught—then you move in accord with Way.

32

Uncarved simplicity² itself has Absence as its mind, Absence before names. And so, if you want to master Way, there's nothing like abiding in uncarved simplicity. . . . This uncarved simplicity itself is a confusion without affinities. It's the realm between Absence and Presence. That's why Lao Tzu says *it's subject to nothing in all beneath heaven*. To embrace uncarved simplicity, practice Absence-action—then the things of this world never tangle wild thusness all clarity-absolute, and the desires of this world never harm spirit-lightning awareness. In this, you are yourself a guest of the ten thousand things and a master of Way.

38

How do you realize Way wholly? Depend on Absence for your actualization. If you depend on Absence for your actualization, there's nothing you cannot sustain. . . . However vast its expanses, heaven-and-earth has Absence as its mind.

The source-tissue root resides in Absence-action. The mother resides in the nameless.

You may treasure using Absence as actualization, but you can't cast aside Absence as potency. If you cast aside Absence as potency, you lose all its vastness. . . . If you use Absence as actualization, you attain the mother.

Only by using the nameless can you true-up the names of things, and only by using the formless can you perfect the forms of things.

40

Everything in all beneath heaven is born of Presence. And Absence is the source-tissue root at the origin of Presence. Presence only comes to completion when it returns back to Absence.

42

The ten thousand forms of the ten thousand things all return home to primal-unity. What kind of emergence allows that return to primal-unity? They emerge from Absence. And because primal-unity is the first emergence from Absence, we can call it *Absence*.

I don't tell people to follow some teaching I've made up. I just tell them to abide in occurrence-appearing-of-itself, for that is to inhabit the inner-pattern.

54

How do I understand all beneath heaven? I understand it by looking within, not by searching elsewhere. That's why Lao Tzu says it's when you don't step out your door that you can understand all beneath heaven.

55

Mind is an accord of Absence and Presence. It deploys *ch'i*, and thereby grows strong.

63

Cultivate the dwelling of Absence-action. Cultivate the teaching of wordlessness. Cultivate the flavor of tranquility. Here lies the furthest depths of healing.

64

Occurrence-appearing-of-itself: that's what ignorance makes possible for you.

65

Sage illumination means full of insight—and so, cleverness and delusion obscure uncarved simplicity. *Simple-minded* means free of understanding—and so, attentiveness and thusness-clarity abide in occurrence-appearing-of-itself.

Commentary on the *I Ching*

1

To dwell deeply, ride the hidden dragon. To set out, ride the flying dragon. This is why the text says *Ride six dragons in the proper season.* If you ride the transformations of change, you wander the great vessel of heaven through rapt stillness and forthright movement.

24

Return means turning back to the source-tissue, and that source-tissue is the very mind of all heaven-and-earth itself. Wherever movement ceases, stillness begins—but there's no opposition between movement and stillness. Wherever words end, silence begins—but there's no opposition between silence and words. And it's the same with heaven-and-earth. Heaven-and-earth is vast, rich with the ten thousand things that thunder moves and wind drives through the ten thousand transformations in the revolving seasons of change—but the tranquility of Absence remains the source-tissue of all that. And so, it's when earth's movement ceases that the mind of heaven becomes visible. If Presence were its mind, that source-tissue would be lost among all those different kinds of things.

ADDENDUM

You can't use Absence to illuminate Absence. For that, you must search into Presence. If you search assiduously into the furthest depths of Presence and its ten thousand things, you will illuminate that source-ancestral from which things all arise. [60–61]

郭象

Kuo Hsiang (252–312)

ALTHOUGH HE DIFFERED IN EMPHASIS AND DETAIL,
Kuo Hsiang (literary name: Adept Dark-Enigma) shared Wang Pi's
overall framework and approach. Kuo Hsiang wrote the defining commentary on the third of the "Dark-Enigma Three": the *Chuang Tzu*
(p. 38). Indeed, he actually created the canonical version of that text by
editing and compiling it from a much larger body of material. It was
in this commentary that he developed his system of thought. Wang Pi
focused on Absence, on ontological ground. Kuo Hsiang focused on
Presence, on the particularity of things: *tzu-jan*, occurrence-appearing-of-itself as the ten thousand things in their vast transformations.
In this, he anticipates Ch'an's emphasis on immediate experience as the
open door to sage insight.

To begin with fundamentals: both Wang Pi and Kuo Hsiang very
importantly asserted the identity of Absence and Presence, silence
and thought/words, empty-mind tranquility and everyday struggles—
that is, the identity of seemingly unenlightened and seemingly enlightened. Kuo used *tzu-jan* as the key to his own formulation of this
identity: he proposed that every aspect of reality is equally *tzu-jan*, no
exceptions. In this, he (like Wang Pi) anticipated Ch'an's insistence
that we are always already enlightened, always already Buddhas, and
that there is therefore no need for practice (in fact, practice only gets
in the way).

For Kuo, sage insight is most essentially to "wander boundless and free," selfless and integral to the Great Transformation of Way (see Key Terms, p. 334). This idea begins in the *Chuang Tzu*, where it recurs (1.10, 1.16, 6.6, 6.11), and Kuo Hsiang explores its importance at length (pp. 65 [2 refs.], 66 [2 refs.], 68). In this, he essentially established the terms of awakening for the Ch'an tradition, where we find this idea echoed in many key passages describing awakening (pp. 143, 192, 291).

Already here in Kuo Hsiang, we find fully developed the mature Ch'an concepts of empty-mind and *no-mind* that are central to this awakening, awakening as more than the simple emptiness and tranquility that had arrived with Buddhism—for a fuller translation of *no-mind* (無心) is "Absence no-mind," because of the ever-productive double-meaning of 無: "no" and "Absence." No-mind allows one to abide as integral to the *inner-pattern*—a central concept in Ch'an thought that we have already seen briefly, but which Kuo Hsiang develops into a major concept. Anticipating Ch'an further, Kuo identifies no-mind with dark-enigma itself. Inhabiting this dark-enigma mind, an enlightened sage operates at Tao's generative origin-moment/place, the "hinge of Tao" where our "movements range free" because we move as the Cosmos (Tao) itself unfurling inexhaustibly through its boundless transformations:

> *No-mind* inhabits the mystery of things. . . . This is the importance of being at the hinge of Way. There, you can know dark-enigma's furthest depths. There, your movements range free.

And Kuo further establishes the nature of Ch'an awakening when he describes it in terms of *tzu-jan* and *wu-wei*, concepts that will continue as philosophical touchstones in Taoist/Ch'an cosmology/ontology:

> The ten thousand things can only take *tzu-jan* as their source. It is *wu-wei* action that makes *tzu-jan tzu-jan*. . . . If you move as *wu-wei*, you're self-reliant; and so, act as source.

And indeed, Kuo Hsiang also anticipates one of the most distinctive characteristics of the Ch'an tradition, that Ch'an insight and awakening is "a separate transmission outside all teaching" (p. 123): empty- or no-mind itself, rather than the words and doctrines imparted by a teacher. He states it simply: "Absence no-mind is the source-ancestral teacher."

NOTE

For translation comparison: there is no full translation of Kuo Hsiang's *Chuang Tzu* commentary.

Commentary on the *Chuang Tzu*

The principle thought in Chuang Tzu is *wandering boundless and free*, that liberation in Absence-action through which we find the furthest depths of self-realization.

Heaven-and-earth is a simple name for the ten thousand things in their vast transformations. Heaven-and-earth takes the ten thousand things as its potency, and the source of those ten thousand things is occurrence-appearing-of-itself. Occurrence never *takes action*—that's why it's simply occurrence-appearing-of-itself. . . . So, to mount the source of heaven-and-earth is to abide by the original-nature of the ten thousand things, yielding and devoted as a river. And to ride the six seasons of *ch'i* in their endless dispute is to wander the blur of change and transformation. If you set out like that, how could you not set out into the inexhaustible? Embrace this, mount the source of heaven-and-earth, depending on nothing at all—then you've mastered that *wandering boundless and free*, a sage of heart-sight clarity merging self and other in dark-enigma.

If you shade away into things, they're so kindred you can never leave them. This is no-mind's dark-enigma. And it feels just like drifting free, cut loose from the mooring of self, a boat ranging here and there, east and west.

Perfect a sage's mind and you penetrate the furthest depths of *yin* and *yang*, fathom wholly the wondrous mystery of the ten thousand things in their vast transformations. Then you live integral to change, merged with transformation. Wherever you go, you're everything everywhere. And in all the ten thousand things, there isn't one that isn't the exact thusness that it is. Once you perfect Absence no-mind, you can find yourself anywhere, even in the chaos of our human world. And in Absence no-mind, how could you ever fail to live in harmony with our human world? Indeed, you live integral to dark-enigma, penetrating the furthest depths of wondrous mystery. You fathom clear through the original-nature of the ten thousand things in their vast transformations, and delight in knowing yourself coined by the transformations of all beneath heaven....

When there's tranquility anywhere you go, wherever you are is arrival. Death and life cannot change this self you are, much less seething flood or fire. Possessing sage wisdom, you're never tangled in hardship and calamity. But it isn't because you avoid such things. It's because you see through inner-pattern with absolute and immediate clarity. It's because you know that whatever form it takes, occurrence-appearing-of-itself is always great good fortune.

A mind full of bramble never sees through it all with absolute and immediate clarity. . . . Things each have their inherent accord. Once you realize your inherent accord, how can anything you do not be *wandering boundless and free*?

Once occurrences great and small are free of the complexities we struggle to illuminate, the inner-pattern of profit and ruin reveals that whatever occurs is equally perfect. And then, it's all *wandering boundless and free*.

Being integral to heaven itself . . . , Adept Dark-Weave merged self and other together. . . . *Withered wood* and *dead ash* describe how perfectly still and passionless he is. Hence, he abides by occurrence-appearing-of-itself, and forgets *yes this* and *no that*.[3]

Here below illuminates boundless occurrence-appearing-of-itself. Each thing is occurrence-appearing-of-itself. Who knows why it occurs? It just does. As forms, things are utterly different. But as occurrence-appearing-of-itself, they are utterly the same. . . . Everything other is occurrence-appearing-of-itself, and occurrence-appearing-of-itself also gave birth to me. Because I am born of occurrence-appearing-of-itself, I am occurrence-appearing-of-itself. So, how could I ever be distant from it?

. . . Absence no-mind inhabits the mystery of things. . . . This is the importance of being at the hinge of Way. There, you can know dark-enigma's furthest depths. There, your movements range free.

. . . forget all heaven-and-earth, abandon the ten thousand things. Don't go searching through our seed-time and breath-space home,[4] or struggle to fathom the self. Then you can wander boundless expanses unfettered, moving in accord with all things.

Things are all self-enlightened and do not try to enlighten others. But if others are not enlightened, we say it is not perfect. . . . For these three masters to try enlightening others by means of their own favorite methods—isn't that foolhardy?

The sage is selfless. Therefore, *steering by the bright light of confusion and doubt* is how the sage dwells.

Once you realize inner-pattern utterly, there are no words. Words identify things, categorize them—and so, we try to use words for inner-pattern.

The mind of a sage is a mirror reflecting perfectly: it hoards nothing, treasures nothing. All boundless expanse, it's without the transformations of full and empty. . . . And when you see how you too emerge from inner-pattern origins, you see occurrence-appearing-of-itself leaves no traces.

Master Absence no-mind, and you live in perfect accord with all things.

Things are all occurrence-appearing-of-itself, and inner-pattern is their furthest depth whole and complete. If you abide in occurrence and inner-pattern, wherever you go is all sight-clarity absolute. Then you shade away into things, and live therefore in whole accord with yourself.

Realize you are heaven's loom-of-origins—then, sitting or moving about, you depend always on nothing. Depending on nothing, you become yourself utterly. And understanding how that is, you understand responsibility to that from which things emerge.

To search and seek: that's what snares the pheasant in a trap. Just gaze above and below throughout all heaven-and-earth, *wander boundless and free* in this world of things realized and content in and of themselves. That's how you nourish the wondrous mystery of life. Why follow some search into a trap, bow down there pecking at a few nourishing crumbs?

Without empty-mind and its accord with things, we're just thought trespassing and struggling against this world. It's a knowing that keeps the self front and center. But there's no tranquility in that, no meditative stillness. Leave knowing outside yourself—only then can you nurture the wild thusness of things all clarity-absolute, only then can you dwell in wondrous mystery.

Exact the forms of this world, and you've emptied mind.

Abandon hearing and sight, ditch mind and thought, then you're in accord with *ch'i*'s original-nature—self-composed, self-realized. And in that emptiness, you move integral to things themselves.... Empty mind, and you embrace Way's gathering of vast transformations.

This life of mine: it doesn't come from me. Here within this one-and-only hundred-year life—sitting and rising, walking and standing, moving and still, everything I adore and detest, original-nature and emotion, thoughts and abilities, everything I have and everything I have not, everything I do and everything I encounter—nothing of all that is me. It all comes from inner-pattern alone. So why agonize over this life? It's simply occurrence-appearing-of-itself. And it's vanishing, vanishing.

Hear what you hear, learn what you learn, and then move on. That is Absence-action.

When masters of Absence no-mind do study, they study occurrence itself. ... Such teachers are self-realized ones, abiding in their enduring nature as occurrence itself. Abandoning self and self-fulfillment, they move integral to the world of things outside themselves.

Occurrence-appearing-of-itself is already everything everywhere. And so, sage-masters never struggle to realize themselves.

Absence no-mind is the source-ancestral teacher.

Whatever heaven and human do, it's all occurrence-appearing-of-itself. Understand that—then within, you are free of self; and without, you shade away into things. You grow indistinguishable from dark-enigma. Master this, and there's nothing that isn't realization's arrival.

Deep roots are final-and-total tranquility, for they return you to primal-unity Absence.

Once you give up analysis and understanding, heaven's loom-of-origins is revealed in and of itself.

Inner-pattern reveals itself final-and-total when you shade the outer and inner together, not when you wander the outer's promise without shading it into the inner. If you can't shade outer into inner, you never really wander the outer. To wander the outer, sage-masters perennially use their inner Absence no-mind—and so, they live in accord with Presence. They see changeless spirit-lightning *ch'i* in the day's myriad restless forms. And gazing above and below, they recognize the loom-of-origins weave.

When I'm open to everything that is not me, dark-enigma merges outer and inner together. In this, I treasure the fresh transformations of passing days, whether lost in antiquity or appearing today. And so, how could I ever understand where I am, where I belong?

When I act with straightforward clarity according to my original-nature, it's occurrence-appearing-of-itself. When I act in violation of my original-nature, it's also occurrence-appearing-of-itself. And so is working to rectify that violation. So what can I understand from occurrence-appearing-of-itself in the form of me?

In their vast transformations, the ten thousand things of this world are all Absence-action occurrence-appearing-of-itself.

In Absence no-mind you trust yourself to change unfurling of itself. . . .

Master Absence no-mind, then you move through life in accord with the Great Transformation of things.

In Absence no-mind, each and every thing in this world is the proprietor of its own fine wisdom.

If you mirror things perfectly, you don't feel them becoming part of you. It's Absence that you feel becoming part of you.

[Inner-pattern is] the ground from which the ten thousand things are born. It includes those things, for origins can only include progeny, and it carries them back to the origin-tissue.

In their vast transformations, the ten thousand things can only take occurrence-appearing-of-itself as their source. It is Absence-action that makes occurrence-appearing-of-itself occurrence-appearing-of-itself. . . . If you move as Absence-action, you're self-reliant; and so, act as source.

PART III

The Birth of Ch'an

(4th–5th centuries C.E.)

MOUNTAINS ARE GREAT CH'AN TEACHERS. THOSE VAST forces of this generative Cosmos are most dramatically manifest in mountain landscapes, and they possess a resounding silence. Ch'an put the wisdom of mountains at the heart of its practice: Ch'an monasteries were typically located in remote mountains (those in cities surrounded themselves with the domesticated landscapes of gardens), and Ch'an masters leading those monasteries generally took the names of local mountains as their own because they so deeply identified with mountain landscape. Meditation empties mind of words and concepts, the preoccupations that distance us from the immediate presence of earth's ten thousand things, replacing them with silence and mirror-deep clarity. And mountain landscape reinforces meditation practice because its dramatic distances and visual drama opened that same mirror-deep empty-mind clarity.[1]

Not surprisingly, a mountain presided over the birth of Ch'an in the early fifth century: Thatch-Hut, in south China, a remarkably beautiful complex of ninety peaks with names like Incense-Burner and Yellow-Dragon, Crane-Song and Twin-Sword, Five-Elders and Spirit-Vulture. Thatch-Hut was a primary center of Buddhist practice in China, boasting many monasteries. There were Ten-Thousand-Cedar and Flourish-Peak Monasteries; White-Crane and Cloud-Gaze; West-Forest and, most illustrious, East-Forest. Here, at East-Forest Monastery on Thatch-Hut

Mountain, Ch'an arose as part of a broad cultural movement establishing mountain landscape as the heart of Chinese spiritual and artistic practice.

Philosophically, Ch'an began as an amalgam of Dark-Enigma Learning Taoism and imported Dhyana Buddhism. This amalgam was forged by four primary figures when their paths crossed early in the fifth century at East-Forest: two Buddhist philosophers, Sangha-Fundament (Seng Chao) and Way-Born (Tao Sheng); and two poets, Hsieh Ling-yün and T'ao Ch'ien. This conjunction was facilitated by Prajna-Distance (Hui Yüan), the abbot at East-Forest, who was also an influential figure. Prajna-Distance, too, aspired to combine Buddhism and Dark-Enigma Learning, focusing practice on meditation that combined the two and aspired not to mere quiescence, but to the integration of consciousness and the generative origin-tissue (Tao/Way, Absence). Under Prajna-Distance's auspices, this remarkable conjunction of mountains and people was the catalyzing moment from which Ch'an emerged as an independent cultural entity.

Ch'an is not a religious project; it is a philosophical one. For all four of these figures, as for virtually all artist-intellectuals at the time, Dark-Enigma Learning operated as the body of assumptions defining their intellectual framework. The two philosophers explicitly reinvented Buddhist principles as Taoist principles, forging Ch'an by transforming Dhyana Buddhism into an extension of Dark-Enigma Learning. This philosophical project continues Dark-Enigma Learning's focus on deep cosmological/ontological dimensions of consciousness and Cosmos, combining it with Buddhist thought and practice. Like Dark-Enigma Learning itself, it is sometimes challenging, sentence after sentence reading like complex philosophical aphorisms requiring sustained attention. But this complexity opens depths that allow later Ch'an to develop more accessible ways of cultivating those depths as immediate everyday experience.

Hsieh Ling-yün played a crucial role in this philosophical project, as we will see. But in addition, he and T'ao Ch'ien gave form in their poems to this proto-Ch'an amalgam as immediate experience. They both described their lives in mountain landscape as a return to *tzu-jan*, "occurrence-appearing-of-itself," that concept central to Taoist and Dark-Enigma Learning cosmology/ontology. In this, they began investing daily experience with Ch'an depths, which became the essential project of the Chinese poetic tradition to follow (see the sample of T'ang Dynasty poetry below, p. 245ff.). And so, a poetry that operates as Ch'an's native language.

It seems remarkable that Ch'an and mature Chinese poetry arose simultaneously, but it makes perfect sense. Ch'an insight famously resides outside words and texts. Normal prose discourse remains always at an explanatory distance from the immediate actualization of that insight. Poetry is as close to that wordless insight as words can come, for it is a language of immediate experience rather than explanation. As such, it was practiced by virtually all Ch'an adepts as a way of cultivating and articulating understanding, and it plays a large role in the Ch'an textual tradition. And so, there at Thatch-Hut Mountain, the poetic cultivation of Taoist cosmology/ontology by Hsieh and T'ao represents the beginning of China's mainstream poetic tradition, which was most essentially a tradition of Ch'an-inspired rivers-and-mountains poetry (山水: often translated as "landscape").

僧肇

Sangha-Fundament (Seng Chao, 374–414)

LIKE ALL CHINESE ARTIST-INTELLECTUALS OF HIS TIME, Sangha-Fundament was well-versed in Taoist Dark-Enigma Learning, but when he read the Indian *Vimalakirti Sutra* he discovered insights he believed deepened the understanding of Dark-Enigma Learning's insights. This led him to seek out Kumarajiva and become his disciple in Peace-Perpetua (Ch'ang-an), the northern capital. Kumarajiva (344–409/413), a Buddhist scholar who came from India, became the most influential among all translators of Buddhist texts into Chinese: his translations remain even today the most widely read and influential. Working with a large team, he introduced no less than seventy-four texts to China, many quite large. Sangha-Fundament was a key member of that translation team. Kumarajiva would explain a passage to him, and he would compose the Chinese text. It is said that the accuracy of Kumarajiva's translations is proven by the fact that when he was cremated, his tongue remained unburned. However, that would seem to be an oversight of the literature gods, for Sangha-Fundament interpreted many of the fundamental concepts from those texts as Dark-Engima Learning concepts. In other words, he understood Buddhism as a different formulation of Dark-Enigma Learning. And this misunderstanding/mistranslation was crucial to the formation of Ch'an.

Sangha-Fundament articulated his mongrel understanding in a number of essays, the most widely influential of which was his "Prajna

Absence-Knowing Discourse," written in 404. This essay was broadly recognized as a whole new approach to Buddhism, a brilliant blending of Buddhist concepts with native Chinese understanding. It therefore circulated widely among Kumarajiva's community and beyond in the intellectual community of the northern capital. Way-Born (whom we will meet more fully in the next chapter) was briefly part of that community, but he spent most of his life in the south, at Thatch-Hut Mountain's East-Forest Monastery and in the southern capital. When he left Peace-Perpetua and returned to Thatch-Hut Mountain in 408, he carried with him Sangha-Fundament's "Prajna Absence-Knowing Discourse," which he shared with East-Forest's community of adepts.

The essay had a great impact on Way-Born and the East-Forest sangha, where it was intensely discussed. As part of that discussion, the monks there sent a series of responses and questions to Sangha-Fundament. These were incorporated into the essay, together with Sangha-Fundament's responses (seen in the excerpt below under the heading "Response to the Letter from Peopled-Bequest"). The essay no doubt circulated far beyond the East-Forest sangha to the other monasteries on Thatch-Hut and throughout the south, both among Buddhist adepts and artist-intellectuals more generally. In particular, Way-Born surely took it with him when he moved in 409 to the southern capital, where there were no less than thirty monasteries. And the essay's influence continued large throughout the Ch'an tradition. Indeed, a number of Ch'an masters over many centuries described achieving enlightenment while reading Sangha-Fundament's essays.

Especially revealing examples of Sangha-Fundament's reconfiguration of the Buddhist concepts into China's native Taoist/Dark-Enigma Learning framework are *sunyata* and *prajna*. Sangha-Fundament devotes an entire essay to each of these concepts, so the reconfiguration is visible in extensive detail. He uses 空 (*emptiness*: see Key Terms, p. 330) to translate the Sanskrit *sunyata*. In its original Indian Buddhist context, *sunyata* does mean "emptiness"—but "emptiness" in the sense that things have no intrinsic nature or self-existence, that they are illusory or delusions conjured by the mind. Here, *sunyata* is closely associated with nirvana as a state of selfless and transcendental extinction or *emptiness*. This *sunyata* emptiness is essentially metaphysical, suggesting some kind of "ultimate reality" behind or beyond the physical world we inhabit. But that atmosphere of metaphysics is quite foreign to the Chinese sensibility and Ch'an. Indeed, there was no word in Chinese with the meaning of *sunyata*. The character 空 (emptiness), with its apparent similarity, was quite simply the only possibility. And in the Taoist/Ch'an context, emptiness is virtually synonymous with Absence, reality seen as a single formless and generative tissue that is the source of all things—a concept altogether different from the Buddhist *sunyata*. And etymologically, the ideogram's elements are *cave* + *labor*. Hence, a hollow space in earth where the work of gestation happens: emptiness as both earthly and generative. (See also Key Terms, p. 341.)

In his essay on *sunyata*, Sangha-Fundament reconceives *sunyata* within the Taoist/Dark-Enigma Learning framework, saying of it: "Emptiness perfectly unborn, perfectly Absence-alive—it's the insight of *prajna*'s dark-enigma mirror," where "dark-enigma mirror" echoes *Tao Te Ching* 10: "Can you polish the dark-enigma mirror / to a clarity beyond stain?" The proposition is quite precise and rich with the generative life of earth and our everyday existence (and of course, Ch'an locates nirvana here in the everyday world we inhabit). Indeed, Sangha-Fundament's essay on *sunyata* begins with a mélange of concepts from Taoist/Dark-Enigma Learning cosmology/ontology:

> Emptiness perfectly unborn, perfectly Absence-alive—it's the insight of *prajna*'s dark-enigma mirror. Master that, and you master the wondrous mystery of source-ancestral enlightenment understanding things themselves clear through to the end. Without this extraordinary and radiant enlightenment of a sage—how can you cultivate yourself spirit-lightning whole, at the boundary between Presence and Absence? This is how the self-realized fathom spirit-lightning mind in the inexhaustible, how they exhaust what moves without obstruction.
>
> In that enlightenment clear through to the end, ear and eye reside in the very acts of seeing and hearing. When you stop trying to define and regulate this beautiful world of sights and sounds, isn't it clear that the ten thousand things

are inherently empty? Then things can never tether spirit-lightning enlightenment in tangles of thought and learning. This is how a sage's thusness-clarity mind accords with inner-pattern. In that accord, there's no obstruction and no penetrating insight. And gazing into all transformation, you explore *ch'i*'s primal-unity breath-force. . . .

And so, this translation of *sunyata* into 空 is a crucial and emblematic moment in the transformation of Indian Buddhism into Ch'an as a reconfiguration of Taoism. And near the end of the tradition we are tracing in this book, in the *Blue-Cliff Record*, we find again this insistence on the distinction between *sunyata* and 空 continuing:

> Rich confusions of grasses
> among hazy veils of mist:
>
> there, you're emptiness-born amid cliffwall paths, wildflower profusions, and a mere snap of the finger erases old *sunyata*.

In Indian Buddhism, *prajna* refered to a transcendental state of perfect wisdom in which one directly sees or even becomes the fundamental emptiness (*sunyata*) of things. Reconceived in the entirely empirical terms of Taoist cosmology/ontology, it is defined in a host of related ways in the Ch'an tradition, but a good working definition is mind returned to its original-nature as "Absence," which we just saw Sangha-Fundament equate with empty-mind as a "dark-enigma mirror." And indeed, the Chinese ideograms used to transliterate *prajna* mean "accord-pleasure": hence, the pleasure of being in accord with Tao/Way. This reveals a profound shift from Sanskrit/Buddhism to Chinese/Ch'an, for *prajna* has been reconfigured into a Taoist concept. Again, metaphysics replaced by the Great Transformation itself: this wild earth we inhabit day-by-day, moment-by-moment.

This redefinition is encapsulated in the title of the essay about *prajna* excerpted below: *prajna* + *not/Absence* + *know*. Here, yet again, is the philosophically rich double-meaning of 無 (not/Absence), allowing the title to be read two ways, both of which reveal aspects of *prajna* in its Ch'an conception: "*Prajna* Is Not-Knowing" and "*Prajna* Is

Absence-Knowing." This double-meaning is exploited throughout the essay, every instance translated "Absence-knowing" simultaneously meaning "not-knowing." As usual, these two meanings are complementary, providing a full description of *prajna* as the nature of a "sage mind."

Thus, although the idea of enlightenment and its cultivation through meditation came from Dhyana Buddhism, the content of enlightenment was entirely Taoist. Rather than a kind of transcendental nirvana-tranquility, it is consciousness integral to the tissue of Tao's Great Transformation. Sangha-Fundament summarizes this enlightenment in a remarkable and clearly Taoist distillation: "This heaven-and-earth Cosmos and I share the same root. The ten thousand things and I share the same original potency," where *potency* is Wang Pi's concept of an inherent nature giving shape to the emergence of things (see Key Terms, p. 326). And further anticipating Ch'an, Sangha-Fundament identifies enlightenment with meditation itself (rather than some sacred or transcendental state meditation is leading to), for he transforms meditation from the pursuit of nirvana-tranquility to Taoist understanding: "Meditation is the Way of a sage mind moving in accord with each moment," mind identified with *tzu-jan* (occurrence-appearing-of-itself) and the unfurling of Absence into Presence.

NOTE

For translation comparison: Bracketed numbers refer to page numbers in Walter Liebenthal's *Chao Lun: The Treatises of Seng-chao* (1948/1968).

Prajna Absence-Knowing Discourse

Prajna is dark-enigma emptiness, and isn't that the deepest source-ancestral of the Three Vehicles?[2] It is, in truth, primal-unity thusness all clarity-absolute and without distinctions—but it's long been lost in a confusion of strange discourses. [62]

The *Light-Accord Sutra* says: *Prajna is something without form and appearance, without even the birth or death of form and appearance.* And the *Buddha-Way Cultivation Sutra* says: *Prajna is something you cannot know and cannot see.* People exhaust explanation and wisdom and illumination—but in the end, *prajna* remains the Absence of form and appearance, the Absence of knowing. So then, what is it? And to finally know the Absence of form and appearance: that is the illumination of not knowing, the radiant enlightenment of it. But what could that be?

There are things we know, and things we don't know. If you perfect the Absence-knowing of sage mind, there's nothing you don't know. The knowing of not knowing: that is called *complete knowing.* And so, the sutra says: *There's nothing a sage mind knows, and nothing it doesn't know.* Exactly! That's why a sage empties mind and grounds illumination in the actual. Master that and, free of knowing, you know perfectly all day long.

Soon you can hide *prajna*-radiance in dark splendor, and mirror dark-enigma in empty-mind. Closing off wisdom and shutting out intelligence, you're awakened alone in depths of shadowed mystery. There, Absence-knowing wisdom mirrors origin-dark quiet utterly. There, spirit moves in accord with each moment, free of anxiety. In the Absence of anxiety, spirit can rule itself within our human affairs; and in the Absence of knowing, wisdom can illuminate dark-enigma outside our pursuits and struggles. But even though outside our pursuits and struggles, wisdom lacks nothing of our pursuits and struggles. And even though within our human affairs, spirit dwells all day on home-ground.

Examining everything above and below, moving in accord with change, you touch the inexhaustible. If you can't see into Absence's origin-dark quiet, you'll illuminate nothing. And so, what Absence-knowing knows is the insight of a sage's spirit—and from that comes action integral to things. Actuality, not Presence; emptiness, not Absence: a sage's wisdom is something you can nurture but never talk through. So what is it? Try to explain it as Presence, and you find no shape, no name. Try to explain it as Absence, and you find sage awareness itself. Sage awareness itself: it's an emptiness that lacks no illumination. Without shape and without name, it's an illumination that lacks no emptiness. An illumination that lacks no emptiness, hence muddy confusion beyond clarification. An emptiness that lacks no illumination, hence simple movement within the everyday.

This is the actualization of a sage's wisdom. Don't give it up for a moment. Search it out through this entire world of form and appearance, because it won't come easily. That's why the *Treasure-Store Sutra* instructs: *Use no-mind's ch'i-weave insight to cultivate whatever appears, shimmering.* And the *Light-Accord Sutra* says: *All dharmas are established in the awakening of those who remain motionless.*

The ten thousand affairs of a sage's life: they all share the same primal-unity. That's how *prajna* illuminates emptiness. Forget thusness all reality absolute itself, and you find knowing. Perfect arrival in all ten thousand movements, and you find stillness. Find Absence in sage accord, and you perfect action.[3] And so, free of knowing, you know yourself. And free of action, you enact yourself. Then, how could you ever return to what knowing once was? And how could you ever return to what action once was? [66–70]

RESPONSE TO THE LETTER FROM
PEOPLED-BEQUEST

You write, quoting me: "Understood fully, a sage mind is dark and silent. Enlightened to inner-pattern understood clear through to the end, it is Absence itself. And though dwelling in the midst of named things, it is far away, is indeed the nameless itself."

Here lies the inner-pattern's dark-enigma, dark-enigma grounded always in blackness. Nurturing it, you can forget the understanding within words. And in that forgetting is the heart's meditative stillness. Things confuse people. And how can you use the strange marvels of that confusion to search out the strange marvels of a sage mind?

You write: "Considering your discourse, talking through it, we suspect that to exhaust wordless enlightenment clear through to the end is to fulfill the wondrous mysteries of dark accord. That's another name for silent-illumination, for the potency of *prajna*-meditation. If mind, in its potency, is occurrence-appearing-of-itself, occurrence become aware and responsive, then people and all sentient life exist at rest in the loom-of-origins."

In my view, "to fulfill the wondrous mysteries of dark accord" is not what *prajna*-meditation names. And "become aware and responsive" is not what *people and all sentient life exist at rest* describes. Although these two definitions seem different, in the actualization of wondrous mystery they are always one and the same.

We leave such traces, but not the sage. Why? Because a sage's dark-enigma mind is blackness illuminated. Enlightened to inner-pattern understood clear through to the end, it is Absence itself. We say it's Absence, but to say that precludes enlightenment clear through to the end. So long as we use names for *prajna*-meditation, how can there be Absence understood clear through to the end? If we use names for *prajna*-meditation, we're describing something that's outer. If we describe the things of this world as inner, whatever we describe is no longer inner. And if we describe the things of this world as outer, whatever we describe is other than us.

And there's more. A sage mind is emptiness emergent, is wondrous mystery beyond all bounds. It responds to Absence without answering, knows Absence without understanding. It follows the dark loom-of-origins through its unfurling transformations, but never moves. How can it respond to this sentient world and remain at rest? Well, mind is defined by Presence, but that Presence is never its own. And so, a sage mind is not defined by Presence. Not defined by Presence, it's defined by the Presence of Absence. Defined by the Presence of Absence, it's not

Absence. Not Absence, a sage is neither Presence nor Absence, neither defined nor not defined. Neither Presence nor Absence, neither defined nor not defined—that is spirit-lightning emptiness.

What does that mean? Presence and Absence: They are two more of mind's images and sounds. And words and ideas are the origin-tissue of those images and sounds. Throw away Presence and Absence, and mind is free of images and sounds. When images and sounds sink away, words and ideas grow unfathomable. When words and ideas grow unfathomable, they belong to Way beyond this peopled realm. And when they belong to Way beyond this peopled realm, you can exhaust wordless enlightenment clear through to the end. To exhaust wordless enlightenment clear through to the end is called *wondrous mystery fulfilled*. Being wondrous mystery fulfilled, Way resides in Absence. Residing in Absence, a sage mind is dark and silent—and when darkness is beyond all bounds, emptiness understands it. Wondrous mystery fulfilled nurtures our understanding of this sentient world clear through to the end. When this sentient world is understood clear through to the end, this sentient world answers. And when this sentient world answers, you are in motion among events that you know through and through.

When you use emptiness to understand, Way leaps beyond names. When Way leaps beyond names, we call it *Absence*. When you are in motion among events you know through and through, we call it *Presence*. And what we call *Presence*: that is thusness all clarity-absolute. Forced to say more, I call it *occurrence*, though that has nothing to do with occurrence itself.

A sutra says: *If you perfect the Absence-knowing of sage wisdom, there's nothing you don't know. And if you perfect the Absence-action of sage wisdom, there's nothing you don't enact.* This is the still and blank Way beyond words and beyond forms. How can we say Presence, and also *be* Presence; say Absence, and also *be* Absence?

Your practice is motion hoping to achieve tranquility, but that's tranquility stripped of actualization. In considering my discourse, it seems you too easily trust words to capture the wordless teaching of meditation. Instead, you should search through the world's vast regions and small corners, and embrace everything that appears before you, recognize them all as bright streamers of dark-enigma.

Nurture what nurturing requires. Understand how a sage knows Presence, and you understand Presence-mind. But understand how a sage knows Absence, and you understand vast emptiness. There at the boundary between Presence and Absence, you can recognize what nurtures. And in that, you dwell at the center of undifferentiated Way.

What does all this mean? Although the ten thousand things are myriad, they are in their ancestral Buddha-nature a single source-tissue. To say there are no individuated things doesn't mean there are no things in the world. When things are individual things, names have differentiated them as forms and appearances. When things aren't individual things, they remain thusness all clarity-absolute. That's why things aren't individual things for a sage, and they aren't not individual things. When things aren't individual things, they aren't Presence. And when things are individual things, they aren't Absence. Not Presence: that is free of choosing. Not Absence: that is free of clinging.

If you're free of clinging, wondrous mystery nurtures thusness all clarity-absolute. If you're free of choosing, names are separated from forms. When names and forms are separated, it's Presence-knowing. And when wondrous mystery nurtures thusness all clarity-absolute, it's Absence-knowing. And so the sutra says, *Prajna is there in all dharmas: just don't choose or cling, know or not-know.* To venture beyond this origin-tissue, to mind's far-off boundaries, and there investigate Presence and Absence—isn't that to live at a terrible distance from this life? Listen, investigate the patterns Presence and Absence take right here in this world. That is wisdom here in this life, enlightenment clear through to the end here in this world of forms.

But original source-tissue dharma is without form and appearance, so how does sage wisdom know it? If you just label and describe this world of things, you'll never know that dharma. If you just say things like *tree* and *rock, supreme emptiness*—then you're just flowing past and things seen never become part of you. Wordless enlightenment mirror, candle-flame in origin-dark quiet, appearances without signs and omens: Way is Absence all mystery deep in the loom-of-origins, and how can we speak of Absence-knowing? Absence-knowing begins in the Absence of knowing. Otherwise, you don't know Absence, and you don't know Presence. If you don't know Presence, you live without Presence. And if you don't know Absence, you live without Absence.

Emptiness is never without illumination, and illumination never without emptiness. And so, occurrence itself is forever silent. It scatters beyond our clinging, our grasping. Who can command Presence in their movements, and employ Absence in their stillness? The sutra says: *Thusness-clarity prajna is not Presence and not Absence. It doesn't arise or vanish. And talk will never reveal it to people.* So, how can we approach it? You can say it's not Presence and not anywhere in the realm of Presence, but that doesn't prove it's in some realm of non-Presence. And to say it's not Absence and not anywhere in the realm of Absence, but that doesn't prove it's in some realm of non-Absence. Not Presence and not non-Presence, not Absence and not non-Absence: that's why Bodhi Instant-Awakening[4] taught *prajna* all day long, but said only what cannot be said. This Way of silencing words: it's transmission. But of what? All you dark-enigma masters there—you must understand it through and through.

You write: "You say *meditation is the Way of a sage mind moving in accord with each moment.* Does that come from illuminating the formless, or from looking utterly into the perennial transformations of things?"

In considering my discourse, you seem to doubt that the wordless teachings of formlessness and transformation are one and the same. If you only look at the perennial transformation of things, it seems different than formlessness. And if you only illuminate formlessness, it seems you cannot respond in harmony with those transformations moment-by-moment. But there remains the inner-pattern of thusness all clarity-absolute, and doubting it is the great obstruction.

The *Mind Sutra* says:

> this beautiful world of things,
> this world is no different than emptiness,
> and emptiness no different than this world,
> this world exactly emptiness,
> emptiness exactly this world.[5]

If you master the wordless teaching of Buddha Existence-Tissue Arrival, you can gaze into this beautiful world of things as emptiness—which means primal-unity mind seeing this beautiful world and emptiness together. If primal-unity mind sees this beautiful world of things deeply, it finds this world only appears different than emptiness. And if primal-unity mind sees emptiness deeply, it finds emptiness only appears different than this world. Emptiness and this beautiful world of things: at its source-tissue root, meditation reveals that they are not two separate aspects.

So when the sutra says *not this beautiful world of things*, it really considers that non-world to be this beautiful world, rather than merely some non-world. If this non-world were merely non-world, and supreme emptiness were merely non-world—how could they reveal radiant enlightenment in this actual world? But if you consider that non-world to be this beautiful world of things, then non-world is no different than world. And if non-world is no different than world, this beautiful world of things enacts that non-world. In this, you can know transformation in the formless, and the formless in transformation.

People each have their own nature and circumstance, so there are many different teachings. But inquire into dark-enigma records, and you find the original source-tissue of sage thought. Then you'll never leave thusness-clarity for a false and strange mind. Emptiness has its own singular illumination, the illumination of formlessness, and with it you never lose the ability to respond in harmony with the situation. Look into the movements of perennial transformation, and don't rely on some wordless teaching of formlessness. Begin with Presence no different than Absence, and Absence no different than Presence—then you'll never live without Presence, and never live without Absence.

Hence the saying, *Master motionless awareness, and you abide in all dharmas.* If you use this to move forward, to actualize stillness, what can stop you? And then, why talk about what we know when we look into perennial transformation, or how it's any different than the illumination of formlessness?

In considering my discourse, I'm afraid you've neglected to mention how emptiness encompasses two different minds—tranquil and headlong. And so, you talk about what we know when we look into perennial transformation, but you never say what that knowing does not encompass. If you can get free of that old mind cloistered within you—then you can search through dark-enigma's loom-of-origins outside our human realm, balance the ten thousand things in primal-unity emptiness, and understand with lit clarity how to dwell in that emptiness excluding nothing. Then you can speak of moving all day in accord with each moment, moving and changing with things, mounting the turning seasons and responding in harmony with transformation. Never clinging to anything: that is sage mind. How can we cling and grasp at things, and then talk about the inner-pattern of never grasping and never letting go?

You write: "Absence exists, and thusness all clarity-absolute exists. Absence inheres, and everything that comes to pass inheres."

That sounds like Buddha Existence-Tissue Arrival talking. But if Absence no-mind inhabits what exists, and what exists inhabits Absence no-mind; if Absence no-mind inhabits what inheres, and what inheres inhabits Absence no-mind—then all day long you exist without needing Absence to *exist*; and all day long you inhere without needing Absence to *inhere*. Just fear existing where Absence exists, inhering where Absence inheres. That's how trouble starts. Why? When you say thusness all clarity-absolute *exists*, when you say everything that comes to pass *inheres*—you've replaced the actual with the appearances of names.

This life is lovely one moment, foul the next—and it's terrifying how suddenly the days of a lifetime slip away. Who can stop it? That's why a sage cherishes emptiness vast as sky, emptiness without even the Absence of knowing. If you master that, you can work at everyday business, and yet abide in the realm of Absence-action. You can wander the inner realm of names, and yet inhabit wildlands far from words. Still and solitary, empty and boundless—the appearances names conjure have nothing to do with you. You are exactly what you are, and nothing else.

So when you say "thusness all clarity-absolute *exists*" and "everything that comes to pass *inheres*," it's not wordless and elegant insight. I'm afraid once *exists* and *inheres* arise, they replace the reality of things themselves. They have no reality, so how could they fulfill the reality of things themselves? Once that word-trace begins, you've set out on a different path altogether. But words include everything wordless, and that path includes everything pathless. This is using words to make words whole, searching words for what is beyond words. It's taking the path to make the path whole, searching the path for what is beyond the path.

Just master dark-enigma's inner-pattern emptiness—then you realize mind is itself already fallacy, especially when it's caught in words. Then realization's just something twisting in the distance, I'm afraid. But if you possess a mind that penetrates the whole—you dwell out beyond silver-tongued sutras, trusting instead to the actual and immediate. [93–100]

道生　謝靈運

Way-Born (Tao Sheng, ca. 360–434)
and Hsieh Ling-yün (385–433)

As we have seen in the discussion of Sangha-Fundament (p. 78), Way-Born was instrumental in disseminating Sangha-Fundament's insights. But he was also a profound and influential philosopher himself. Although we know he wrote extensively, little of his original thinking survived. He is generally known in fragments and secondary sources for his emphasis on a number of concepts important to Ch'an: instantaneous enlightenment, a revolutionary idea completely original to Way-Born; and two concepts adapted from Indian sutras: all beings have Buddha-nature, and nirvana is *samsara* (this realm of our everyday lives). But perhaps more important is how Way-Born continued the reconfiguration of Dhyana Buddhism as Dark-Enigma Learning. The most dramatic example may be how, in his preface to a translation of the *Nirvana Sutra*, Way-Born states directly that awakening means dwelling integral to *tzu-jan* (occurrence-appearing-of-itself), which he identifies with inner-pattern.

The particular clarities of Way-Born's innovations survive primarily in Hsieh Ling-yün's "Source-Ancestral Discourse," which attempts to think through the teachings of Way-Born, the "master of Way with a new doctrine" that the essay mentions several times. Hsieh Ling-yün first visited Thatch-Hut Mountain sometime around 412. Although he never lived there, Hsieh visited numerous times and remained close to the East-

Forest sangha, especially Way-Born. Typical of artist-intellectuals in his day, Hsieh's conceptual world was defined by Dark-Engima Learning's cosmology/ontology. Through his association with the East-Forest sangha, most notably his friendship with Way-Born, he absorbed the proto-Ch'an thinking initiated by Sangha-Fundament and elaborated by Way-Born, thinking that infused his Dark-Enigma Learning framework with profound new dimensions.

In addition to being the most renowned poet of the age and a celebrated calligrapher, Hsieh was the patriarch of China's most illustrious family. As such, he was very involved in politics, which took him often to the southern capital, where Way-Born was living. Because of disputes with the emperor, he was exiled in 422 to the coastal mountains of southeast China. Living in seclusion there, he devoted himself to Buddhist and poetic practice, and in a few months transformed himself completely. Hsieh's proto-Ch'an understanding had surely been deepening steadily since his first visit to Thatch-Hut Mountain, including no doubt some awakening experiences, but he apparently underwent an intense Ch'an awakening in those coastal mountains, and that awakening shaped his epochal poetry. At the same time, it led Hsieh to write "Source-Ancestral Discourse." Although the basic approach came from Way-Born (and Sangha-Fundament), Hsieh elaborated and shaped the ideas according to his own understanding.

If we could locate the birth of Ch'an in any single moment, "Source-Ancestral Discourse" would be that moment. (It has, nonetheless, never before been translated into English.) Ch'an deconstruction is already complete here in Hsieh's essay, and all the elements of Ch'an awakening are in play. Among the panoply of Taoist concepts he employs—Tao/Way, Absence, Presence, *tzu-jan*—Hsieh focuses especially on two: the source-ancestral (宗) of the title, and inner-pattern (理), both of which we have already encountered in Sangha-Fundament's "*Prajna Absence-Knowing Discourse.*"

In the blur of concepts at deep cosmological/ontological levels, *source-ancestral* seems virtually indistinguishable from Way or Absence, and it is elsewhere described as equivalent to Absence-action (*wu-wei*). The full dimensions of this concept are revealed dramatically in the etymologies of its two pictographic elements: 宀 and 示. 宀 simply means "roof" and is a stylized version of 𝖓, the early form that portrays a side-view of the traditional Chinese roof with its prominent ridgeline and curved form. 示 derives from 川 and the more ancient oracle-bone form 𝕿, showing heaven as the line above, with three streams of light emanating earthward from the three types of heavenly bodies: sun, moon, and stars. These three sources of light were considered bright distillations of, or embryonic origins of *ch'i*, the breath-force that pulses through the Cosmos as both matter and energy simultaneously. Hence, 宗 is the cosmological source of *ch'i* as a dwelling-place, a dwelling-place that is the very source of the Cosmos.

The common meaning of 示 was simply "altar," suggesting a spiritual space in which one can be in the presence of those celestial *ch'i*-sources. And indeed, enlightenment for Hsieh was to inhabit this dwelling-place altar, as it was for Chuang Tzu, who described a sage as one who "holds fast to the source-ancestral." But there's more, a variation on the Ch'an insight that we are always already enlightened, an insight already present here in "Source-Ancestral Discourse." When enlightenment is understood this way, practice only delays final-and-total awakening—and indeed, the common meaning of 宗 is "ancestor," which suggests a remarkable sense of the source as ancestral to us, as kindred. And so, we find the source-ancestral is always already our very nature.

At these levels, source-ancestral is scarcely distinguished from inner-pattern—a primary concept in "Source-Ancestral Discourse," but also a major presence in the Ch'an literature to follow, where it is already central to practice and awakening in the teachings of Bodhidharma at the legendary beginning of Ch'an a century after Hsieh. Originally referring to the veins and markings in a precious piece of jade, inner-pattern is the system of principles according to which the ten thousand things burgeon forth spontaneously from the generative tissue of Absence. In the thought of Way-Born and Hsieh, inner-pattern is scarcely distinguishable from Tao/Way, *tzu-jan*, Absence, Absence-action (*wu-wei*), source-ancestral, and such Buddhist concepts as *sunyata*, Buddha, and dharma. It simply emphasizes the mysterious organizing capacity of reality as a single generative tissue. This is indicative of the Ch'an blur of cosmological/ontological concepts already present in the tradition, a blur that entails a reconfiguration of Buddhist concepts: Buddha, for instance, is here identical with the ten thousand things in their vast transformations, *tzu-jan*, Tao/Way, and Absence.

For Way-Born and Hsieh, awakening is dwelling as integral to inner-pattern. Hsieh incorporates this into landscape practice, recognizing that inner-pattern is revealed most immediately and dramatically in rivers-and-mountains landscape. For Hsieh, this awakening is available through *adoration* (賞)—a concept not mentioned in the essay, but that recurs in the poems. *Adoration* denotes an aesthetic experience of the wild rivers-and-mountains realm "mirrored" as a single overwhelming whole. It is this aesthetic experience that Hsieh's poems try to evoke in the reader (pp. 104–6). Here we find another seminal dimension of Hsieh's work: the deep philosophical connection of Ch'an and land-scape, Ch'an as essentially landscape practice. And indeed, after his awakening in 422, Hsieh made his home in the remote mountain land-scape of southeast China.

With their grandiose language, headlong movement, and shifting perspective, Hsieh's poems were especially celebrated for possessing an elemental power that captures the dynamic spirit and inner rhythms infusing the numinous realm of rivers-and-mountains. In this, they replace narrow human concerns with a mirror-still mind that sees its truest self in the vast and complex dimensions of mountain wilderness. This mirroring, which we have already seen multiple times, will become central to Ch'an, where it is cultivated in meditation practice. And as rivers-and-mountains landscape is the most magisterial manifestation of Tao/Way, Hsieh's inner-pattern awakening is essentially the awake-ning of Lao Tzu and Chuang Tzu, wherein self is integral to the ongoing cosmological/ontological process of Tao/Way. Indeed, another espe-cially crucial innovation in Hsieh is the identification of empty-mind with the generative tissue of Absence, emblematic of how Buddhism's abstract or metaphysical approach becomes in Ch'an earthy and empir-ical. And of course it is conceived in terms of landscape practice in which that empty-mind "mirrors the whole":

> Only by becoming Absence and mirroring the whole can you
> return to the final-and-total enlightenment of inner-pattern's
> primal-unity.

Hsieh Ling-yün represents a remarkable origin moment for Ch'an and Chinese culture, a condensary where so much converges and comes alive transformed: Taoist Dark-Enigma Learning, Ch'an, poetry, landscape. Hsieh's "Source-Ancestral Discourse" is, again, perhaps *the* formative moment in Ch'an's development. Broadly influential among the intellectual community during and after Hsieh's time—including, as we will see, Bodhidharma a century later (p. 122)—it is the earliest surviving text to describe Ch'an's famously distinctive idea of awakening as instantaneous and complete, and only achievable outside language and teaching. As with Sangha-Fundament and Way-Born before him, native Taoism provides the conceptual framework for Ch'an practice and awakening for Hsieh. And further, he places his discussion clearly within the classical Chinese tradition, casting Confucius and Lao Tzu as exemplars. At the same time, he explicitly rejects the approach of imported Indian Buddhism.

But Hsieh is primarily remembered as a giant of Chinese poetry.[6] He and his contemporary T'ao Ch'ien invented the operating assumptions that shaped mainstream poetry through the centuries and dynasties that followed. First among these is a direct and personal voice speaking of immediate experience. No less important, they took rivers-and-mountains landscape as the essential context for poetic insight. Both of these characteristics are associated with the Ch'an understanding that was taking shape at the time: that awakening comes from empty-mind mirroring of immediate everyday things, and the understanding that such mirroring is most intensely called into play by the drama of mountain landscape. This marks the beginning of poetry seen as a form of Ch'an practice and teaching, an assumption that would define virtually all poetry to follow. In this, Ch'an and poetry share a single origin and remain inextricably linked throughout their histories.

NOTE

For translation comparison: there is no translation of Hsieh Ling-yün's "Source-Ancestral Discourse."

Source-Ancestral Discourse

I often wander these coastal mountains with friends, monks and masters of Way. Karmic transformations brought us together here, mind and spirit, searching for the insight beyond words that understands Way. Sick in bed, no official work, I've got time on my hands—so I'll try to recreate the evolution of our *ch'i*-weave thought, and perhaps settle the search for source-ancestral awakening.

According to Buddha's teaching, the Way of a sage may be remote, but through earnest study it can be realized—for he taught that ending the tangles of thought and bringing the mirror to life, you come to a gradual awakening. According to Confucius's teaching, the Way of a sage is so mysterious even Sunset-Peak Return[7] never quite mastered it—for he taught that only by becoming Absence and mirroring the whole can you return to the final-and-total enlightenment of inner-pattern's primal-unity.[8]

But there is a master of Way with a new doctrine that says the tranquil mirror is all mystery and shadowed-emergence, and without partial stages or degrees. There are no limits to where earnest study can lead, so where could it complete itself? Here today, I reject Buddha's gradual awakening, and choose instead realization itself. And I reject Confucius's never-quite-mastered, and choose instead the final-and-total enlightenment of primal-unity.

This final-and-total enlightenment of primal-unity is altogether different than gradual awakening, and realization is not at all never-quite-mastered. An understanding of inner-pattern rejects both and yet chooses each. In this, it's far from either Buddha or Confucius. I think the two of them only taught as they did because they were trying to rescue sentient beings. But the teachings of this Taoist master explain insight *ch'i*-deep.

My friends and I ventured to analyze this new doctrine, and explain just what it is. We humbly tried to unravel its implications *ch'i*-deep, and slowly discover what awakening might be.

Dharma-Entire asked: "In this doctrine of reverent mirror-clarity, primal-unity awakening instantaneous and whole comes when you fathom with illuminated insight the source-ancestral, final-and-total just there where things emerge. However delighted I am with this new discovery, there are still things I wonder about.

"To fathom with illuminated insight and all the way through, you must become inner-pattern and cut off desires that want things different. We long and long because we're tangled in confusion and doubt. But once you see the source-tissue inner-pattern, you've cut off those desires. We're only tangled in confusion and doubt because we've turned away from the source-ancestral.

"But how can we talk about this? Don't the sutras say that if you chase ever new studies you're far from *prajna*-awakening, illuminated insight lost completely? Absence itself teaches us how to embrace inner-pattern. So it's all perfectly evident here before us—but we're restless and unsure, and once you set out on some gradual search for the great source-ancestral, there's nothing to rely on. If you're still tangled in the tawdry dust of this world, you can struggle for countless *kalpas* and only end up further away, further away and full of sad longing for the contentment of embracing inner-pattern itself.

"I bow and await the sage river of your thought."

I answered: "Way and our everyday lives: without inner-pattern, they seem unrelated. And that's how it is when teachings use words and concepts. Words and concepts only teach the illusions names conjure, but without words and concepts there's no illusion. Wisdom is made of wild thusness all clarity-absolute itself, but there's nothing of that in expedient teaching meant to nurture sentient beings. No-clarity can't diminish clarity, of course, and the source-tissue root is there in expedient teaching. But no-illusion never follows from illusion, and nurturing sentient beings precludes knowing the source-tissue root. You can chase words and concepts for endless *kalpas*, and never become emptiness itself; but with diligent attention, you can know the shimmer of this existence-tissue world brilliant as sunlight."

Dharma-Entire asked again: "Doesn't it follow, then, that the Ways of Confucius and Buddha are the same, that because they both use the illusions names conjure to rescue sentient beings, there's no real difference between them? But in the spirit-Way realm, Sunset-Peak Return alone didn't need instruction from Confucius. And in the appearance-and-reality mystery, simple-minded people all needed instruction from Buddha. Those two sage-masters established profound teachings in words, and how could we ever turn away from them?"

I answered again: "Those two teachings aren't the same. Principles and practices adapted to the individual needs of sentient beings are different in different places. In broad comparison: those differences depend on the people. We Chinese easily see the inner-pattern directly, but find it difficult to pursue teachings. So we close off the tangles of learning and open up final-and-total primal-unity. Indians, on the other hand, easily pursue teachings, but find it difficult to see inner-pattern directly. In this, they close off sudden awakening and open up gradual awakening. In gradual awakening, you live blind to the substance of sudden awakening. But in the final-and-total enlightenment of primal-unity, you cut off the very thirst behind tangles of learning. That's exactly how we Chinese achieve inner-pattern awakening—not through the misguided Way of gradual practice, and not through learning. But Indians imagine inner-pattern awakening comes through learning and the misguided Way of gradual practice.

"So even if sudden and gradual seem the same in substance, teachings using words and concepts are in practice always different. The old masters considered primal-unity itself to be the Way of learning, so how could the teachings of Confucius and Lao Tzu not be the same? Both probe the source-ancestral, and more: the very substance of things, that wild thusness all clarity-absolute itself!"

Dharma-Entire asked a third time: "How deeply your answers search! Whether Chinese or Indian, people by nature find insight both difficult and easy. That's why the teachings of Confucius and Buddha are both alike and different. We admire keeping deep principles and practices close to the commonplace, but the superior practice is to make the dark final-and-total abyss into a bright and clear mirror. Simple-minded people following along dull and blind—that's inferior. It leads to the precept of teaching according to people's needs, and the faith that people just following along will certainly realize the source-ancestral.

"Confucius abandoned the road of sage learning; Buddha opened the path of gradual awakening. But the traps and snares⁹ of words trying to capture insight: they're all confusion and error. So how can the people return to wild thusness all clarity-absolute itself?"

I answered a third time: "Winter and summer are different in nature, but they share spring and autumn in their beginnings and endings. Day and night are different in reality, but they share dusk and dawn in their departures and returns. It's like that for the essential inner-pattern, too—but how can coarse people come to realize it?

"Those who don't trust gradual awakening nurture silence to fashion sudden liberation. Those who trust reverent teachings obscure themselves to become masters of learning. Masters of learning never leave the six classics, as if classics could lead to sudden liberation. And they don't see *Tripitaka* scriptures are just traps and snares one after another. Who can doubt it's all confusion and error? Only after you've got fish and rabbit, only then can you nurture the people."

Sangha-Allied asked: "According to this dharma teacher's new doctrine, the final-and-total source-ancestral is all mystery and shadowed-emergence, and without partial stages or degrees. But surely we can understand Presence final-and-total through learning. As for Absence— if occurrence-appearing-of-itself is Absence and Presence in perfect accord, how could you speak of Absence alone? And if you depend on Absence to understand Presence exhaustively, how can we not call that gradual awakening?"

I answered: "If you haven't ended the tangles of thought and learning, you cannot realize Absence. To realize Absence, you must end those tangles through to the last trace. All those tangles of thought and learning extinguished: that is itself Absence.

"To be sincere in that perfect accord of Absence and Presence, and thereby clear away those tangles, you must stay free of all teachings. Here in the seasons of Presence, you'll never reach awakening through learning. It's only outside learning that you'll realize awakening. Teachings with partial stages or degrees: that's just talk for simple-minded people. It's the doctrine of primal-unity awakening that understands *ch'i*-deep."

Sangha-Allied asked again: "This new doctrine says that awakening is outside Presence and not gradual. But those who seek the source-ancestral through learning—couldn't they get closer to its illumination day-by-day? Maybe that's nothing like source-ancestral illumination itself, illumination you can't reach day-by-day because it's altogether different than words—but people can get closer through day-by-day practice, can't they? And isn't that gradual awakening?"

I answered again: "Source-ancestral illumination is not realized gradually. Only faith comes from teachings, for you can't talk about illumination. Because this faith comes from teachings, it fosters the illusion that there's some merit in day-by-day practice, that practice will bring you closer to illumination. But because source-ancestral illumination is not gradual, entry into its radiance cannot be partial or divided. Indeed, that radiant illumination is where mind whole in the presence of Way arises.

"Suppress the tangles of thought and learning, and you suppress delusion. That suppression alone seems like Absence, and a mind whole seems simple as turning away from the broken and confused. But even this practice is not at all like Absence no-mind altogether source-tissue without a tangle of thought or learning anywhere. And that is the primal-unity awakening that ends at once all ten thousand obstructions."

Sangha-Allied asked a third time: "You just said *Because this faith comes from teachings, it fosters the illusion that there's some merit in day-by-day practice, that practice will bring you closer to illumination. And because source-ancestral illumination is not gradual, entry into its radiance cannot be partial or divided.* But suppose someone venerates teachings and through them explores the source-ancestral. It may not last forever—but can't they, at least for a few moments during that exploration, become integral to Absence? Assuming such momentary integration exists, surely it offers more wisdom than no integration at all. And how could it happen without gradual practice?"

I answered a third time: "Momentary integration is an illusion names conjure. Wild thusness all clarity-absolute itself: that's what endures. Illusion-understanding is not enduring, and understanding that endures is not illusion. Now, how can anyone use momentary illusion-understanding to cross over into the thusness-clarity understanding that endures? . . ."

Prajna-Piebald asked: "The primal-unity integration that comes of illusion-understanding: is it the same as thusness-clarity understanding, or different?"

I answered: "It's different than thusness-clarity understanding."

Prajna-Piebald asked again: "How is it different?"

I answered again: "If you come to illusion-understanding by suppressing the tangles of thought and learning, you only find inner-pattern's momentary actualization. Because inner-pattern's actualization is only momentary, illusion-understanding is not enduring. But if you come to thusness-clarity understanding by illuminating the tranquil mirror, you find inner-pattern's enduring actualization. And because inner-pattern's actualization is enduring, thusness-clarity understanding is perennial."

Prajna-Piebald asked a third time: "Tangles of thought and learning can't clear themselves away, and so we search out inner-pattern to clear them away. In the primal-unity integration that comes of illusion-understanding, inner-pattern's substance is there in the mind. But even with it there in the mind, the tangles of thought and learning aren't rooted out. How do you root them out?"

I answered a third time: "According to the gradual method, when tangles of thought arise, mind begins. And once mind is involved, more tangles appear. When the tangles of thought endure in that involvement, mind is just dark confusion day after day. Trust teachings, and you can suppress mind day after day. And by suppressing the tangles of thought completely and for a long time, you can extinguish those tangles. And so, in this method, those tangles are extinguished only after suppressing them.

"But however much they may seem the same, suppressing the tangles of thought is altogether different than extinguishing them. We need to understand this deeply. With those tangles extinguished—self and things are together forgotten, and you gaze into Absence and Presence as a single primal-unity. With those tangles merely suppressed—self and others still seem distinct, and you see emptiness and reality as different. When reality and emptiness are different, self and others distinct, you've gone inward into obstruction. But when Absence and Presence are a single primal-unity, self and things integral, you've gone outward into radiant illumination."

Poems of Hsieh Ling-yün

Stone-House Mountain

Searching out new realms all origin-dark quiet,
I sail in morning clarity out beyond farmlands,

swept along past shallows crowded with orchids,
moss-covered peaks towering vast and majestic.

Here, Stone-House floats above outland forests,
a waterfall tumbling down from the rocky dome,

its empty cascade drifting through millennia
below summits outlasting the shift of dynasties.

Nowhere near village sights and sounds, distant
wind and mist keep even woodland foragers away,

but after longing to climb peaks since childhood,
I'll keep these close through the dusk of old age.

A sacred land long since wrapped in solitude:
it seems to share this mind adoration conjures,

and come to this accord that's empty of all words,
I gather its blossoms, savor thickets in cold bloom.

Crossing the Lake from South Mountain to North Mountain

I set out from sunlit shores just after dawn
and stopped among shadowy peaks at dusk,

leaving the boat to gaze at far-off islands.
Pausing to rest high among thriving pines

where the pitched trail enters recluse depths
above ringed dragon-jade isles all ashimmer,

I see treetops tangling away into sky below,
hear rivers above flooding the Great Valley.[10]

Streams branch past rocks and flow away.
Forest paths are grown over, tracks gone.

Isn't this how heaven-and-earth touches us,
this exquisite burgeoning forth of things:

young bamboo still wrapped in green slips
and new rushes fluttering purple flowers,

seagulls frolicking along springtime shores
and pheasants at play among gentle breezes?

Embracing change, the mind never tires,
and gazing deep, our love for things grows.

I have no regrets this far from humankind.
It's true there are no kindred spirits here,

but wandering alone I feel only adoration,
and without it, who plumbs the inner-pattern?

Following Axe-Bamboo Stream, I Cross Over
a Ridge and Hike on Along the River

Though the cry of gibbons means sunrise,
its radiance hasn't touched this valley all

origin-dark quiet. Clouds gather below cliffs,
and there's still dew glistening on blossoms

when I set out along a wandering stream,
climbing into narrow canyons far and high.

Ignoring my robe to wade through creeks,
I scale cliff-ladders and cross distant ridges

to the river beyond. It snakes and twists,
but I follow it, happy just meandering along

past pepperwort and duckweed drifting deep,
rushes and wild rice in crystalline shallows.

Reaching tiptoe to ladle sips from waterfalls
and picking still unfurled leaves in forests,

I can almost see that lovely mountain spirit
in a robe of fig leaves and sash of wisteria.

Gathering orchids brings no dear friends
and picking hemp-flower no open warmth,

but the heart finds its beauty in adoration,
and you can't talk out such shadowy things:

in the eye's depths you're past worry here,
awakened into things all wandering away.

陶潛

T'ao Ch'ien (365–427)

AFTER TRYING FOR YEARS TO LIVE THE CONVENTIONAL and secure life of a government bureaucrat, T'ao Ch'ien left for his family farm on Thatch-Hut Mountain, where he lived out his life as a poor farmer. He was drawn to that life by a commitment to inhabiting the Taoist/Ch'an cosmology in his everyday life, the same commitment that was coming to define Ch'an. And indeed, like Hsieh Ling-yün, he described his homecoming as a return to *tzu-jan*, occurrence-appearing-of-itself. T'ao's Thatch-Hut Mountain farm was close to East-Forest Monastery, and he associated with the sangha there. He no doubt knew of the formative Ch'an project centered at East-Forest, but he chose to remain an outsider. According to legend, he was often invited to participate in the sangha, but refused because wine was not allowed.

T'ao was the first in a long line of poets for whom wine was as good as Ch'an for enlightenment. They saw that wine, too, can be a great teacher—sipping wine as a way of easing self-consciousness, thereby clarifying awareness of the ten thousand things by dissolving the separation between inside and outside. So with the help of wine, T'ao cultivated the insight of Thatch-Hut Mountain itself. And there was a second dimension to wine as a teacher: getting thoroughly drunk as a way of opening oneself to Absence-action, action as the wild and selfless energy of the Cosmos, which is the other aspect of enlightenment for ancient

Ch'an. The practice of wine therefore reveals in simple outlines the two aspects of Ch'an awakening: emptiness and wildness.

There is always a testy relationship between Ch'an wisdom and the Ch'an institution, for that wisdom is invariably described as outside teaching. T'ao is an early exemplar of the Ch'an figure who understands that we are always already enlightened, with no need for long institutional practice. In this, his life at the margins of a proto-Ch'an community became a legendary archetype. His poetry embodies Ch'an's insistence that awakening inheres in our everyday immediate experience. In stark contrast to the abstract philosophies of Dark-Enigma Learning and contemporaneous Buddhist philosophers, philosophies he no doubt knew well, T'ao was the first writer to make a fully achieved poetry of his natural voice and immediate experience. In this, he anticipates Hsieh Ling-yün by perhaps twenty years. Although the two may have met, it's unlikely Hsieh knew T'ao's poetry because it was entirely unrecognized in T'ao's lifetime. The two poets seemingly came to this innovative way of writing independently, which suggests that it grew out of the formative-Ch'an thinking of their time.

As we have seen, this Ch'an-inspired personal lyricism became the hallmark of Chinese poetry. So T'ao Ch'ien, with his Ch'an-inspired poetry, effectively stands at the head of the great Chinese poetic tradition like a revered grandfather: profoundly wise, self-possessed, quiet, comforting. And in this, he was a great Ch'an teacher who established poetry as a primary form of Ch'an teaching and practice, an assumption shared by virtually all great Chinese poets to follow.

Unlike Hsieh Ling-yün, whose poems are animated by the need to establish an enlightened relationship with a grand alpine wilderness, T'ao effortlessly lived everyday life on a mountain farm as an utterly sufficient experience of dwelling. And though this dwelling meant confronting death and the existential realities of human experience (notably his own poverty) without delusion—a central preoccupation in T'ao Ch'ien and all Chinese poets—the spiritual ecology of Taoist/Ch'an cosmology/ontology provided ample solace. If T'ao's poems seem bland, a quality much admired in them by later poets, it's because they are never animated by the struggle for understanding. Instead, they always begin with the deepest wisdom. Huang T'ing-chien, the great Sung Dynasty calligrapher and Ch'an master, said of T'ao's poetry: "When you've just come of age, reading these poems seems like gnawing on withered wood. But reading them after long experience in the world, it seems the decisions of your life were all made in ignorance."

Drinking Wine

3

Way's been ruins a thousand years.
People all hoard their hearts away:

so busy scrambling after esteemed
position, they'd never touch wine.

But whatever makes living precious
occurs in this one life, and this life

never lasts. It's startling, sudden as
lightning, a hundred years offering

all abundance. Take it! What more
could you hope to make of yourself?

5

I live here in this busy village without
all that racket horses and carts stir up,

and you wonder how that could ever be.
Wherever the mind dwells apart is itself

a distant place. Picking chrysanthemums
at my east fence, I see South Mountain

far off: air lovely at dusk, birds in flight
going home. All this means something,

something absolute: whenever I start
to explain it, I forget words altogether.

After Kuo Chu-pu's Poems

We had warm, wet weather all spring. Now,
white autumn is clear and cold. Dew frozen,

drifting mists gone, bottomless heavens
open over this vast landscape of clarity,

and mountains stretch away, their towering
peaks an unearthly treasure of distance.

These fragrant woodland chrysanthemums
ablaze, green pines lining the clifftops:

isn't this the immaculate heart of beauty,
this frost-deepened austerity? Sipping wine,

I think of recluse masters. A century away,
I nurture your secrets. Your true nature

eludes me here, but taken by quiet, I can
linger this exquisite moon out to the end.

Cha *Festival Day*

Seeing off the year's final day, windblown
snow can't slow this warm weather. Already,

at our gate planted with plum and willow,
there's a branch flaunting lovely blossoms.

If I chant, words come clear. And in wine
I touch countless distances. So much still

eludes me here. Who knows how much with
all this unearthly Manifest Mountain song?

Written One Morning in the 5th Month,
After Assistant-Magistrate Sustain's Poem

It's all an empty boat, oars dangling free,
but return goes on without end. The year

begins, and suddenly, in a moment's glance,
midyear stars come back around, bright

sun and moon bringing all things to such
abundance. North woods lush, blossoming,

rain falls in season from hallowed depths.
Dawn opens. Summer breezes rise. No one

comes into this world without leaving soon.
It's our inner-pattern, which never falters.

At home here in what lasts, I wait out life,
A bent arm my pillow, I keep empty whole.

Follow change through rough and smooth,
and life's never up or down. If you can see

how much height fills whatever you do,
why climb peaks like Flourish and Exalt?

Untitled

Days and months never take their time.
The four seasons keep bustling each other

away. Cold winds churn lifeless branches.
Fallen leaves cover long paths. We're frail,

crumbling more with each turning year.
Our temples turn white early, and once

your hair flaunts that bleached streamer,
the road ahead starts closing steadily in.

This house is an inn awaiting travelers,
and I yet another guest leaving. All this

leaving and leaving—where will I ever
end up? My old home's on South Mountain.

PART IV

Early Ch'an

(6th–7th centuries C.E.)

CH'AN CONTINUED TO DEVELOP UNDER THE AURA OF a mountain: Exalt-Peaks, where according to legend Bodhidharma practiced the "wall-gaze" meditation that led to his final enlightenment. Bodhidharma is traditionally considered the beginning of Ch'an. But that claim emerged from the Ch'an institution's desire to claim a lineage back to Buddha himself. That is, later Ch'an figures created an imaginary Bodhidharma who came from India, where he was in a direct line of lineage reaching back to Buddha, thereby establishing Ch'an as the "true Buddhism." This impulse continued in the creation of a lineage of four more patriarchs following Bodhidharma, leading to the more historically represented (however embellished) Sixth Patriarch (p. 160).

It's odd. After centuries of historically unproblematic figures—Wang Pi and Kuo Hsiang from the Dark-Enigma Learning period; Sangha-Fundament, Way-Born, and Hsieh Ling-yün amalgamating Dark-Enigma Learning and Dhyana Buddhism to form Ch'an—suddenly a kind of legendary period seems interjected from outside the actual evolution of ideas. This legendary beginning of Ch'an—Bodhidharma and the patriarchs linking him directly to the Sixth Patriarch—obscures Ch'an's true lineage as an extension of native Taoism. And as this legendary origin-story for Ch'an is widely adopted in the Ch'an/Zen community, that true lineage is lost to view.

All of this is not to say those early patriarchs didn't exist. They no doubt did in some sense. But the legend is a superficial veneer that obscures their true natures. For as we will see, the texts associated with those figures, the actual ideas and teachings that define them at a deep philosophical level, reveal them to be wholly part of Taoism's evolution into Ch'an. Here we encounter a structure of Ch'an so large and foundational that we barely notice how remarkable it is: the tradition of Ch'an masters as native Chinese sages who were equal to Buddha in their enlightenment, and a "separate transmission outside all teaching" (Bodhidharma) that was passed down through a lineage of those Ch'an masters. This becomes Ch'an's essential historical framework, beginning in a more textually/historically verifiable form with the Sixth Patriarch in the T'ang Dynasty, and followed by a plethora of singular and fully realized sage-masters (part V, pp. 155–244). Here lies the philosophical core of Ch'an: even if institutional Ch'an wanted the imprimatur of a lineage connecting to a quasi-deified Buddha and the whole Buddhist edifice that surrounded him (represented in the massive library of sacred texts translated from Sanskrit), the actual teaching and practice of enlightenment depended only on native and very human Ch'an masters meeting students face-to-face generation after generation.

菩提達磨

Bodhidharma (active ca. 500–540)

IN THE TRADITIONAL ACCOUNT, BODHIDHARMA IS THE great beginning of Ch'an, the First Patriarch—and as we will see, his Ch'an too emerged from the landscape of a great mountain: Exalt-Peaks Mountain in northern China, one of China's "five sacred mountains." Bodhidharma's name says it all, for it means "awakened dharma." In the Ch'an legend, Bodhidharma was the twenty-eighth Indian patriarch in a lineage descending directly from Shakyamuni Buddha himself. He crossed the seas from India to southern China, where he encountered the emperor who ruled southern China (the country was divided into northern and southern dynasties). This emperor was a devout Buddhist, avidly studying scriptures and donating vast fortunes to support Buddhist institutions. In his earnestness, the emperor asked his exotic and sage visitor about Buddhist principles, and Bodhidharma flatly denied any value in Buddhist teachings or good works. He further denied knowing even who he himself was. Given that an emperor was revered and feared as the infallible and all powerful "son of heaven," this was dangerously audacious behavior, and the emperor wasn't pleased. Bodhidharma thereupon crossed the Yangtze River standing on a reed and traveled into the north. There, at Rare-Shrine Forest Monastery (Shao-lin) on Exalt-Peaks Mountain, he sat gazing at a wall in silent meditation for nine years—an echo of the legend in which Buddha attained enlightenment by sitting for seven weeks under the Bodhi tree.

Of this legend, only the association with Rare-Shrine Forest and Exalt-Peaks seems reliable. Otherwise, there is another Bodhidharma, the one we find breathing and speaking in a group of texts gathered under his name and full of Ch'an teaching at a very deep level. Although these texts are of various and unknowable authenticity, they represent the actual Bodhidharma whose teachings had such an outsized influence within the Ch'an tradition. And they reveal a Bodhidharma quite different from the Indian patriarch of Ch'an legend.

China's artist-intellectual class, including Ch'an teachers, would have understood the Bodhidharma legend for what it is: an institutional invention meant to give the Ch'an school a pedigree proving it to be the most authentic school of Buddhism, or a revealing bit of philosophical storytelling. (This in a tradition where philosophy was mostly storytelling, for its purpose was understanding how to live rather than abstract "truth.") They would have seen that Bodhidharma's teachings describe practice and awakening entirely within the Taoist cosmological/ontological framework, summarized in his routine use of key concepts like Tao/Way, Absence and Presence, *tzu-jan* (occurrence-appearing-of-itself), *wu-wei* (Absence-action), inner-pattern, loom-of-origins, potency and actualization (two highly specialized concepts from Dark-Enigma Learning), etc. Indeed, "Outline of the Great Vehicle for Entering Way . . . ," long considered the most authentic of the Bodhidharma texts, begins with the two core concepts from Hsieh Ling-yün's "Source-Ancestral Discourse": *source-ancestral* and *inner-pattern*. Clearly, Bodhidharma knew this essay well. Rather than an Indian sage newly arrived with a body of foreign wisdom, Bodhidharma operated wholly within the framework of philosophical assumptions that had been shared by Chinese artist-intellectuals for centuries.

Typical of Ch'an teachers, Bodhidharma uses some Buddhist terminology in his attempt to engage people trained in conventional Buddhism. But rather than advocating conventional Buddhism, he in fact consistently dismantles it: Ch'an here at its official beginning as thoroughly anti-Buddhist. This begins in the legendary encounter with the emperor, where he dismisses conventional Buddhist practices and knowledge. And it continues in Bodhidharma's teachings, where he replaces a distant demigod Buddha with mind or original-nature as the object of Ch'an cultivation. Further, he condemns traditional practices (the six paramitas,[1] for example) and sutra learning, describes the purpose of practice as "entering Way," redefines karma in Taoist terms as Way unfurling one fact following inevitably after another, effectively replaces all Mahayana (Great Vehicle) teaching with his own wild and anti-Buddhist teachings when he titles his essay "Outline of the Great Vehicle for Entering Way. . . ." And it hardly stops with these examples.

Bodhidharma's "awakened dharma" is perhaps nowhere so clear as in the small poem we encountered in the general introduction (p. 8):

> A separate transmission outside all teaching
> and nowhere founded in eloquent scriptures,
>
> it's simple: pointing directly at mind. There,
> seeing original-nature, you become Buddha.

This is the archetypal distillation of Ch'an's essential elements, each line expressing one of its key ideas. Here, Bodhidharma establishes the terms of Ch'an awakening when he calls it 見性 "seeing original-nature," where "original-nature" is synonymous with "mind" or "empty-mind": consciousness emptied of all content. This phrase was codified as a single term (*chien-hsing*; Japanese: *kensho*) that became one of the two primary terms meaning "enlightenment" or "awakening" in the Ch'an lexicon. This is Bodhidharma's core teaching of radical self-sufficiency and wonder: that awakening is simply seeing the true nature of your own mind, that you are always already an enlightened Buddha and have no need to search elsewhere for enlightenment or Buddhahood. Or in more contemporary terms, that in your original-nature as empty-mind, you are yourself a stunning locale in the topography of the Cosmos, a place where the Cosmos is miraculously open to itself, aware of itself. Radical, and radically exhilarating!

Bodhidharma's great innovation may be that he completed the reconfiguration of what was primarily a philosophical system (Taoism) into a system of spiritual practice (Ch'an). And he established the historical structure through which practice and awakening could be "transmitted" through time as a tradition. Hsieh Ling-yün declared that insight and awakening have nothing to do with words and teachings. Bodhidharma extended this central Ch'an principle, fashioning it into a tradition—a tradition without, in a sense, a tradition. He declared Ch'an is transmitted directly, mind-to-mind and outside of all teaching and texts, and he represents the first teacher operating within that tradition.

In legend, he received transmission through the line of Indian patriarchs stretching back to the first transmission where Buddha held up a flower and Mahakasyapa smiled (see the introduction, p. 6). Though the facts remain shadowy, it is clearly more accurate to say that direct transmission began with Bodhidharma's mind-to-mind transmission to Prajna-Prospect (Hui K'o), the Second Patriarch. Here it is, retold seven hundred years later as a sangha-case (koan) in the great *No-Gate Gateway* collection (p. 285):

> Bodhidharma sat facing a wall. The Second Patriarch stood outside in the snow. To prove his determined sincerity, he cut off his arm and presented it to Bodhidharma, then said: "Your disciple's mind is not yet silent. Please, master, silence this mind."
>
> "Bring your mind here," replied Bodhidharma, "and I'll silence it for you."
>
> "I've searched and searched, but I can't find my mind."
>
> "There, you see, I've silenced your mind through and through."

NOTE

For translation comparison: The poem on the following page appears in D. T. Suzuki's *Zen Buddhism: Selected Writings of D. T. Suzuki* (1956: p. 11) and Heinrich Dumoulin's *Zen Buddhism: A History*, volume 1, *India and China* (1988: p. 85). This poem is discussed in my *China Root: Taoism, Ch'an, and Original Zen*, pp. 13, 126–27.

There are many translations of the seminal "Outline of the Great Vehicle for Entering Way...." The most noteworthy appear in: D. T. Suzuki's *Manual of Zen Buddhism* (1935: p. 73) and *Essays in Zen Buddhism: First Series* (1949: p. 180); Red Pine's *The Zen Teaching of Bodhidharma* (1989:

p. 3); J. C. Cleary's *Zen Dawn* (1991: p. 33); Nelson Foster's *The Roaring Stream* (1996: p. 3); and Jeffrey Broughton's *The Bodhidharma Anthology* (1999: p. 9).

Bracketed numbers in the "Blood-Kin Pulse Discourse" and "Original-Nature Awaken Discourse" refer to page numbers in Red Pine's *The Zen Teaching of Bodhidharma*.

A separate transmission outside all teaching
and nowhere founded in eloquent scriptures,

it's simple: pointing directly at mind. There,
seeing original-nature, you become Buddha.

Outline of the Great Vehicle for Entering Way through the Four Practices and Wall-Gaze Meditation[2]

To enter Way, there are many paths. But in essence, there are only two. One is to enter through inner-pattern, and the other is to enter through practice.

Entering through inner-pattern refers to awakening to the source-ancestral through direct teachings. It begins with a deep trust that everything sentient, everything that cherishes life, it all shares the same original-nature all clarity-absolute. The only reason this original-nature cannot shine forth is because each thing survives in the dust of this world by wanting and scheming. If you cast aside wanting and scheming, you can return to that clarity-absolute. And if you sit gazing at a wall, dwelling in stillness—no self and no other, no difference between commoner and sage-master—if you dwell there resolute and free of scriptural teachings, you can reach deep and mysterious concord with inner-pattern. It's the place where that distinction between Absence and Presence arises,[3] and there you can master the tranquility of Absence-action. That is called *entering through inner-pattern*.

Entering through practice refers to four separate practices. All other practices enter through them. And these four—what are they? The first practice is accepting adversity. The second is abiding in origin-tissue. Third is seeking nothing. And fourth is moving in accord with dharma. Fine, but what on earth is all this, really?

First practice, accepting adversity.
If you have cultivated Way, when sorrow comes, you just think to yourself: "Since distant times, I've wandered countless *kalpas*, abandoning source-tissue roots to follow twigs and branches tangling away, carried along on the ripples and swells of Presence. When adversity has arisen, so often I've despised it, and my struggle against suffering has known no bounds. I've done nothing wrong: this is simply retribution from long

ago. Evil karma comes to fruition, but neither human nor heaven understand how or why. Mind cheerful, I accept adversity without complaint."

The sutra says: *Why grieve when sorrow comes? How can there be a reason for it, or a way to fathom it?* Once you see this, you live integral to inner-pattern. And so, the body's adversity brings mind closer to Way. That's why I talk about the practice of accepting adversity.

Second practice, abiding in origin-tissue.

Everything born is without self, is turned and wheeled in the seasons of origin-tissue karma. Accept joy and grief equally, for both are born of origin-tissue. If I find myself blessed with glory and fame, it's the result of things I went through eons ago. And when any configuration of origin-tissue ends, it all disappears back into Absence. Why delight in its Presence? Success and failure, gain and loss—it all arises from origin-tissue, so how can it enhance or diminish mind? If you're unmoved by the winds of delight, you live belonging to Way, belonging mysterious as a flowing river. That's why I talk about the practice of abiding in origin-tissue.

Third practice, seeking nothing.

People of the world live in confusion. Wherever they go, whatever they do, they long and long. I call this *seeking*. But sages awaken to the wild thusness of things all clarity-absolute. They adopt the inner-pattern and return to the commonplace. Their tranquil minds abide in Absence-action, while their bodies abide in the turning and wheeling seasons.

Presence, the ten thousand things in their vast transformations—it's perfectly empty. There's no joy in longing for something else. The goddesses of prosperity and destitution take turns coming and going, forever arriving and following each other away. Even after you ascend through *samsara*'s three realms, it's all still a house on fire. To have a body is to suffer. How can anyone find peace? Once you understand this world through and through, you stop clinging to things. Just give up all this dreaming and seeking. The sutra says:

> Seek, and there's always grief.
> Seek not, and you realize joy.

Seek not: master that, and you
wander Way all clarity-absolute.

That's why I talk about the practice of seeking nothing.

Fourth practice, moving in accord with dharma.
The inner-pattern of original-nature pure: just recognize that is itself
dharma. In this inner-pattern, all forms and appearances are perfectly
empty: no renunciation and no attachment; no me and no you; no here
and there, now and then. And the sutra says: *In dharma, there is no
individually born thing—for there's no delusion that things are individually born. In dharma, there is no I, no self—for there's no delusion that
individual selves exist.*

A sage trusts that this inner-pattern is itself liberation—and so, moves
in accord with dharma. And dharma's potency isn't stingy. To enrich
your life, offer it all up and give it away. This is first among the six paramitas. Don't be miserly of mind, and you're freed into the liberation of
threefold emptiness: emptiness of the giver, emptiness of the gift, emptiness of the recipient. No reliance and no attachment: that's how you get
free of delusion. In accord with everything born in constant transformation, you're done welcoming some forms and rejecting others. This is a
practice of self-cultivation—but it's also how you profit others. And how
you adorn the majestic Way of *bodhi*-awakening. Offer it all up, just that,
and you'll clear away the other five paramitas as mere fantasy. Then, to
practice the six paramitas is to practice nothing at all. That's the practice
of moving in according with dharma.

Blood-Kin Pulse Discourse

"The blur of everything arising throughout *samsara*'s three realms: it all comes back to primal-unity mind. Buddhas past and future all use mind itself to transmit mind. It's a transmission absolutely not founded in eloquent scriptures."

"If it's a transmission not founded in eloquent scriptures," someone asked, "how do those Buddhas reveal mind?"

Bodhidharma answered: "When you question me—that is your mind exactly. And when I answer—that is my mind exactly. If I didn't have mind, how could I be liberated enough to answer? If you didn't have mind, how could you be liberated enough to question? That questioning: it's your mind exactly. Throughout vast *kalpas* all beginningless distances, throughout all the times and places of your life and everything you do— there's always your original source-tissue mind, always your original source-tissue Buddha.

"*Mind itself is Buddha* amounts to the same thing. Outside of this mind, there is absolutely no other Buddha to find. Outside of this mind, there's nowhere to find *bodhi*-awakening or nirvana. Your own original-nature is the very substance of things, that wild thusness all clarity-absolute itself: free of cause, free of result. Dharma is exactly mind's karma, and your own mind is nirvana—so don't say Buddhas find *bodhi*-awakening somewhere outside of mind. Where would that be?

"Then where is it Buddhas find *bodhi*-awakening? That's like asking if someone can catch hold of empty sky. Empty sky has a name, *mountain-tiger emptiness*, but no actual form. You can't take hold of it, and you can't give it away. You'll never catch hold of empty sky, and you'll never see Buddha outside of mind. Never. You'll only find Buddha in the workings of your own mind. So why go searching anywhere else?

"Buddhas past and future speak only of this mind. Mind is exactly Buddha, and Buddha is exactly mind. Outside of mind there is no Buddha, and outside of Buddha there is no mind. If you say there is Buddha outside of mind, where is your Buddha? There's never been a Buddha outside of mind. How could such a thing have appeared?

"Rapt in imaginings and delusions like that, you'll never comprehend original source-tissue mind. Enthralled by a lifeless mirage, you're never free. If you don't believe that, you're just deluding yourself. And that won't get you anywhere. Buddha is never wrong. The problem is that everyone born into this world is turned upside down. Unenlightened, they don't know their own mind is itself Buddha. If they knew their own mind is Buddha, they wouldn't search outside their mind for Buddha. Buddhas don't pass beyond Buddhas. Use mind to search for Buddha, and you never recognize Buddha. You're just someone gone searching outside for Buddha, someone that's completely failed to recognize your own mind is Buddha.

"Don't use Buddha to worship Buddha, and don't use mind to imagine Buddha. Buddhas don't chant sutras. Buddhas don't keep precepts, and they don't break precepts. Buddhas don't keep or break anything, and they don't do good or evil. If you want to find Buddha, the only way is to see your original-nature. See original-nature, and you are yourself Buddha. Imagining Buddhas and chanting sutras, keeping fasts and precepts: if you don't *see original-nature*, all that won't get you anywhere." [9–11]

"*Buddha* is a term from the language of India. Here in this country, we speak of *original-nature awareness*, pure awareness miraculous beyond words. Moving in accord with the loom-of-origins or integral to the ten thousand things in their vast transformations, eyes open wide in astonishment or glancing quickly, hand twisting or foot stepping: it's all the miraculous pure awareness of your own original-nature.

"That original-nature is exactly mind, and mind is exactly Buddha. Buddha is exactly Way, and Way is exactly Ch'an. And Ch'an—it's just one little word, but no one can fathom it, not commoners and not sages. And we also say that to see original source-tissue nature is itself Ch'an. If you don't see original source-tissue nature, there's no Ch'an. You may be able to explain the thousand sutras and ten thousand discourses thoroughly—but if you don't see your original source-tissue nature, you're just another commoner. Explanations have nothing to do with Buddha-dharma.

"To delve into the depths of Way's origin-dark quiet—it's wisdom no talk can touch. Depending on holy scriptures: that leads nowhere. Just see original source-tissue nature, and you'll realize that wisdom even if you can't read a single word. To see original source-tissue nature is itself Buddha. A sage's potency is from the beginning pure clarity. Without that, it's all tangled confusion. With it, whatever you say is the actualization of mind itself. Potency and its actualization are from the beginning empty. Names and talk will never reach them. And how could even all those sutras in the Twelve Collections reach them? Way is originally perfect and complete: its actualization has nothing to do with evidence or proof. . . .

"Once you see original source-tissue nature, you recognize how the Twelve-Collection sutras are simply idleness given eloquent voice, how the thousand sutras and ten thousand discourses are simply mind radiant in illumination. But when words end, wisdom is whole again. So what good are teachings? You only realize inner-pattern when words fall silent. Teaching is words and stories, and that's certainly not Way. Source-tissue Way has nothing to do with words. Words are illusions." [29–31]

"We sentient beings—if we can only see our original source-tissue nature, all trace of our little obsessions is instantaneously extinguished. Then awareness itself is never obscured. Then you see things with absolute and immediate clarity, and understanding becomes easy. It's simply this wild existence-tissue thusness here before you right now. If you want to understand Way all clarity-absolute, don't cling to any dharma whatsoever. Give up karma and nurture awareness itself. Then all trace of our little obsessions vanishes, and occurrence-appearing-of-itself becomes such radiant illumination.

"Don't strain and struggle. If you search outside of Way itself, you'll never understand Buddha's *ch'i*-weave insight. The more you strain and struggle, the further away you get. If you scurry around all day contemplating Buddha and unrolling sutra scrolls, you're blind to original-nature awareness. You'll never escape the wheel of reincarnation.

"Buddha is all idleness. He didn't scurry around the wide world trying to prove himself and turn a profit. So why should we all these years later? It's so simple, but people fail to *see original-nature*. So they read sutras and contemplate Buddhas, study long and hard, purify and progress. They practice Buddha-Way all day and night, sit in long meditation without sleep, study throughout the wide world, listen to countless teachings. They think that's Buddha-dharma. But people like that only malign Buddha and dharma both. Among Buddhas past and future, there's only one teaching: *seeing original-nature*." [35]

Original-Nature Awaken Discourse

No thought: that is dharma whole and complete. I call this meditation, *ch'an*⁴ *stillness*. Once you comprehend this completely, everything in your life is ch'an stillness—whether you're walking or standing, sitting or sleeping.

To understand mind is empty: I call this *seeing Buddha*. Why? All Buddhas throughout the ten distances of time and space: they're all essentially Absence no-mind. And failing to see this Buddha-Absence in mind: I call this, too, *seeing Buddha*.

To give yourself away without regret: I call this *alms-giving of vast generosity*. To dwell far from all movement and all stillness: I call *this sitting in vast ch'an meditation*. Why? Commoners know only movement, adepts of Indian Lesser-Vehicle Buddhism know only stillness—and sitting in ch'an meditation leaves both commoner and adept far behind. I call this *sitting in vast ch'an meditation*. If you're among those who abide by this wisdom, you're completely done searching this world of form and appearance in hope of finding liberation. And you're completely done trying to heal illnesses in hope of setting out unburdened. All of this is the power of vast meditation, vast ch'an stillness. [49]

Wield mind to study dharma, and you're confused about mind and dharma both. Don't wield mind to study dharma, and you're awakened to mind and dharma both. The confused are confused even in awakening, but the awakened are awakened even in confusion. When you see absolutely, you understand mind is Absence empty—and so, you step beyond confusion and awakening. When you're done with confusion and done with awakening—that's where absolute liberation begins. [55]

Those who cultivate Way never search outside themselves for Way. Why? Because they understand mind is itself Way. To fathom mind, you must fathom Absence no-mind. To fathom Way, you must fathom Absence no-Way. And if you speak of using mind in the search to fathom Way, you've twisted seeing itself into tangles.

When you're confused, there's Buddha and there's dharma. When you're awakened, there's no Buddha and no dharma. Why? Because awakening is itself the Buddha and dharma of Buddha-dharma. [59]

There's absolutely nothing anyone can say that isn't Buddha-dharma exactly. If you inhabit Absence and talk all day long—it's Way. If you inhabit Presence and keep silent all day long—it's not Way. That's why, for Buddha Existence-Tissue Arrival, words didn't need silence, and silence didn't need words. Words and silence: there's no difference. Once you're awakened to this, you inhabit *samadhi*'s three-shadowed earth.

When you understand all this and speak, your words are liberation. When you don't understand and stay silent, silence only ties you down. And so, if they are free of form and appearance, words are liberation. But if it's attached to form and appearance, silence ties you down. The liberation of original source-tissue nature: it's there even in eloquent scriptures. How could eloquent scriptures ever tie it down? Those ties that hold you down: they're not anywhere in eloquent scriptures. [65]

鑑智僧璨

Mirror-Wisdom Sangha-Jewel
(Seng Ts'an, ca. 529–613)

EVEN THOUGH THE CH'AN TRADITION ENSHRINES MIRROR-Wisdom Sangha-Jewel as its Third Patriarch, very little is known about his life. But it seems mountains played a major role—for it is said that he lived with the Second Patriarch in obscurity among remote mountains to avoid political turmoil and persecution of Buddhists. Nevertheless, the nature of Sangha-Jewel's understanding survives with clarity in his long poem "Fact-Mind Inscription" (信心銘). This poem is broadly influential: often quoted by later teachers in the Chinese tradition, and now widely translated and chanted by practitioners in the modern West.

This "Fact-Mind Inscription" reveals itself as integral to the native Chinese intellectual tradition in a number of ways. It is written in the austere four-words-per-line form of *The Book of Songs*, the most ancient of China's poetic texts. This form was employed in the poetic tradition to give a work the aura of ancient wisdom. More generally, poetry was commonly used in ancient China to allow the most direct and concise statement of ideas. And "Fact-Mind Inscription" is indeed a remarkably distilled philosophical presentation of Ch'an practice and insight, as well as the conceptual framework underpinning that practice and insight. And that framework is Taoist through and through.

Remarkably, if we didn't know the author's identity, we might guess it was written by a sage in the neo-Taoist Dark-Enigma Learning school, or perhaps even Lao Tzu himself. While Buddhist terminology appears only twice in the poem (*One Vehicle* and *dharma*), all of the foundational terms in Taoist cosmology/ontology appear, often numerous times: *Tao/Way, Absence, Presence, tzu-jan, wu-wei, dark-enigma*. In addition, the poem is woven from themes borrowed from the seminal Taoist sages Lao Tzu and Chuang Tzu. One example is undifferentiated mind—essentially Ch'an empty-mind, consciousness prior to the distinctions created by words and concepts. Lao Tzu uses the metaphor of "uncarved wood" or "uncarved simplicity" for this undivided mind. Both he and Chuang Tzu denounce words and concepts, as well as judgments/choices (*"yes this* and *no that"*), as violations of undifferentiated mind. It is a theme that pervades the "Fact-Mind Inscription" and Ch'an more broadly, for it is a fundamental example of how the conceptualizations of "differentiated mind" alienate consciousness from the tissue of existence.

The poem's title, 信心銘, is layered with readings made possible by the range of meanings contained in 信: faith, belief, trust, truth, accurate, sincerity, empirical fact/evidence. (The other two ideograms are relatively straightforward: "mind" + "inscription.") The title is often translated with some formulation translating 信 as "faith/belief": "Inscribed on the Believing Mind" (R. H. Blyth and D. T. Suzuki) or various formulations of "Belief/Faith in Mind" (D. T. Suzuki's second version, Thomas Cleary, Andy Ferguson, Sheng Yen). But using the religious language of Christianity injects a foreign conceptual framework that only confuses our understanding of Ch'an. "Trust" is better, as the poem emphasizes mind itself as the center of Ch'an understanding and practice: "On Trust in Mind" (Arthur Waley, Burton Watson).

In any case, these translations open nothing of the philosophical dimensions at play here. "Sincerity" is a better translation: "Sincerity-Mind Inscription." This begins to address those philosophical dimensions, the actual content of the poem, which define a mind of "sincerity" as an undifferentiated mind. But there is a deeper sense of "sincerity": a correlation between mind and reality, portrayed in the ideogram's pictographic structure showing a person (人, a person seen from the side) standing beside words (言, sounds rising out of a mouth). Hence, the spoken content of mind correlating with the reality of action or fact. This idea of an integration of mind and empirical fact leads to the final layer of meaning for 信: "empirical facts" or "that which provides empirical evidence." Hence the translation used here: "Fact-Mind Inscription." This represents the deepest realization of mind undifferentiated. Rather than mind simply undifferentiated within, as we might expect in the traditional Buddhist context, it is mind also undifferentiated from the empirical world of *facts*. And indeed, mind must first be undifferentiated within itself as empty mirror-mind if it is to be undifferentiated from the world of empirical fact.

信 appears in two passages of the poem itself, the first of which is line 112

正	信	調	直
utter/pure	sincerity/fact	harmonize	sight-clarity

Translating 信 as "sincerity" gives us something like "[mind] utter sincerity become sight-clarity absolute." Here *sincerity* describes mind undifferentiated, and therefore without conceptual distinctions: hence, the tissue of reality known as a single organic whole. But reading 信 more properly as "fact" gives us something like "facts themselves sight-clarity pure." This reading is especially suggested because the pictographic etymology of 直 renders an eye seeing with direct immediacy: ⽬. Hence, "the eye seeing straight," from which came "straight, honest, direct" and eventually "real, actual, perfectly true." But its deeper meaning suggests sight mirroring things wholly, filling mind wholly with "facts." This gives a deeper meaning of the "absolute clarity of sight seeing deeply and purely" (and indeed, another meaning of 信 is "accurate").

The second appearance of 信 in the poem is lines 143–44, where it appears in a phrase with 心 (mind), exactly as in the title:

信	心	不	二
fact	mind	not	two

不	二	信	心
not	two	fact	mind

Rendering 信 as "sincerity," we get "sincerity-mind is undifferentiated; / undifferentiated is sincerity-mind." These lines are essentially the end of the poem, for the two lines that follow them simply say there is nothing more to say. And it is the title's source in the poem, so it is clearly the heart of the poem. And when 信 is rendered as "fact," we can see why—for it opens the idea of "sincerity-mind" undifferentiated within, the theme developed throughout the poem, to its most complete realization as undifferentiation with the world outside. Here it is clear the two terms 信 and 心 are nouns contrasted to each other, nouns commonly considered radically separate. Hence the Ch'an surprise of declaring them not separate:

> Fact and mind not two things,
> not two things fact and mind.

And this integration happens through empty mirror-mind perception, which in Ch'an is summarized as sight: hence the "sight clarity-absolute" that recurs in the poem, as in line 112 where 信 first appears. This integration of fact and mind is the final fulfillment of the first reading of 信 as "undifferentiated sincerity." And the poem goes on in the final couplet to say that this integration of fact and mind is where words and explanations end.

NOTE

For translation comparison: There are many translations of the "Fact-Mind Inscription," under titles that are variations on "Faith/Belief/ Trust in Mind." The most noteworthy are: D. T. Suzuki's *Manual of Zen Buddhism* (1935: p. 91) and *Essays in Zen Buddhism: First Series* (1949: p. 196); Arthur Waley in Edward Conze's *Buddhist Texts through the Ages* (1954: p. 295); R. H. Blyth's *Zen and Zen Classics*, volume 1 (1960: p. 46); Burton Watson in Samuel Bercholz and Sherab Chodzin Kohn's *Entering the Stream: An Introduction to the Buddha and His Teachings* (1993: p. 147); Sheng Yen's *Faith in Mind* (2006: p. 5); Andy Ferguson's *Zen's Chinese Heritage* (2011: p. 499).

Fact-Mind Inscription

It isn't hard to inhabit Tao's Way.
Just stop picking and choosing,

stop hating this and loving that,
and you're there bright and clear.

A hair-width distinction is error
enough to split heaven-and-earth:

to face Tao's shimmering Way
simply give up like and dislike,

for battling things you dislike
is mind's great disease. It hides   10

wordless dark-enigma depths,
turns tranquil thought into toil.

Emptiness where all things begin,
never too little or too much, Tao's

Way is one existence-tissue whole.
In choosing and refusing, you lose

it absolutely. Don't chase origins
or struggle to dwell in emptiness:

make mind one tranquil embrace
itself complete in that wholeness.   20

Still movement to find stillness,
and stillness keeps on moving,

and stuck in those two options
who knows that one wholeness,

one wholeness you never fathom,
making those two ways useless?

Deny Presence, and it sinks you;
seize emptiness, and it flees you.

Full of talk and clever schemes,
you're confused without a clue: 30

but cut off talk, cut off schemes,
and insight opens clear through.

Returned to root, you find depths.
Chasing light, you lose the source-

ancestral; but turning to your own
light, you see through this empty

world all transformation opening
our illusions. Don't use emptiness

to find the wild thusness in things:
just give up trying to see original-   40

nature this way or that. Take care!
Don't pose even two alternatives:

once *yes this* and *no that*⁵ arise, it's
pure confusion, mind utterly lost.

Any two arise from primal-unity,
primal-unity you cannot inhabit,

for primal-unity mind is unborn.
It keeps all ten thousand dharmas

flawless: no flaw and no dharma,
no birth, no mind. Primal-unity: 50

self ending when factuality ends,
factuality ending when self ends,

self making factuality factuality,
and factuality making self self.

Understand the two, and you see
they are at origin one emptiness,

one emptiness no other than two
containing all ten thousand forms.

Don't insist on muddled or clear-
eyed, then you see things whole.   60

Magisterial Way is a vast potency
nowhere easy, nowhere difficult:

seeing it small is fox-suspicion
churning more and moving less,

clinging to its unfurling, stalled,
tangled in twisty paths. Let it go

and occurrence appears of itself,
potency never staying or leaving.

In original-nature, we wander Way
boundless and free without a care.　　70

Mind fettered, wild thusness lost,
you sink into dark, loving nothing,

and loving nothing kills the spirit,
keeps things distant. Why do that?

To master our One Vehicle, never
resist this world-dust of the senses.

Never resist world-dust: that alone
returns you to pure enlightenment.

Sage-masters live Absence-action;
simpletons tie themselves in knots.　　80

Dharma hasn't different dharmas.
Attachment to this or that: it's our

own illusion. And using mind to
seize mind: isn't that great error?

Stillness and confusion delusion's
invention, love and hate nowhere

in awakening: all such divisions,
they're contemplation's illusions,

dreamt mirage of flowers empty.
Why struggle to grab hold of it?　　90

Success, failure; *yes this*, *no that*:
you can throw them out at once,

for in this eye that never sleeps
dreams all vanish of themselves.

Mind undivided, the ten thousand
dharmas are one existence-tissue,

existence-tissue all dark-enigma
potency, emptiness too forgotten.

Seeing those dharmas whole, you
return to occurrence-appearing-of-   100

itself, without reasons and causes,
without comparison and judgment.

Motion stilled is Absence moving;
stillness moving is Absence stilled:

unless you see both are complete,
how can you know primal-unity?

In clear-through-to-the-very-end
enlightenment, rules utterly gone,

integral mind is wholly uniform
and everything done simple ease,   110

fox-suspicion rinsed clean, mind
facts themselves sight-clarity pure:

it lets things go, clings at nothing,
remembers nothing. Such empty

sage radiance illuminating itself,
mind never exhausts its strength,

never thinks, ponders, fathoms
things seen becoming part of us,

dharma-world all wild existence-
tissue thusness of things: no self,   120

no other. Compelled to explain,
we simply say *not two*. Not two:

so all things everywhere integral.
Throughout the ten distances of

time and space, sages all plumb
this source-ancestral, ancestral

source where time has no scale:
one thought ten thousand years.

There's no here or not here. All
ten distances of time and space   130

appear before you. Tiny is vast
if you forget those separations

boundaries define, and vast tiny
if you stop seeing from outside.

Presence is nothing but Absence,
Absence is nothing but Presence:

until you understand it like this,
how can you ever abide in them?

Primal-unity is every last thing,
every last thing is primal-unity: 140

if you can just know it like this,
how could anything worry you?

Fact and mind not two things,
not two things fact and mind:

this is Way nowhere in words,[6]
no more past, future, or present.

般若波羅蜜多心經

Wisdom-Beyond-Wisdom Mind Sutra (ca. 649)

GENERALLY TRANSLATED UNDER THE ABBREVIATED AND erroneous title *Heart Sutra* (see below), the *Wisdom-Beyond-Wisdom Mind Sutra* is chanted in virtually all Zen sanghas, a practice that began soon after its appearance. Indeed, it seems likely the poem was constructed for that very purpose. Its core philosophical section is borrowed from a much larger sutra translated from Sanskrit by Kumarajiva (see p. 78) in ca. 425, the actual Chinese text very possibly written by Sangha-Fundament (p. 78), who was Kumarajiva's co-translator. Sangha-Fundament cited lines 6–10 in his "*Prajna* Absence-Knowing Discourse" (p. 89), which was widely influential and may indeed be why the core section was later chosen as the basis for this sutra. The framing sections at the beginning and end appear to come from an unknown Chinese source—even if at first glance they seem the most Indian, with Sanskrit terminology and names.[7]

These kinds of reference were common practice for Chinese-composed Buddhist texts, to give them the exotic veneer of early Buddhist texts from India. The poem's setting and characters also come from ancient India. Bodhisattva-Gaze Composure-Free is Avalokiteshvara, a mythological bodhisattva from the vast *kalpas* of time preceding Shakyamuni Buddha and said to have originated as a beam of light radiating from the forehead of Amitābha, the Buddha of boundless radiance. Adept Bestow-Bounty is Sariputra, one of Shakyamuni Buddha's most accomplished disciples. And a third character doesn't appear, but is the most likely speaker of the poem: Shakyamuni Buddha himself, describing Bodhisattva-Gaze Composure-Free's insights as a way of teaching his student.

But classical Chinese, with its open grammar, leaves open the possibility that Bodhisattva-Gaze Composure-Free is himself the speaker. A much larger version of the poem describes a more elaborate setting: the great sangha-assembly on Vulture Peak, Shakyamuni Buddha's favored teaching site. There, with Buddha deep in meditation, it is Bodhisattva-Gaze Composure-Free that teaches Adept Bestow-Bounty. Adapting this grand setting for our short version of the poem locates it in the realm of vast cosmic time and wisdom.

Although ostensibly a translation from Sanskrit, the poem's philosophical core is also essentially Chinese. For it is an especially dramatic example of a Sanskrit text (mis)translated into the Taoist/Ch'an conceptual framework—dramatic because the poem focuses so resolutely on deep cosmological/ontological understanding. In this, we see at the deepest most essential levels how mistranslation effectively transforms a Sanskrit text into a native Chinese text. And also how, operating under the assumption that Ch'an is an extension of Indian Buddhism, translators have failed to render the poem's native philosophical dimensions in English, replacing it instead with the conceptual world of Indian Buddhism with its abstraction and metaphysics.

The poem distills Ch'an insight to its barest and most profound essentials—the reason it is ritually chanted over and over. And nothing is more essential to Ch'an than mind: 心 (see Key Terms, p. 331). Hence the abbreviated title 心經 (*Mind Sutra*). 心 actually means "heart" and "mind" as a single entity, and the title is generally mistranslated into English as the *Heart Sutra*—either for the emotional/poetic appeal, or because *heart* is given its English meaning "essence of" (hence *Sutra of the Essence of Wisdom-Beyond-Wisdom*), a meaning it does not have in classical Chinese. For Ch'an and poetry, 心 should almost always be translated "mind" because the emphasis is on consciousness empty of all contents (though the emotional dimension is never absent). And indeed, the *Mind Sutra* focuses with great concision on the essential nature of mind that must be understood for awakening, and the term's one appearance in the poem itself clearly refers to this awakened mind.

That essential nature of mind is defined as *prajnaparamita* (wisdom-beyond-wisdom). Here, *prajna* literally means "before knowing," and as "wisdom" it refers to original empty-mind. *Paramita* means "perfection" (hence, *prajnaparamita* as the "perfection of wisdom"), or "arrived beyond," and so the compound *prajnaparamita* emphasizes the idea of a wisdom beyond knowing: that is, again, empty-mind. Mind is further defined by means of two terms that positively permeate the *Mind Sutra*: Absence (無) and its Ch'an synonym *emptiness* (空). These terms dominate the poem's two incantatory passages: emptiness the first, Absence the second.

As we saw in the chapter on Sangha-Fundament (p. 78ff.), *emptiness* translates the Sanskrit *sunyata*—but instead of Indian Buddhism's sense that reality is somehow illusory, with its metaphysical implications, *emptiness* is synonymous with 無 (Absence), reality seen as a single generative tissue to which we belong (a tissue *empty* of individual forms). We find a parallel misconception obscuring the other repeated term in this passage: 色. 色 translates the Sanskrit *rupam*, and *rupam* means "that which is formed," in the sense of "outward appearance." In the Buddhist context, this again suggests a more real dimension behind the "outward appearance" of this world's ten thousand things, a metaphysical scheme in which the world around us is mere illusion. Quite to the contrary, 色 means "color" or "beauty/appearance," as in a beautiful and even seductive woman. Hence, the sense is very physical and tangible and sensual, without any metaphysical suggestion: "this beautiful world of things," or perhaps "the beautiful things of this world." Again reading Ch'an with the assumption that it is using Indian concepts unchanged, English translations always translate 色 as "form," which creates an atmosphere of abstraction commensurate to the vague metaphysics of the Sanskrit's Buddhist sense. In one of the standard translations, Roshi Robert Aitken renders it as:

> form is no different than emptiness,
> and emptiness no different than form,
> form exactly emptiness,
> emptiness exactly form.

But read with its native Chinese meaning, this passage becomes fundamentally different:

> this beautiful world of things,
> this world is no different than emptiness,
> and emptiness no different than this world,
> this world exactly emptiness,
> emptiness exactly this world.

The emptiness sequence is followed by an even more incantatory sequence where 無 functions as the rhythmic drumbeat. 無 translates the Sanskrit *na*, which simply means "no/not." There are two words in Chinese that simply mean "no/not"—不 and 非—and they would seem to be the logical translation choice. But 無 was chosen instead, and its philosophically rich double-meaning transforms this Indian text into a native Chinese Ch'an text, for it allows 無 to be read throughout in both its simple meaning of "not" and in its cosmological/ontological meaning "Absence." Reading 無 as "not," which is how English translators have always rendered it, the passage becomes a series of negations:

> There is no world of beautiful things,
> no perception, thought, intention, awareness,
> no eyes and ears, nose and tongue, self and *ch'i*-weave intelligence,
> no beautiful world of dharma's
> color and sound, smell and taste and touch,
> no sight expanses and no *ch'i*-weave awareness expanses,
> no Absence-illumination and no Absence-illumination extinguished,
> no old age and death
> and no old-age and death extinguished.

Or in Aitken's translation:

> Therefore, in emptiness there is no form, no sensation, thought,
> impulse, consciousness;
> no eye, ear, nose, tongue, body, mind;

no color, sound, smell, taste, touch, object of thought;
no realm of sight to no realm of thought;
no ignorance and also no ending of ignorance
to no old age and death and also no ending of old age and death.

But read this way, the passage describes some kind of imagined metaphysical realm that is known through awakening and is truer than the physical world. The empirical-minded Chinese would have no patience for such claims. Nor should we today. And they have nothing to do with Ch'an.

Hence, we are encouraged to read 無 as the this-worldly Taoist concept of Absence, the physical world seen as a single generative tissue. This reading is also suggested because between the poem's two incantatory sections (emptiness and Absence) there is a sentence full of negations (including the same Sanskrit *na*) in which the more common negation word 不 is used in the Chinese. So, the sudden switch to 無 rather than continuing reasonably with 不 further encourages us to read 無 as "Absence." In addition: the more the passage is read as poetic incantation—and remember the *Mind Sutra* is routinely chanted by Ch'an practitioners—the more 無 resonates poetically as "Absence," which is how it appears in this translation. But as it would have been read by the ancient Chinese masters, the two readings (no and Absence) exist simultaneously. And in fact the two are complementary—for when the world is seen as Absence, all of the negations in the "no" reading make empirical (and not the Sanskrit's metaphysical) sense. Again, read with its native Chinese meaning, this passage is transformed:

this beautiful world of things Absence,
perception Absence, thought, intention, and awareness.
Absence eyes and ears, nose and tongue, self and *ch'i*-weave intelligence.
Absence this beautiful world of dharma's
color and sound, smell and taste and touch.
Sight expanses Absence all the way into *ch'i*-weave awareness expanses.
Absence illumination-Absence and no-illumination-Absence[8]
all the way into old-age-and-death Absence
and no-old-age-and-death Absence.

Finally, there is a philosophically remarkable and beautiful aspect of the poem's mythological dimensions that coincides with our reading of 無 as Absence. For *Prajnaparamita* (Wisdom-Beyond-Wisdom) was not only an awakened state of consciousness but also simultaneously a sage goddess. This goddess was revered for her profound generative power (attractive to the Chinese mind because it corresponds to Lao Tzu's Way, which was described as "female" and "mother")—for she was no less than the sage mother of all Buddhas. Hence, the poem's title might almost be rendered: *Buddha-Mother Wisdom-Goddess Mind Sutra*. As we have seen, empty-mind is itself a form of 無 (Absence), the generative source. And etymologically, this 無 is an image of a woman dancing, her swirling movements enhanced by fox tails streaming out from her hands: 舞.

NOTE

For translation comparison: There are many translations of the *Mind Sutra* under the title *Heart Sutra*. The most noteworthy are found in: Robert Aitken's *Taking the Path of Zen* (1982: p. 110); Red Pine's *The Heart Sutra* (2004: p. 2); and Kazuaki Tanahashi's *The Heart Sutra* (2014: p. 3).

Wisdom-Beyond-Wisdom Mind Sutra

When Bodhisattva-Gaze Composure-Free[9]
practiced deep Wisdom-Beyond-Wisdom meditation,
he saw with radiant insight how the five dimensions of consciousness[10]
are perfectly empty.
O Adept Bestow-Bounty,
this beautiful world of things,
this world is no different than emptiness,
and emptiness no different than this world,
this world exactly emptiness,
emptiness exactly this world.
Our perception and thought, intention and awareness,
they too are like this.
O Adept Bestow-Bounty,
all these dharmas together are empty:
no birth and no death, no stain and no purity, no increase and no decrease.
It's all the ancient heart of emptiness:

this beautiful world of things Absence,
perception Absence, thought, intention, and awareness.
Absence eyes and ears, nose and tongue, self and *ch'i*-weave intelligence.
Absence this beautiful world of dharma's
color and sound, smell and taste and touch.
Sight expanses Absence all the way into *ch'i*-weave awareness expanses.
Absence illumination-Absence and no-illumination-Absence[11]
all the way into old-age-and-death Absence
and no-old-age-and-death Absence.
Absence all bitter sorrow and gathering together, all vanishing and Way itself.
Knowledge Absence, realization Absence,
and everything that brings realization Absence too.

Bodhisattvas take refuge in this Goddess Wisdom-Beyond-Wisdom—
and so, their minds are free of all hindrance.

Free of hindrance—and so, free of fear.
They stay far from topsy-turvy fantasy
and tranquil-final nirvana too.
All Buddhas in *kalpas* past, present, and future
take refuge in this Buddha-Mother Wisdom-Beyond-Wisdom—
and so, they realize enlightenment whole, whole deep and star-shimmered.

Know then this Wisdom-Beyond-Wisdom is the great spirit-lightning mantra,
is the great illumination mantra,
is the Absence-rising mantra,
the Absence-all-patience mantra
able to resolve all bitter sorrow.
It isn't empty talk. It's the true thusness of things all clarity-absolute.
And so, let us chant this Wisdom-Beyond-Wisdom mantra,
this Buddha-Mother Wisdom-Goddess mantra:
Gone! Gone! Gone beyond! Gone so utterly beyond,
all bodhi-awakening and rejoicing, rejoicing!

PART V

Realized Ch'an:
T'ang Dynasty Masters

(7th–10th centuries C.E.)

THE T'ANG DYNASTY WAS CHINA'S GREAT MOMENT OF
cultural renaissance. As Ch'an is integral to broader Chinese culture, it
is no surprise that this is also the moment when Ch'an came into full
fruition. Indeed, Ch'an was a major catalyst driving the T'ang renaissance, providing the philosophical framework for artistic endeavor and
personal self-cultivation. And in this, it continued to operate in the cos-
mological/ontological framework we have been tracing. That framework
operates more and more as the unspoken assumption shaping Ch'an insight and practice, and the central philosophical concepts often appear
explicitly, as in this exchange with Fathom Mountain (Tung Shan, 807–
869) that hearkens back to Dark-Enigma Learning and beyond that to
the phrase "dark-enigma deep within dark-enigma" at the end of *Tao Te
Ching* I (p. 27):

> A monk asked: "What is dark-enigma deep in the midst of
> dark-enigma?"
> Fathom Mountain replied: "Tongue of a corpse."

This was the era when Ch'an masters emerged as fully realized figures,
more or less historical individuals whose teachings and actions are extensively documented. These masters put into actual practice all the essential characteristics of Ch'an, and conjured the radical teaching strategies
that have been used ever since. Integral to this appearance of distinctive

individuals was a defining transformation known as the Ch'an of "wild words and woolly actions" (奇言畸行): striking and illogical remarks, zany antics, paradox, wordless and violent teaching methods like shouts and slaps and stick-blows (the Ch'an that held such appeal when it arrived in the United States as Japanese Zen).

It may seem inexplicable that students would subject themselves to such treatment. They so often seem shockingly over-dependent on the master and the Buddhist teachings Ch'an dismantles, and they seem so willing to invite abusive treatment. To some extent, this is simply a literary construction serving the narrative: the need for students asking questions so that the master can teach. But there's more: Ch'an understanding is very difficult to fully absorb, and this is what the students are trying to do. They surely had a deep conceptual understanding of Ch'an, but Ch'an demands an immediate experiential understanding, and that is much more difficult. The point of asking seemingly simple questions like "What is Buddha?" or "What is Way?" is to invite a breakthrough into levels of Ch'an more profound and experiential than the theoretical. And it worked. Such teaching created a lineage of mind-transmission that proliferated dramatically, with teachers often sanctioning scores of heirs who spread out and taught. In this, Ch'an's cultural presence became widespread among the educated population.

Mountain landscape continued as a major influence. The famous split in the Sixth Patriarch's time between northern and southern Ch'an (see below pp. 160–61) was less about gradual versus sudden enlightenment, as so often portrayed, than about a cultured and institutionalized Ch'an of the glamorous northern cities versus a wild and independent Ch'an of the southern mountains. The Sixth Patriarch represented the latter, and it was this wild-mountain tradition that came to dominate the deep dimensions of Ch'an. Virtually all major Ch'an figures practiced and came to enlightenment in the mountains. Monasteries were called "forests," and many Ch'an masters so identified with the mountains where they lived that they adopted the mountains' names as their own. The examples are countless, including a host of Ch'an masters who appear in the selections below: Yellow-Bitterroot Mountain, Cold Mountain, Cloud-Gate Mountain, Incense Mountain (Po Chü-i), Twofold-Creek Mountain, Fathom Mountain, Wellspring-South Mountain, Plum-Vast

Mountain, Hundred-Elder Mountain, South Mountain, River-Act Mountain, Reliance Mountain.

This cultivation of mountain landscape is reflected in the T'ang's Ch'an-inspired poetic tradition, which grew out of a passion to inhabit the Taoist Cosmos at the deepest and most immediate levels. It makes sense, for Ch'an continued to operate within the same Taoist cosmological/ontological framework that is by now familiar—as a way to cultivate mind as integral to the generative source-tissue that burgeons forth in its most majestically enthralling form as dramatic and ever-changing mountain landscape. And mountains often appear explicitly in Ch'an teaching itself, as here in this answer to the oft-repeated question essentially asking about the nature of enlightenment:

> Someone asked: "What is the *ch'i*-weave mind Bodhidharma brought from the West?"
>
> Cloud-Gate Mountain replied: "Gazing at a mountain in broad daylight."

慧能

Sixth Patriarch Prajna-Able
(Hui Neng, 638–713)

Sixth Patriarch Prajna-Able initiates the prolif-eration of Ch'an masters in the T'ang, and it is in him that the full dimensions of Ch'an understanding and practice first come together in a single figure, as recorded in the seminal *Platform Sutra of the Sixth Patriarch* (六祖壇經). This includes, notably, the first instance of the "wild words and woolly actions" Ch'an of shouts and blows that will become so central in the tradition. Prajna-Able is the first figure in the Ch'an tradition rendered as a real flesh-and-blood human. Unlike Bodhidharma, whose life is only sketched in mythic outlines, Prajna-Able is portrayed in the *Platform Sutra* through a series of life-events meant to bring Ch'an into everyday experience. Indeed, Prajna-Able is portrayed as the most ordinary of people, an illiterate peasant. But the record of his life is the only Ch'an text honored with the title *Sutra*, thereby dignifying this commoner with the nobility of Buddha himself, the original subject of sutras in the Buddhist tradition.

The *Platform Sutra* was composed sometime after Prajna-Able's death, and it apparently fabricates aspects of the Prajna-Able character in ways useful to the development of Ch'an's self-image. Much of this was conjured by Prajna-Able's dharma-heir Spirit-Lightning Gather (Shen Hui), who also invented the split between northern (gradual) and southern (sudden) schools, then argued that Prajna-Able's southern school was the true Ch'an (pp. 4, 158). Prajna-Able is described as an illiterate peasant to illustrate two central Ch'an tenets. First, that we are all, in our original-nature, inherently enlightened. That is, we are all Buddhas. This means that awakening has nothing to do with diligent practice, for it is simply recognizing one's originally awakened nature, and must therefore be instantaneous and complete. And second, that awakening isn't a question of learning, for deep insight is outside of knowledge and texts and teaching: Bodhidharma's "separate transmission outside all teaching."

Although we have seen these ideas developing centuries earlier, they are famously associated with Prajna-Able and his enlightenment poem in the story that begins the *Platform Sutra* (pp. 165–66). In this story, the Fifth Patriarch asks the monks of his sangha to each demonstrate their understanding by writing a poem. Only the head monk dares venture a poem, and in it he writes that awakening comes from assiduously polishing the mind-mirror. In response, the illiterate Prajna-Able writes a poem saying there is no mirror to polish, for mind is always already awakened. This becomes a kind of historical origin moment in Ch'an. When the Fifth Patriarch declares Prajna-Able his true heir, Prajna-Able flees the danger posed by a sangha of jealous monks. He travels to the mountain wildlands of the south and founds a Ch'an of instantaneous awakening outside of words and teachings. In stark contrast to the illiterate peasant Prajna-Able, the head monk Spirit-Lightning Flourish (Shen Hsiu) is from the aristocratic class. He travels to the capital cities of the north, cultural center of China, and there leads a cultivated Ch'an of urban sophisticates wherein awakening is a gradual process of study and practice. The distinction between sudden and gradual was perhaps more a matter of emphasis than real difference—for both sides accepted the necessity of learning and practice as preparation for the sudden transformation of enlightenment itself. The more salient distinction is perhaps between institutional orthodoxy and independent iconoclasm, between cities and wild mountains, between a more conventional Buddhist approach and a more Taoist wrecking-crew approach. In any case, it is the "southern" Ch'an of Prajna-Able that became the prevailing and enduring Ch'an.

There is a further, unnoticed, revelation in the legend of Prajna-Able as an illiterate peasant. Similar to Bodhidharma—in Ch'an legend,

a foreigner bringing a foreign system of understanding to China—
we see Prajna-Able in the *Platform Sutra* operating within the Taoist
cosmological/ontological framework, deploying the full panoply of
Taoist concepts, even though as an unlearned illiterate he should know
nothing of such things (or of Buddhist scripture, which he also seems
to know well). And again as with Bodhidharma, this shows how deeply
the Taoist framework functioned as the unthought assumptions shaping
Ch'an thought and practice, for later teachers and students apparently
saw nothing unusual in Prajna-Able slinging around these profound
cosmological/ontological concepts.

But it's often more subtle than direct references to those foundational
cosmological/ontological concepts. One good example comes in Prajna-
Able's introduction to his enlightenment poems (pp. 166–67). There, describing the nature of awakening, he equates understanding *ch'i*-weave
mind (see Key Terms, pp. 331–32) with Bodhidharma's "seeing original-
nature." This identifies the Taoist concept of *ch'i*-weave mind with the
Buddhist concept of one's own original-nature. Original-nature is of
course no different from empty mirror-mind (subject of Prajna-Able's
enlightenment poem)—and so, Prajna-Able here invests consciousness
with the full dimensions of Taoism's generative cosmology: mind woven
into *ch'i*, the Cosmos seen as a single breath-force tissue in constant
transformation.

This continues in the poems themselves, which became the models for
enlightenment poems that are a routine part of Ch'an, a way for teachers
to confirm the enlightenment of students. There in Prajna-Able's rewriting of the head monk's poem, we find enlightenment operating entirely
in terms of the generative cosmology of Tao/Way. The first couplet of
Prajna-Able's first poem reads in the original:

菩 bodhi-awakening	提 original	本 not/Absence	無 tree	樹 source-tissue

明 brilliant	鏡 mirror	亦 absolutely	無 not/Absence	臺 stand

A first translation is:

> Original source-tissue *bodhi*-awakening
> isn't a tree. Nowhere stands the brilliant mirror.

But this couplet at its depths turns on the double reading for 無 (not/Absence) that we so often see, giving the lines this second, much more deeply cosmological/ontological reading:

> Original *bodhi*-awakening is an Absence tree,
> and the brilliant mirror stands in that Absence.

明 (brilliant) at the beginning of the second line also means "wisdom" or even "enlightenment." And indeed, that enlightenment follows immediately in the line. For here we find an archetypal restatement of the crucial association of mirror-mind and Absence that we have seen evolving in the tradition, beginning with the Dark-Enigma Learning philosophers: crucial because here Taoist cosmology/ontology invests empty-mind with empirical and cosmic proportions, perhaps the most salient aspect of Ch'an enlightenment.

Wang Wei, the quintessential Ch'an rivers-and-mountains poet and painter (pp. 249–50), describes in his memorial inscription for the Sixth Patriarch how Prajna-Able taught that Ch'an insight means to be "unborn and therefore without an I," and that "*prajna*-wisdom is to depend on nothing." Wang describes *wu-wei* (Absence-action) as the essence of awakening for Prajna-Able. He further describes Prajna-Able as a master of *wu-wei* who has seen through the distinction between Absence and Presence. In sum, this describes Prajna-Able and awakening itself in the Taoist sense of unborn dwelling integral to the Great Transformation of Tao's ongoing process. And in his memorial inscription, Wang describes the actual experience of this awakening in terms by now familiar:

> Done giving up Presence, we
> penetrate the source of Presence.
> Done dwelling in emptiness, we
> fathom the origin of emptiness.

When movement is all stillness
we ride transformation perennial,
inhabiting the hundred dharmas endlessly,
suffusing the ten thousand things boundlessly.

NOTE

For translation comparison: Bracketed numbers refer to page numbers in Philip Yampolsky's *The Platform Sutra of the Sixth Patriarch* (1967) and Red Pine's *The Platform Sutra: The Zen Teaching of Hui-neng* (2006). Other translations include Thomas Cleary's *The Sutra of Hui-Neng* (1998) and John McRae's *The Platform Sutra of the Sixth Patriarch* (2000). Readers may also want to consult Morten Schlütter and Stephen Teiser's *Readings of the Platform Sutra* (2012).

The Platform Sutra of the Sixth Patriarch

One day, the Fifth Patriarch suddenly summoned everyone in the sangha. Once the sangha had gathered, he said: "I've told you life and death are matters of the greatest importance for people. But you just fuss over offerings, searching day after day through the fields of Buddha and dharma and sangha blessings, and not freedom from the bitter seas of life and death. Instead of relying on your own original-nature, you rely on the gates of those blessings. How will you ever save yourselves?

"Go back to your rooms and look inside yourselves. If any of you are wise enough to grasp the *prajna*-awakening of your original source-tissue nature, write a *gatha* and present it to me. I'll read them, and if anyone reveals an awakening to the vastness of *ch'i*-weave mind, I'll give them the dharma-robe and appoint them Sixth Patriarch.

"Hurry! The house is on fire! Hurry! Hurry!"

The monks returned to their rooms, saying to each other: "How can we clarify our minds and write gathas revealing *ch'i*-weave mind? Head monk Spirit-Lightning Flourish is the master teacher here. Once he has received the dharma, we can rely on him. Why pretend we can reveal *ch'i*-weave mind?" Their minds were at ease, and they didn't risk presenting gathas.

Deep into the third watch,[1] Spirit-Lightning Flourish took a candle and went down to the central wall of the south corridor. There, he wrote a gatha on the wall. No one knew what he had done. The gatha read:

> Body is the *bodhi*-awakening tree
> where mind stands like a brilliant
>
> mirror. Polish it clean day after day,
> never let the least dust gather there.

The great master summoned the sangha, then lit incense before the gatha. When the monks entered and saw the gatha, their minds were filled with reverence.

"From now on, I want you all to chant this gatha," declared the Fifth Patriarch. "It will reveal to you the awakening of *seeing original-nature*."[2]

A young monk came through the mill-room chanting Spirit-Lightning's gatha. Hearing it, I immediately knew it didn't reveal the awakening of *seeing original-nature* or fathoming the vastness of *ch'i*-weave mind.

"That gatha you were just chanting, where did it come from?" I asked the monk.

"Don't you know?" the monk replied. "Our great master said that life and death are matters of the greatest importance, and that he wanted to transmit the dharma-robe. So he told everyone in the sangha to write a gatha and present it to him. He said whoever reveals an awakening to the vastness of *ch'i*-weave mind would be given the dharma-robe and appointed patriarch of the sixth generation.

"Head monk Spirit-Lightning Flourish went down to the south corridor and wrote that Absence gatha empty of all form and appearance. The Fifth Patriarch told everyone in the sangha to start chanting it, because it could reveal to us the awakening of *seeing* our own *original-nature*. He said that if we relied on it for our practice, we could attain liberation."

"I've been peddling this millstone for over eight months," I said, "and I've never visited the Dharma Hall. Please, take me down to the south corridor so I can see the gatha and bow in reverence to it. I want to chant it like everyone else, so in my future life I too will be reborn in the Buddha-land."

The monk took me down to the south corridor, and I there bowed in reverence to the gatha. I couldn't decipher the words, so I asked someone to read them to me. When I heard them, I fathomed the vastness of *ch'i*-weave mind. Then I too wrote a gatha and asked someone to write it on the west-corridor wall, so I could present my own original source-tissue mind.

If you don't fathom original source-tissue mind, studying dharma won't get you anywhere. But if you fathom mind, if you *see original-*

*nature*³—you're awakened to the vastness of *ch'i*-weave mind. And so, my gatha said:

> Original source-tissue *bodhi*-awakening
> isn't a tree. Nowhere stands the brilliant
>
> mirror. Buddha-nature perennially such
> pure clarity—where could dust gather?

Then I composed a second:

> Mind is the *bodhi*-awakening tree,
> body where a brilliant mirror stands,
>
> original source-tissue mirror such
> pure clarity—what could dust stain?⁴ [128–32; 5–8]

My wise and understanding friends, this dharma-gate of mine takes meditation and *prajna*-awakening as the ancestral root. First and foremost: never make the mistake of saying meditation and *prajna* are different. They are one thing in essence, not two: meditation is the potency of *prajna*, and *prajna* is the actualization of meditation. When you abide in *prajna*, meditation is there within *prajna*. When you abide in meditation, *prajna* is there within meditation. The principle here, my wise and understanding friends, is that meditation and *prajna* are one and the same. [135; 10]

To make *samadhi*'s three-shadowed earth a practice devoted to the primal-unity tissue day in and day out—whether walking or standing still, sitting or lying down: that is to cultivate straightforward mind all sight-clarity absolute, perennial mind that sees through things with absolute and immediate clarity. The *Vimalakirti Sutra* says: *Straightforward mind all sight-clarity absolute is the fieldland of Way* and *straightforward mind all sight-clarity absolute is the ground of purity.* Without this mind, practice is just fawning talk about rules and regulations, chatter about the straightforward dharma of sight-clarity absolute, about the primal-unity practice of *samadhi*'s three-shadowed earth. That is exactly not the practice of straightforward mind, of a disciple to Buddha. Just make straightforward mind all sight-clarity absolute your practice throughout all dharmas. And let go of attachments; don't cling to anything at all. That is what we call *the primal-unity practice of samadhi's three-shadowed earth*.

Confused people clutch at attachments to the forms and appearances of dharma. They cling to the primal-unity practice of *samadhi*'s three-shadowed earth, to straightforward mind all sight-clarity absolute. They sit all stillness, clear away delusions and quash emerging thoughts. And they think that is the primal-unity practice of *samadhi*'s three-shadowed earth. But in that dharma you're dead to the world. And you block the movement of Way. But Way always flows through. Why try to hold it back? If mind doesn't dwell in dharma, Way flows through. If mind dwells in dharma, we say it's tangled itself in knots.

If sitting all stillness is the secret, why did Vimalakirti scold Sariputra for sitting in quiet meditation amid forest trees? My wise and understanding friends, I see there are still teachers who tell people to sit all stillness and quash emerging thoughts, to sit gazing at mind, gazing at purity. And people devote themselves to this, thinking they will achieve great things. But it only confuses people. It never awakens them. Clinging to teachings like that, they're soon turned upside down. And there are hundreds of teachers who claim all that confusion is Way. No wonder there's so much delusion everywhere. [136–37; 11–12]

My wise and understanding friends, everything in my dharma-gate from the very beginning is founded on no-thought Absence as the source-ancestral essence, no-form Absence as the ancestral potency, no-dwelling Absence[5] as the ancestral root. Once you master no-form Absence, even amid forms and appearances you are far from forms and appearances. Once you master no-thought Absence, even amid thoughts you are without thought. And once you master no-dwelling Absence, you move as original source-tissue nature. [137–38; 12]

Thought thinks the original-nature of this existence-tissue all thusness-clarity absolute. This existence-tissue all thusness-clarity absolute is the original potency of thought, and thought is the actualization of this existence-tissue. In its own original-nature, this existence-tissue all thusness-clarity absolute rises into thought—and even tangled through perception like sight and hearing, it never stains the ten thousand mirrored things. So, you move always composed and free. The *Vimala-kirti Sutra* says: *Outside attending precisely to dharma's every form and appearance; inside devoting yourself all stillness to the first and foremost inner-pattern Way.* [139; 13]

My wise and understanding friends, in this dharma-gate, sitting in ch'an meditation at origins has nothing to do with mind and nothing to do with purity. And I never talk about stillness. People speak of gazing at mind, but mind is at origins illusion. And since illusions are mere mirage, what is there to see? People speak of gazing at purity, but our original-nature is itself source-tissue purity—even when illusory thoughts hide from us this existence-tissue all thusness-clarity absolute. And far from those illusory thoughts, original source-tissue nature is itself also purity. If you don't see your own original-nature is itself source-tissue purity, you invent mind to gaze at purity, and then you've also conjured an illusory purity. [139; 13–14]

. . . Gazing at mind, gazing at purity: that just blocks the movement of Way.

So what is sitting *ch'an*[6] in this dharma-gate of mine? It means to be completely free of obstruction. Outwardly, *sitting* is no-thought arising anywhere border to border. And inwardly, *ch'an* is gazing at your original source-tissue nature without any confusion. [140; 14]

My wise and understanding friends, our original-nature is source-tissue purity. So the ten thousand dharmas are there in your own original-nature. . . . You can see the ten thousand dharmas within your own original-nature, for every dharma is there of itself in original-nature. [141–42; 15–16]

Mind's measure is a vast expanse. It's like the emptiness of empty sky. But if you just sit concentrating your mind, you'll fall away into blank emptiness. The emptiness of empty sky contains sun and moon, stars and planets, this vast rivers-and-mountains earth, all grasses and trees, vile people and good people, vile dharmas and good dharmas, heavens and hells. They're all there in empty sky. And the emptiness of our original-nature—it's exactly like that.

Don't listen to me talk about emptiness, and then just devote yourself to emptiness. This is the most important of all things: don't just devote yourself to emptiness. If you just empty the mind and sit in serene tranquility, you're devoting yourself to a blank and traceless emptiness.

Your own original-nature contains the ten thousand dharmas.[7] It is vast indeed. And the ten thousand dharmas, they're nothing but your own original-nature. [146; 20]

Once you *see original-nature*—you dwell in neither inner nor outer, and of yourself come and go freely; you cast aside the mind that clings to this or that, and so move unhindered through the unfurling of things. [150; 23–24]

To recognize in your own mind the most wise and understanding teacher: that is liberation. . . . To realize in sight's clarity-absolute the most wise and understanding teacher: that is the one awakening in which you know Buddha completely.

    When the insight of your own original-nature and mind-ground[8] sees with deep illumination, penetrating the sage radiance of inner and outer, you recognize your own original source-tissue mind. And to recognize your source-tissue mind—that is liberation itself. This liberation is the accord-pleasure *prajna* of *samadhi*'s three-shadowed earth. And awakening to the *prajna* of *samadhi*'s three-shadowed earth: that is no-thought Absence itself. . . . Once you awaken to the dharma of no-thought Absence, you move through the ten thousand dharmas utterly, and you see this thousand-Buddha-realm Cosmos border-to-border. Once you awaken to the sudden dharma of no-thought Absence, you inhabit the mind-ground as Buddha's equal. [152–53; 25–26]

> Teachers offer ten thousand forms of *prajna*-awakening,
> but inhabit inner-pattern and you return to primal-unity.
>
> . . .
>
> *Bodhi*-awakening is source-tissue clarity crystalline pure.
> To invent mind is to invent an illusion, though even there
>
> in the midst of that illusion, original-nature remains pure.
> . . .
> [160; 31–32]

. . . confusion and worry—they too are *bodhi*-awakening, are indeed nothing other than existence-tissue itself. [164; 35]

The great master said: "Listen to what I say, and you will see the place of awakening. The mind-ground is without flaw, and is therefore itself the precept of your own original-nature. The mind-ground is without confusion, and is therefore itself the meditation of your own original-nature. The mind-ground is without ignorance, and is therefore itself the *prajna*-awakening of your own original-nature."

And great master Prajna-Able continued: "Your precepts and meditation and *prajna*-awakening cultivate commoners with shallow roots. Mine cultivate those who have grown tall and strong. Just awaken to your own original-nature, and don't revere answers like precepts or meditation or *prajna*-awakening."

"Please, master," asked Resolve-Sincere, "how do I not *revere answers*"?

"Your own original-nature is without flaw, without confusion, without ignorance. In every thought, you see deeply into the radiance of *prajna*-awakening. And in the forms and appearances of the wordless Absence-tissue dharma, what answers are there to revere? Awakening of yourself to your own original-nature, the sudden cultivation of sudden awakening: there's absolutely nothing gradual about it. It is therefore the dharma complete without answers to revere." [164–65; 35–36]

There was a monk named Spirit-Lightning Gather⁹ from South-Brights. He came to Twofold-Creek Mountain, bowed reverently and asked: "When you sit *ch'an*, master, do you *see original-nature* or not *see original-nature*?"

The great master got up and struck Spirit-Lightning three blows. . . .

"You certainly haven't seen your own original-nature. How dare you come here and play games like this?"

Spirit-Lightning Gather was speechless. He bowed reverently again.

"Your mind's a confusion," continued the great master. "You don't see your original-nature. So you seek the path from wise and understanding teachers. You use mind to find the awakening of *seeing original-nature*, depend on dharmas and the rituals and practices of self-cultivation. You're confused and don't see your own mind, and now you come asking me if I *see original-nature* or not! If I understand how to see my own original-nature, that will never replace your confusion. And if you see your own original-nature, that will never replace my confusion. Why don't you try a little self-cultivation first, then ask if I *see original-nature* or not?" [169; 39–40]

On the third sun of the eighth moon in the second year of the Ancestral-Heaven reign, our great master crossed over into extinction. On the eighth sun of the seventh moon, he summoned the sangha and bid them farewell:

"If you understood where I am going, there would be no tears of grief. In the dharma, original-nature is never born and never dies, never leaves and never arrives. [174; 43]

"There's no need to hand down the dharma-robe of transmission. Don't believe me? I'll chant for you the gathas written by our first five patriarchs when they were entrusted with the dharma-robe. If you understand even First Patriarch Bodhidharma's gatha about coming here to China, if you make it's *ch'i*-weave mind your own, you'll see there's no need to transmit a dharma-robe. Here, I'll chant them for you. Listen.

Gatha of First Patriarch Bodhidharma

At the origin, I came here to transmit insight,
end the confusion of things outside not felt

inside. One flower five petals, and the fruit
occurrence-appearing-of-itself grown whole.

Gatha of Second Patriarch Prajna-Prospect

At those origins, it was origin-tissue came,
ground where the seed-sown flower is born.

If at those origins dark-enigma were not
ground, where would the flower be born?

Gatha of Third Patriarch Sangha-Jewel

A flower seed needs ground, but ground is
itself a seed from which the flower is born.

And so, the flower seed's original-nature is
unborn, and the very ground too is unborn.

Gatha of Fourth Patriarch Way-Sincere

In seed is born the flower's original-nature.
Seed needs ground for the flower to be born,

and even with ancestral origin-tissue total
confusion, we're entirely Absence unborn.

Gatha of Fifth Patriarch Patience-Expanse

Things outside felt inside: that is the seed
he brought. No outside inside, there is born

the flower. No outside felt inside, no seed:
so what? Mind-ground is always unborn.

Gatha of Sixth Patriarch Prajna-Able

Things outside felt inside: it's mind-ground holds
the seed. And the outside-felt-inside flower is born

in dharma-rain. Awakening of yourself is the seed,
and occurrence of itself the *bodhi*-awakening fruit.
[176–78; 45–46]

My mind is its own Buddha, my own Buddha
the Buddha of reality itself all clarity-absolute:

if I don't carry within my own Buddha-mind,
where would I ever go searching for Buddha?
[180; 48]

"Continue practicing as you did when I was here, devote yourselves to
sitting in meditation without motion and without stillness, without
birth and without death, without leaving and without coming, without

good and without bad, without dwelling and without setting out—all in the simplest stillness and quiet. That is the majestic Way." ...

Once he was done speaking, as the clappers of night's third watch sounded, our great master returned fully to the Great Transformation of things. He had passed through seventy-six springs and autumns.

On the day our great master crossed over into extinction, a strange fragrance of earth's life-bringing source of change filled the monastery and lingered for days. Mountains tumbled into ruins, and the earth trembled. Forest trees turned white. Sun and moon stopped shining. Wind and cloud lost their colors. [181–82; 50]

馬祖道一

Patriarch Sudden-Horse Way-Entire
(Ma Tsu, 709–788)

IN THE CH'AN TRADITION, PATRIARCH SUDDEN-HORSE Way-Entire is considered hardly less seminal a figure than Bodhidharma or Prajna-Able. After the legendary six patriarchs from Bodhidharma through Prajna-Able, Way-Entire is the only teacher called a "patriarch"— and indeed, Way-Entire is the only teacher whose name actually includes the term *Patriarch* (祖). He too lived on the fringes of institutional structures, wandering both as a student and teacher from monastery to monastery among China's rivers-and-mountains. Way-Entire is the first Ch'an master possessing all the characteristics that typify Ch'an teachers throughout the tradition to follow. We have seen much teaching in the form of direct philosophical explanation, and that is necessary to prepare practitioners for the immediate realization of Ch'an insight. In this dimension of Ch'an teaching, Way-Entire reveals himself to be an incisive and deeply probing philosophical mind capable of pushing thought almost beyond the thinkable. But to this traditional teaching strategy, he initiated a new dimension (glimpsed in *The Platform Sutra of the Sixth Patriarch*, p. 165) that came to be known as "wild words and woolly actions." This takes the form of teaching by means of shouts and blows and illogical statements. And it turns out Way-Entire's methods were remarkably successful: he taught over a hundred dharma-heirs who fanned out across the country to teach, a major factor in the proliferation of Ch'an in China.

Way-Entire's strategy is to reveal the "separate transmission outside all teaching" directly through actions. This is the performative dimension of Ch'an teaching: rather than talking about insight, Way-Entire *enacts* it, thereby making it available to students as direct immediate experience. This strategy traces its source back to Buddha holding the flower up before Mahakasyapa, the first transmission according to Ch'an legend, but even more fundamentally to Chuang Tzu's zany sages. As such, it is a dramatic manifestation of Absence-action (*wu-wei*: see Key Terms, p. 328), essence of Ch'an awakening. And this wild-and-woolly Ch'an comes more and more to the fore in the tradition to follow, until three hundred years later it comes to define the essential nature of Ch'an in Sung Dynasty sangha-case collections (see part VI, pp. 257–298).

Throughout Way-Entire's teaching, we find Ch'an continuing to function as an extension of native Taoism—not least, the name he took as a monk: Way-Entire. An alternate translation adds even more depths: Primal-Unity Way. Way-Entire deploys the full Taoist cosmological/ontological framework: it is the explicit content of his traditional explanatory teaching; and though rarely mentioned, it is the implicit assumption within which his wild-and-woolly teaching takes place. In stark contrast to the quietude of traditional Buddhist meditation as the path to awakening, Way-Entire's antics are enactments of *wu-wei* (Absence-action), that foundational Taoist principle. That is, those antics reveal Way-Entire acting with the spontaneous energy of the Cosmos, and thereby enacting the essence of awakening.

Patriarch Way-Entire's most influential teaching may be "ordinary mind is Way," which casts Ch'an realization in wholly Taoist terms. *Way* here does mean Ch'an's way of practice, or way to enlightenment. But at the same time, its more philosophically important Taoist meaning describes ordinary everyday mind/self as always already belonging wholly to the cosmological/ontological movement of Lao Tzu's Way (Tao), the Cosmos seen as a single undifferentiated generative tissue. This explains the seeming idealism that appears in some of Way-Entire's teaching. For when Way-Entire says mind is the source of things, he isn't asserting that empirical reality is somehow created by the human intellect. Instead, he is saying first that mind is integral to Tao, and therefore is part of the generative source; and second, that we only see the tissue of the Cosmos as differentiated things when we name them (an idea dating back to Lao Tzu).

Way-Entire's "ordinary mind is Way" became one of Ch'an's central insights. It reappears in the first generations of Way-Entire's lineage. Later, Purport Dark-Enigma (p. 208) quotes Way-Entire's line and suggests it represents the very essence of Ch'an. We find it as the very terms of awakening in the encounter where Visitation-Land (p. 224) is enlightened:

> Visitation-Land asked Wellspring-South Mountain: "What is Way?"
>
> "Ordinary mind is Way," answered Master Wellspring.

And variations of this insight resonate as a bedrock understanding throughout the Ch'an tradition.

But "ordinary mind" never attains more profound dimensions than in Way-Entire's enlightenment story (which begins the selection below). We have seen the idea of the enlightened mind as a perfectly clear mirror in nearly every major figure so far (see *mirror* entry in Key Terms, pp. 333–34, for specific page references). Throughout, the idea of spiritual practice is compared to polishing the mirror. Way-Entire's awakening comes when his teacher dismantles, in grand Ch'an fashion, the whole mirror conceit and replaces it with truly "ordinary mind": a brick that no amount of polishing will turn into some perfect mirror of enlightenment.

NOTE

For translation comparison: Bracketed numbers prefaced by "SFB" refer to page numbers in *Sun-Face Buddha* (1992) by Cheng Chien Bhikshu (a.k.a. Mario Poceski), and when prefaced by "RM" they refer to Poceski's *The Records of Mazu and the Making of Classical Chan Literature* (2015).

Teaching Record of Ch'an Master
Patriarch Sudden-Horse Way-Entire
from River-West

During the Open-Origin reign [713–41], there was a monk named Way-Entire who sat long days in meditation at Dharma-Transmission Monastery. The abbot there, South Mountain,[10] recognized Way-Entire to be a true vessel of the dharma, so one day he walked over to Way-Entire and said: "My great heart-sight clarity adept—meditating all day like this, what are you trying to do?"

"I'm trying to become Buddha," replied Way-Entire.

South Mountain picked up a brick and began grinding it on a stone out front of the shrine.

"What are you doing," asked Way-Entire.

"Polishing this brick into a mirror."

"But how can grinding a brick make a mirror?"

"How can sitting in meditation make a Buddha?" [SFB 59]

. . .

Instructing the assembled sangha, Ch'an master Serene-Vast Way-Entire from River-West said: "To abide in Way, don't bother with cultivation. Just keep free of contamination. What is contamination? Mind hemmed in by life and death, mind fabricating its little certainties: that is contamination. If you want to fathom Way, if you want to see through it with absolute and immediate clarity, it's easy: ordinary mind is Way. In this ordinary mind there is no fabrication, no *yes this* or *no that*,[11] no clinging-to or letting-go, no short-lived or long-lived, no commoner and no sage. The sutra says: *The practice of bodhisattvas is not the practice of commoners and not the practice of sages*. It is instead exactly this here right now. Walking or standing, sitting or sleeping—simply move in accord with whatever moment the loom-of-origins unfurls, integral to the ten thousand things in their vast transformations. That, that is Way.

"And this Way is the entire dharma-realm, realm comprising this world's wondrous forms and appearances numberless as Ganges sands. If there were anything beyond this, how could we say the mind-ground[12] is itself the dharma-gate, is the inexhaustible lamp? For all dharmas are mind-dharmas, and all names are mind-names. The ten thousand dharmas are all born of mind. Mind is their original source-tissue root. The sutra says: *Once they fathom mind in its source-tissue origins, they're called monks.* Names and concepts, that whole kit-and-kaboodle: it's all dharma pure and simple, whole and free of all confusion.

"If you come to realization through the gates of this teaching, you move in accord with each moment, composed and free. Then, founded in this dharma-realm, you exhaust this dharma-realm. Founded in existence-tissue all thusness-clarity absolute, you exhaust existence-tissue all thusness-clarity absolute. Founded in the inner-pattern, you exhaust the inner-pattern throughout all dharmas everywhere. Founded in our human realm, you exhaust our human realm throughout all dharmas everywhere. Try to single out one dharma, and a thousand follow. That's because there's no difference between inner-pattern and our human realm. And so, you exhaust this world's wondrous forms and appearances all no other than inner-pattern." [RM 301–5]

"All the differentiated things of this world arise from the twistings and turnings of mind. It's like the moon's reflections: they're myriad, but the moon itself is not. Springs brimmed with water are myriad, but water in its original-nature is not. And the ten thousand forms in the lavish fabric of things are myriad, but the emptiness of empty space containing them is not. Just so, we can say the inner-pattern Way is myriad, but unhindered *prajna*-wisdom is not. All the myriad things we differentiate in this world: they all arise from that primal-unity mind." [RM 305]

"Whether settled in and dwelling or swept away—it's all wondrous actualization. And in that wondrous actualization, the things of this world are all at home in themselves. Never leave this wild thusness of things all clarity-absolute, then you'll always have a place to dwell. Our dwelling-place can only be this wild thusness of things, this potency at home in itself as it shapes the actualization of things. If you don't inhabit all that, then what are you?" [RM 306]

"The dharma of things everywhere in and of themselves, that is the Buddha-dharma. All those dharmas together are liberation, and that liberation is the existence-tissue itself all thusness-clarity absolute. So, all those dharmas are nothing other than that existence-tissue. Walking and standing, sitting and sleeping—everything you do is unthinkable and unsayable actualization. There is no waiting for some perfect moment. The sutra says: *Dwell where you are, where you are—for there you are yourself Buddha.*" [RM 306]

"Buddhas are capable of open-heartedness, but they possess *prajna*-wisdom and feel things seen becoming part of them, feel the entire loom-of-origins weave becoming part of them. Once a Buddha, you break through the net of doubt everything alive shares, and you leave the tangles of Absence and Presence far behind. Feeling things seen becoming part of you as both commoner and sage do, you know people and dharma are both empty. And turning with the wheel of Absence, you stride beyond all measurement or limit. In this, everything you do is unhindered, so you penetrate through the inner-pattern and this world it shapes. Then you're like a cloud appearing in the sky, suddenly, and then suddenly free of hindrance disappearing without a trace.[13] Or like writing on water.

"Unborn and undying, you know nirvana's great stillness and extinction. When you're caught in life's tangles, we call it *the womb of all existence-tissue arrival.* Free of life's tangles, we call it *the pure self of dharma.* As the dharma-self, you are boundless potency and without increase or decrease. You can be large or small, square or round. Abiding in the forms things take, like a moon in water, you ride the steady flood of actualization: never standing still and never planting roots, never exhausting Presence-action and never dwelling even in Absence-action. Presence-action is the home Absence-action uses in its actualization;

and Absence-action is the home Presence-action depends on. But once a Buddha, you don't dwell even in that dependence. And so, we say you are existence-tissue perfectly empty and depending on nothing."[14] [RM 307–8]

"The mind of birth and death is one aspect. The mind of existence-tissue all thusness-clarity absolute is another aspect. The mind of existence-tissue all thusness-clarity absolute is a luminous mirror radiant with appearances. Here, the mirror equals mind, and appearances equal dharmas. If mind clings to those dharmas, it wades away into conditions and causes—then it's the mind of birth and death. But if mind doesn't cling to those dharmas, it's the mind of existence-tissue all thusness-clarity absolute." [RM 309]

"Those who listen to noise hear about *seeing original-nature*[15] Buddha, about the bodhisattva's eye *seeing original-nature* Buddha. But once you fathom non-duality, you call the ordinary itself *original-nature*. Original-nature includes no distinctions: it's only when we try to use it that differences appear. In confusion, there is comprehension; in awakening, there is wisdom. To abide by the inner-pattern is awakening, and to abide by the tangled consequence of our human realm is confusion. Confusion means confused about your original source-tissue mind at home in itself. Awakening means awakened to your original source-tissue nature at home in itself. And once awakened, you're always awakened: no more confusion ever. It's like mornings after the sun's risen: no relation at all to black night. And when the *prajna*-wisdom sun appears, it's nothing like the darkness of worry and bewilderment." [RM 310]

"Once you understand mind to its furthest boundaries with perfect clarity, even frenetic tangles of thought are unborn. Once frenetic tangles of thought are unborn, you've mastered the patient dharma of Absence born. It was like this at the beginning and it's like this now, so why cultivate Way or sit *ch'an* meditation? No cultivation, no sitting: that is the clear and pure Ch'an of Buddha Existence-Tissue Arrival." [RM 312]

A monk asked: "Master, why do you say mind itself is Buddha?"

"To stop the crying of little children."

"When little children stop crying, what then?"

"Not mind, not Buddha."

"How do you instruct people other than those two types?"

"I tell them it's nothing at all."

"And what if you meet someone who's right there in the middle of that nothing?"

"I teach them how to manifest the majestic Way." [SFB 78]

When he first requested instruction from Patriarch Way-Entire, Ch'an master Dharma-Perpetua from Plum-Vast Mountain asked: "What is Buddha?"

"Mind itself is Buddha," replied Way-Entire.

Perpetua suddenly had a great awakening.

Afterward, he returned to live on Plum-Vast Mountain. When Way-Entire heard he was back living on the mountain, he sent a monk there to ask: "When you visited Patriarch Way-Entire, what did you realize that made you come back to live on this mountain?"

"He told me mind is Buddha. So now I can simply live here with this mountain."

"These days, Way-Entire teaches a different Buddha-dharma," said the monk.

"How is it different?"

"These days he says *not mind, not Buddha*."

"That old guy's been confounding people forever, and he's still at it," declared Perpetua. "You can keep *not mind, not Buddha*. I'm happy looking after *mind itself is Buddha*."

When the monk returned and told Way-Entire what had happened, Way-Entire said: "The plums are ripe." [SFB 73]

"How do you live integral to Way?" asked a monk.

"I long ago stopped living integral to Way," replied Patriarch Way-Entire.

"Then what is the *ch'i*-weave mind Bodhidharma brought from the West?" another monk asked.

Way-Entire struck him a blow, and said: "If I hadn't walloped you, I'd be a laughingstock all through the land." [SFB 79]

"Now that you understand your own original-nature is itself Buddha, so your whole life through—walking or standing, sitting or sleeping—there's never a single dharma anywhere to realize. And this existence-tissue all thusness-clarity absolute—it has nothing to do with any name whatsoever, not even the name *Absence*. That's why the sutra says: *Wisdom cannot fathom Presence and Absence.*

"Don't seek inside, and don't seek outside. Trust your original source-tissue nature, not some original-nature your mind cooks-up. The sutra says: *All these different ch'i-weave insights we invent: I tell you they're just mind measuring things out.* And no-mind mind, Absence-mind mind: that is the unmeasurable measure.

"No-name is the name all clarity-absolute, and no-search the search all clarity-absolute. The sutra says: *To search out dharma, you must have nothing to search out.* That's because there is no Buddha outside of mind, and no mind outside of Buddha." [RM 246]

Reflecting contours of what happens, the mind-ground
speaks, and it's the very tranquility of *bodhi*-awakening.

The inner-pattern and this world it shapes: they move
unhindered, and so it is that everything born is unborn. [SFB 63]

Someone asked: "What is the *ch'i*-weave mind Bodhidharma brought from the West?"

"What is the *ch'i*-weave mind of here right now?" [SFB78]

The great master Patriarch Sudden-Horse Way-Entire said: "You want to know mind? These very words being spoken are your mind—even as they call this mind *Buddha*, or call it *the dharma-self Buddha of the actual throughout all its forms and appearances*. Even as they give it the name *Way*." [RM 248]

Out walking with Patriarch Way-Entire one day, Ch'an master Treasure-Discern from Flax Canyon asked: "What is vast nirvana?"

"Quick!" replied Patriarch.

"Quick what?"

"Look at the streamwater!" [SFB 73]

When Master Stone-Bowl first came for instruction, Patriarch Way-Entire asked: "Where have you come from?"

"From Crow-Bowl," replied Bowl.

"And what does Crow-Bowl talk about these days?"

"How many people are there here in these blank expanses?"

"Okay, forget blank expanses. What can you reveal in perfect quiet?"

Bowl moved three steps closer.

"I'd like to give Crow-Bowl seven blows with my stick," said Patriarch Way-Entire. "Will you do that for me when you return?"

"Sure, once I'm done with you! You need to feel them first!"

Afterward, Stone-Bowl left and returned to Crow-Bowl. [SFB 76]

When Master Elder-River from Whole-Flood first came to Patriarch Way-Entire for instruction, he asked: "What is the *ch'i*-weave mind Bodhidharma brought from the West?"

"First, offer your bows," replied Way-Entire.

When Elder-River bowed reverently, Way-Entire kicked him over. Suddenly, Elder-River had a great awakening. He stood back up clapping his hands and roaring with glorious laughter, then cried out: "How vast and wondrous, vast and wondrous! Three-shadowed earth of *samadhi* a hundred thousand times, inner-pattern Way beyond all measure: it's all revealed on the mere tip of a hair—but now, now I've entered its root and source!"

He then bowed reverently to Way-Entire and left. Later, back home at his monastery, he said to the assembled sangha: "Ever since Patriarch Way-Entire kicked me over, I've been laughing nonstop!" [SFB 77]

"What is the wordless insight of Buddha's teaching?" asked Hundred-Elder Mountain.[16]

"Exactly where you are when you give up that self you happen to be in this grand unfurling of things," Patriarch Way-Entire replied. [SFB 69]

The master ascended to his seat in the Dharma Hall. A long time passed. Hundred-Elder Mountain picked up his sitting-cushion. The master descended from his seat. [RM 226]

It was morning when Master Way-Entire returned to the Great Transformation of things. The evening before, Way-Entire's head monk asked him, "You've seemed unwell, master. How are you feeling tonight?"

"Sun-face Buddha. Moon-face Buddha." [RM 233]

寒山

Cold Mountain (Han Shan, ca. 8th–9th centuries)

CH'AN TEACHING INSISTS WE ARE IN OUR INHERENT nature already enlightened—that if we can only realize this, there is no reason for practice. It also insists that wisdom is outside teaching. In the same mold as T'ao Ch'ien (p. 107), Cold Mountain possessed an effortless mastery of these insights, a mastery embodied in his life as an outsider living on the fringe of a mountain monastery's sangha: monks struggling to attain that enlightenment that was already theirs.

Almost nothing is known about Cold Mountain the person: he exists more as legend than historical fact. It is said that he lived alone on Cold Mountain, a summit in the Heaven-Terrace Mountains of southeast China. There, he often visited that nearby monastery, where a like-minded friend in the kitchen shared leftovers with him, and the resident monks thought him quite insane. There are stories of his antics there, bantering with his friend and ridiculing the monks for their devout pursuit of an enlightenment they already possessed. But mostly he roamed the mountains, a Ch'an sage composing poems with wild abandon: a dramatic embodiment of *wu-wei*, that Absence-action so central to Ch'an practice.

He inscribed these poems on rocks and trees, the water-based ink sure to dissolve away in the mist and rain. They were collected by a local official who, recognizing Cold Mountain's genius, assembled them into a collection that was preserved. This Cold Mountain came to be widely admired in the literary and Ch'an communities of China (cf. the reverence expressed by Ch'an master Visitation-Land, pp. 232–33). This admiration spread to Korea and Japan, and recently to the West, where Gary Snyder's influential translations recreated Cold Mountain as a Ch'an poet for contemporary America.

Cold Mountain is clearly shaped by the Taoist cosmological/ontological framework. He often deploys the grand concepts defining that framework, and he is entirely in the mold of those wild sages that frequent the *Chuang Tzu*. Cold Mountain identifies the empty-mind of Ch'an enlightenment with the mountain itself. And like so many other Ch'an masters, he took as his own the name of the mountain where he lived. He was a sage-master of belonging utterly to the Taoist cosmology, the dynamic spiritual ecology that the mountain realm manifests so dramatically. Indeed, in some of his best poems, we find Cold Mountain magically emptying out the distinction between Cold Mountain the poet and Cold Mountain the mountain.

NOTE

For translation comparison: The Cold Mountain poems are untitled, but poem numbers can be used to locate poems in the many translations of Cold Mountain's poems, several of which include Finding Lists for editions where the sequence differs (notably Gary Snyder's small selection that was originally printed in his first book, *Riprap*, 1959). Major translations include: Burton Watson's *Cold Mountain* (1962); Red Pine's *The Collected Songs of Cold Mountain* (1983/2000); Robert Henricks's *The Poetry of Han-shan* (1990); Paul Rouzer's *The Poetry of Hanshan* (2017); Kazuaki Tanahashi and Peter Levitt's *The Complete Cold Mountain* (2018).

The Collected Poems of
Master Cold Mountain

9

People ask for the Cold Mountain Way.
Cold Mountain Road gives out where

confusions of ice outlast summer heat
and sun can't thin mists of blindness.

So how did someone like me get here?
My mind's just not the same as yours:

if that mind of yours were like mine,
you'd be right here in the midst of it.

81

Springs flowing pure clarity in emerald streams,
moonlight's radiant white bathes Cold Mountain.

Leave wisdom dark: spirit's enlightened of itself.
Empty your gaze and this world's beyond silence.

97

It's like steaming sand to make rice, or
not digging a well until thirsty. You can

exhaust yourself polishing a raw brick,
but how can you ever make it a mirror?[17]

Buddha says everything shares one dark
origin, thusness-clarity existence-tissue

their original-nature. See that, then you
never leave idleness to seek and struggle.

199

Under vast arrays of stars, dazzling depths of night,
I light a lone lamp among cliffs. The moon hasn't set.

It's the unpolished jewel. Incandescence round and full,
it hangs there in blackest-azure skies, my very mind.

211

In jewel-bright water's crystalline clarity,
you can see to the bottom of occurrence-

appearing-of-itself. Animals grace bright
clarity waters in a mind free of concerns,

shimmering. No illusions arising: that is
mind changeless across *kalpa* after *kalpa*.

When you make this your understanding,
your understanding is open—bottomless.

220

Everyone who glimpses Cold Mountain
starts complaining about insane winds,

about a look human eyes can't endure
and a shape nothing but tattered robes.

They can't fathom these words of mine.
Theirs I won't even mention. I just tell

all those busy people bustling around:
come face Cold Mountain for a change.

226

I delight in the everyday Way, myself
among mist and vine, rock and cave,

wildlands feeling so boundlessly free,
white clouds companions in idleness.

Roads don't reach those human realms.
You only climb this high in no-mind:

I sit here on open rock: a lone night,
a full moon drifting up Cold Mountain.

247

I see people leaving home, becoming monks,
but they never search into real home-leaving.

To really leave home means thusness-clarity
perfected, a pellucid mind utterly unfettered,

crystalline alone in dark-enigma's mystery,
existence-tissue accord, relying on nothing.

Then you range *samsara*'s three realms far
and wide, no anchor amid its four-fold birth,

no concern or purpose, Absence-action gone
wandering boundless and free and all delight.

279

I sit silent and alone beneath cliffwalls,
a full moon adrift and dazzling in sky.

No light of its own, it still shimmers
ten thousand things amid its shadows,

awareness illuminating vast expanses,
fathoming in emptiness dark-enigma

mystery. There, look there: this very
moon that is mind's hinge and pivot!

280

It began with a longing for kinship in Way,
kinship in Way—that's what lasts and lasts.

Often now I meet wanderers free of origins,
guests all talking *ch'an* stillness. Together,

we discuss dark-enigma on moonlit nights,
and by dawn we're exploring inner-pattern,

that loom-of-origins weave leaving no trace,
our original source-tissue identity apparent.

282

Amid ten thousand streams up among
thousands of clouds, a man all idleness

wanders blue mountains all day long,
returns at night to sleep below cliffs.

In the whirl of springs and autumns,
to inhabit this calm, no tangles of dust:

it's sheer joy, depending on nothing,
still as an autumn river's quiet water.

309

Sage Cold Mountain
is forever like this:

dwells alone and free,
not alive, not dead.

黃蘗

Yellow-Bitterroot Mountain
(Huang Po, d. 850)

YELLOW-BITTERROOT MOUNTAIN WAS CERTAINLY A master of Way-Entire's "wild words and woolly actions" Ch'an, apparently deploying wild-and-woolly teaching methods often. Indeed, he was Way-Entire's dharma grandson, and he was the teacher of Purport Dark-Enigma, the great master of wild-and-woolly Ch'an whom we will meet in the next chapter. There are striking descriptions of Yellow-Bitterroot's wild-and-woolly Ch'an in the Ch'an literature: Purport Dark-Enigma's enlightenment story, for instance, where Yellow-Bitterroot's wordless blows lead to Purport's awakening (pp. 211–13). But *Transmission of the Mind-Dharma Essence*, the primary record of Yellow-Bitterroot's teaching, contains barely a mention of wild-and-woolly teaching. Instead, it is a series of explanatory dharma-talks—and this is what Yellow-Bitterroot is primarily known for. In a tradition of "separate transmission outside all teaching," *Transmission of the Mind-Dharma Essence*, with its exhaustive explanations of Ch'an insight, is all about teaching—though always with the intent to evoke sudden and wordless transformation in students.

Fully elucidating the body of assumptions within which Ch'an practice operates, Yellow-Bitterroot Mountain is perhaps the culmination of Ch'an's conceptual development. In this, he sets the stage for the drama of direct teaching to follow, when Ch'an's innovations move further into the "wild words and woolly actions" performative teaching that enacts insight, rather than explaining it in words and concepts. That teaching will begin in earnest with Yellow-Bitterroot Mountain's dharma-heir, Purport Dark-Enigma (p. 2) who, depending heavily on shouts and blows and incomprehensible exclamations, became a great exemplar of "wild-and-woolly" Ch'an. In this wordless teaching, Ch'an's dismantling of concepts and certainties takes on a new focus and ferocity. And that will continue on into the Sung Dynasty's sangha-case practice (see part VI, pp. 257–298), intent upon shattering every possible structure of understanding.

But it was Yellow-Bitterroot's place to explain the principles that allow awakening—and as with his predecessors, it was all about deconstruction, especially deconstruction of the conventional Buddhist beliefs that so many of his students seem to be struggling with. As we have seen throughout the Ch'an tradition, awakening for Yellow-Bitterroot is a Taoist sense of mind dwelling as woven at the deepest cosmological/ontological levels into the Great Transformation of earth's ongoing process of change. It is a dwelling suggested by his full name: Rare-Season of Yellow-Bitterroot Mountain. And it is a dwelling summarized in his repeated references to sentient life that always assume a oneness of human and other sentient beings, a oneness in which we all "share the same primal-unity mind," the same Buddha-nature.

For an example of Yellow-Bitterroot Mountain's appearances in sangha-case collections, see p. 270.

NOTE

For translation comparison: Bracketed numbers refer to page numbers in John Blofeld's *The Zen Teaching of Huang Po* (1959).

Transmission of the Mind-Dharma Essence

All Buddhas and all sentient life—we share the same primal-unity mind. There is absolutely no other dharma.

This mind is without beginnings. It is never born, and it never dies.[18] It has no cropland-green and no harvest-yellow, no forms or appearances, and it has nothing to do with Presence and Absence. You can't call it young or old; it isn't long or short, large or small. This mind is beyond all limits, all words and names; it is beyond all trace and all comparison. It simply is what it always is. Even when thought rustles, twisting you away from this mind, mind remains always emptiness empty:[19] without boundary and impossible to measure.

This primal-unity mind—it alone is Buddha. And Buddha is absolutely no different than sentient life. It's just that we must search outside ourselves to live; and so, we start searching for Buddha. But once we do, we've already turned away and lost Buddha. Using Buddha to find Buddha, wielding mind to seize mind—even if you run yourself ragged for *kalpa* after *kalpa*, it will never work.

Don't understand, stop thinking, give up discontent—then Buddha simply appears shimmering before you." [29–30]

This very mind is Buddha, and Buddha all sentient life. As sentient life, this mind loses nothing; and as Buddhas, it gains nothing. People devote themselves to the six paramitas[20] and the ten thousand rituals and sacred practices, piling up merits and virtues numberless as Ganges sands. But you are originally whole and complete: don't imagine all that self-cultivation can add anything.

When you inhabit origin-tissue, move with it. When origin-tissue grows still, inhabit that stillness. If you don't trust with complete certainty that this is itself Buddha, if instead you devote yourself to mere forms and appearances, performing rituals and sacred practices in the quest for merits and virtues—it's just foolhardy dream and delusion twisting you away from Way.

This very mind is Buddha. There is absolutely no other Buddha, and no other mind. This mind is radiant purity, and remains always emptiness empty—not a mote of appearance or form anywhere. When thoughts explaining mind rustle, twisting you away from dharma's potency, it's just forms and appearances. Buddha without beginnings and without the least form or appearance: to practice the six paramitas and perform ten thousand rituals and sacred practices trying to become such a Buddha—that is to advance by stages. But a Buddha without beginnings and without stages is simply awakened to primal-unity mind, not the least dharma anywhere to master. This is the Buddha of reality itself all clarity-absolute. [30–31]

Buddha shares the same primal-unity mind with all sentient life, no difference whatsoever. This mind is like the emptiness of empty sky— no confusion, no ruin. Empty sky where the vast sun wheels around, blazing down from the four heavens. When it rises, illuminating everything throughout all beneath heaven, the empty-sky emptiness is not illuminated. And when it sets, darkening everything throughout all beneath heaven, empty-sky emptiness is not darkened. Illumination and darkness alternate, but the emptiness of empty sky, its vast and expansive nature, never changes.

This mind of Buddhas and all sentient life—it's exactly like this. People see in Buddha the form of tranquil clarity, radiant illumination and liberation; they see in sentient life the form of mud-stain, shadowy darkness and *samsara*'s death and rebirth. But if you indulge in this kind of understanding, you could practice for *kalpas* numerous as Ganges sands and never realize *bodhi*-awakening. That's because you're devoted to forms and appearances.

There is only this primal-unity mind, not the least dust-mote of dharma to be realized anywhere. And this very mind is Buddha. If students of Way today don't awaken to this mind in all its potency, if they just layer mind over mind and search elsewhere for Buddha—they're devoted to forms and appearances, the rituals and practices of self-cultivation. That's dharma wrong through and through, not the Way of *bodhi*-awakening. [31]

Offering sacrifices in homage to all Buddhas throughout the ten distances of time and space? It can't compare with offering homage to a single no-mind master of Way. Why? Because if you master no-mind, your mind is wholly Absence, wholly the existence-tissue's potency. Rocks and trees all stillness inside, unbounded empty-sky emptiness outside: it does nothing and goes nowhere, has no forms or appearances, no success or failure.

People with plans and goals don't dare enter this dharma. They're afraid of tumbling away into its emptiness, nowhere to drop anchor and settle. So they gaze at the cliff-edge and back away. To see through/across such vast expanses, they search knowledge and analysis. But whoever searches knowledge and analysis is weak and flighty as a feather. And whoever awakens to Way is strong and direct as a horn. [31–32]

People all possess the thing great bodhisattvas reveal. It's nothing other than primal-unity mind. Awaken to it, and that's it. These days, students of Way don't look into their own minds for awakening. Instead, they look outside mind, devoting themselves to forms and appearances. In this, they turn their backs on Way.

The expanse of Ganges sands . . . it's like Buddha said: if all Buddhas and bodhisattvas, Indra and Brahma and all those heavenly beings, if they all go parading across, those sands would not feel the least delight. If oxen and sheep, worms and ants go swarming around, those sands would not feel the least anger. And how could they covet the fragrance of precious treasures, how despise the stench of shit and piss? [32–33]

This mind is no-mind, Absence-mind, completely free of forms and appearances. And it's exactly the same for all sentient life and all Buddhas. Just master Absence no-mind, and you're done.

If students of Way don't see into Absence no-mind with absolute and immediate clarity, they'll spend endless *kalpas* devoted to rituals and practices of self-cultivation and never master Way. Tangled in the practices of Three-Vehicle[21] self-perfection, they'll never find liberation.

Still, direct realization of this mind might come slowly or quickly. Some hear the dharma, and in a flash of thought realize Absence no-mind. But some need to work through the ten stages of bodhisattva faith and the ten stages of bodhisattva wisdom, the ten stages of bodhisattva service and the ten stages of bodhisattva conversion—and only then realize Absence no-mind. Others need to work through the ten stages of Buddhahood before realizing Absence no-mind. But whether the time it takes is long or short, once you realize Absence no-mind you've found a dwelling-place.

There's nothing more to cultivate, no further direct realization. In fact, there's really nothing at all to realize, but that nothing is absolutely not empty. Whether you realize it in a single flash of thought or only after working through the ten stages of Buddhahood, the result is equally wondrous. One isn't deep and the other shallow, but why bother with all those *kalpas* of pointless suffering and bitter struggle? [33–34]

A life all about evil acts and righteous acts is a life devoted to forms and appearances. If in your devotion to form and appearance you perform evil acts, you tangle yourself in the pointless suffering of *samsara's* turning wheel. And if you perform righteous acts, you tangle yourself in the pointless suffering of life's bitter struggle. Either way, it's nothing like giving up words and instantaneously understanding on your own the original source-tissue dharma. This dharma is mind itself: outside mind, there is no dharma. And this mind is dharma itself: outside dharma, there is no mind.

Mind is of itself no-mind, is Absence-mind and indeed Absence-mind Absence. If you nurture Absence-mind mind, mind never becomes Presence. That shadowy silence, all thought and deliberation ended: there's nothing more. Hence the saying: "When the Way of words is cut off, mind moves in the serenity of nirvana's blank extinction."

This mind is the pure-clarity source-tissue Buddha of origins. It's there in everyone. Even creatures that wriggle through the dust—in possessing awareness, they are the same as all Buddhas and bodhisattvas. Mind shares always the same potency, no differences anywhere. It's only because we chase fantasy and illusion that distinctions arise, sowing the seeds for every kind of karmic fruit. [34–35]

Original source-tissue Buddha is, in clearest reality, no single thing. It's empty and everywhere expansive, silent and still, luminous and wondrous, tranquil and joyous. That's what it is. And you enter it through deep awakening to yourself. Once you see things with absolute and immediate clarity, that awakening is instantaneous, full-round and deep, and wholly sufficient. How could that ever be a matter of partial stages?

. . .

And the Buddha also said: "This dharma is perfectly uniform throughout: there is no high or low." That dharma's name is *bodhi*-awakening, and it's nothing other than the pure-clarity source-tissue mind of origins. Manifest in all sentient life and all Buddhas, in this whole rivers-and-mountains world, forms and appearances or no forms and appearances, clear through the ten distances of time and space—it's perfectly uniform throughout, no otherness in relation to some I. [35–36]

This pure-clarity source-tissue mind of origins is always of itself full-round and incandescence luminous everywhere. But people not yet awakened to it think mind is just sight and sound, insight and wisdom. Or they think it's hidden by sight and sound, insight and wisdom. And so, they don't look into the luminous purity of mind's original source-tissue potency. But it's simple: seen with absolute and immediate clarity as Absence no-mind, this original source-tissue potency simply appears, shimmering of itself like the vast sun wheeling up through the emptiness of empty sky, illuminating the ten distances of all time and space without the least hindrance.

Simple. Isn't that why students of Way only understand sight and sound, insight and wisdom; why they let that understanding guide them? Casting aside emptiness for sight and sound, insight and wisdom, they cut mind's path short and find nowhere to enter. They only understand original source-tissue mind in terms of sight and sound, insight and wisdom. But original source-tissue mind is nowhere near sight and sound, insight and wisdom; and it isn't far away either. Just don't rely on sight and sound, insight and wisdom to help you see through things, and don't rely on them to help you think through things. Don't roam far from sight and sound, insight and wisdom hoping to find mind, and don't cast them away hoping to grasp dharma. Don't keep them close or far away. Don't dwell in them or devote yourself to them. For throughout the whole length and breadth of this world, there is nothing that is not the Buddha-Way Terrace[22] of enlightenment. [36–37]

When people hear me say Buddhas only transmit mind-dharma, they think there's some dharma other than mind to realize or possess. So they use mind to search for dharma. They don't understand that mind is itself dharma, and dharma mind. And how could you use mind to search for mind? You could waste a thousand ten-thousand *kalpas* trying to find it, but that day would never come. It's nothing like Absence no-mind right now, for Absence no-mind is itself the original source-tissue dharma.

It's like a strong warrior confused about the pearl right there on his forehead. He sets out looking for it, searching through all ten distances of time and space. He'll never find it. But if a sage shows it to him, that warrior would see for himself the original source-tissue pearl was right there all the time. It's the same for students of Way, confused about their own original source-tissue mind: they don't realize it is itself Buddha, so they set out searching. They devote themselves to rituals and practices of self-perfection, hoping to progress through stages of realization. But you could search like that even for countless *kalpas* and never master Way. It's nothing like Absence no-mind right now.

Just understand with absolute certainty that throughout all dharmas there is nothing of Presence and nothing of arrival, nothing to depend on and nowhere to dwell, nothing that masters and nothing that is mastered. If you cease the delusion of thought, you instantly realize *bodhi*-awakening directly. And when you realize Way, you realize Buddha in original source-tissue mind directly. Pursuing self-perfection through countless *kalpas* is just empty cultivation. It's like that warrior: the pearl he finds was always right there on his forehead. Finding it had nothing to do with how much strength he devoted to the search.

And so it is that Buddha said: "In attaining complete and unexcelled *bodhi*-awakening, I truly attained nothing at all." But he was afraid people wouldn't believe that, so he concocted the insights of his five visions and the truths of his five teachings. But what he said was not empty: it's reality seen all clarity-absolute, the first and foremost inner-pattern Way [37–38]

Just see in a sudden flash of absolute and immediate clarity that your mind is from the beginning Buddha, that there is no dharma to attain, no rituals and sacred practices to cultivate: this is the supreme Way, the existence-tissue Buddha all clarity-absolute. Students of Way fear that a single thought will cut them off from Way completely. But thoughts coming one after another are Absence-forms and Absence-actions. And so, they too are Buddha.

Students of Way—if you want to become Buddha, don't imagine Buddha-dharma is something to study. Just study the end of searching and the end of realization. In the end of searching, mind is unborn. And in the end of realization, mind is undying. Unborn and undying: that is Buddha. [40]

. . . if you stop seeing in terms of Absence and Presence, you will see dharma itself. [43]

From the time he arrived here in Middle-Kingdom China, the great master Bodhidharma taught only original source-tissue mind, and he transmitted only primal-unity dharma. He used Buddha to transmit Buddha, and never mentioned any other Buddha. He used dharma to transmit dharma, and never mentioned any other dharma. Dharma is the unsayable dharma, Buddha the ungraspable Buddha. And they're both this pure-clarity source-tissue mind of origins.

Only this is real. Anything more is not clarity-absolute itself. For *prajna* is wisdom, and this *prajna*-wisdom is original source-tissue mind itself the very form of Absence. [44]

Ever since the Buddha Existence-Tissue Arrival entrusted the dharma to Kasyapa, masters have used mind itself to imprint mind: mind after mind, no difference whatsoever. Revealing emptiness itself, this imprint eludes silver-tongued sutras. And revealing things themselves, it eludes even the most profound dharma. That's why masters use mind itself to imprint mind: mind after mind, no difference whatsoever. This mind-imprint of master and student: it's wisdom rendered whole again. And that's impossibly difficult, so almost no one knows realization. How could they? That mind-imprint is Absence no-mind, and realization is no-realization Absence. [50]

. . . This Way is effortless reality itself all clarity-absolute. Originally it had no name, but that just made it impossible for people to understand. They were confused about what it was both within themselves and without. So the Buddhas appeared, hoping to smash that confusion with their teachings. Afraid people like you wouldn't understand completely, they named it *Way*.[23] But you can't kindle liberation by clinging to such names. That's why Chuang Tzu said: "Once you've got the fish, you can forget the trap."[24]

When body and mind move as occurrence-appearing-of-itself, you fathom Way and understand mind, which is to fathom all source-tissue origins. If you do that, you can be called a monk. And the fruit of being a monk is to live whole, without any uneasiness about what is to come.

But such realization won't come from book-learning. If you use mind to search for mind, traveling here and there to study under sage teachers, certain that it will all be revealed through learning—when will realization ever come? The ancients had razor-sharp minds all wild bounty. Hearing even a single word, they gave up learning. That's what we call *a master who has given up learning for the Absence-action idleness of Way*. [55–56]

"What is relative reality?" someone asked.

The master answered: "Talk's just a tangle of bramble-vines. What good is it? This Cosmos is always, from the very beginning, such clarity crystalline pure. Why bother with wise teachings, questions and answers? Simply trust Absence no-mind whole. I call that *nirvana-wisdom*. You walk and stand still day after day, sit and lie down—but through it all, wise teachings haunt you. Just don't devote yourself to them, don't think they are the dharma.

Words appear and disappear in the blink of an eye—and that too is nirvana-wisdom. But these days, if people set out on the dharma path, they mostly study the Way of Ch'an as if it were seductive music and beautiful women. Why can't they set out on our mind-path, sharing this mind all emptiness empty? It's like setting out all withered wood and raw stone, all cold ash and dead fire. If you do this, you'll have a clean record. If you don't, you'll face old Yama when you die, and that demon of hell will beat a confession out of you!

It's simple: just don't go anywhere near all those dharmas of Absence and Presence. Then your mind will be like the emptiness of empty sky with the sun wheeling around through it: radiant illumination occurring of itself, not luminous and yet luminous. It's effortless, isn't it? When you master it, there's no harbor where you can drop anchor and settle. Then you practice the sacred practice of all Buddhas, dwelling nowhere and therefore bringing their mind to life. And it's your dharma-self all clarity crystalline pure. I call it *complete and unexcelled bodhi-awakening*."

. . .

People end like arrows fallen to earth, their energy spent. If somehow they hit the target in some future life, it won't come of clever insights.

Insights are nothing like Absence-action, that gate of the actual itself: there, it's a single leap into Buddha's land of existence-tissue arrival.
[61–62]

... when Bodhidharma came from the West, he simply pointed at mind: it's in mind itself that you *see original-nature*²⁵ and become Buddha, not in words and talk. [66]

Someone asked: "For a sage, Absence no-mind is Buddha. And for a commoner, is Absence no-mind also profound and empty silence?"

The master answered: "In dharma there is no sage and no commoner, and there's no profound silence. Original source-tissue dharma is not about Presence, and it isn't about seeing into Absence. Original source-tissue dharma is not about Absence, and it isn't about seeing into Presence. Presence blurring into Absence: that's where things seen become part of us. Part of us, and yet vanishing mirage. Hence the saying: *Sight and hearing are vanishing mirage. And it's like that for all sentient life.*

"Inside Bodhidharma's gate, there was a single teaching: Give up the loom-of-origins unfurling this world and forget seeing into things. Forget even the loom-of-origins itself, and you live exalted in the Buddha-Way's lofty abundance. Fuss over the distinctions of explanation, and you live burned by an army of demons." [68–69]

Mind is undifferentiated, and dharma too is undifferentiated. Mind is Absence-action, and dharma too is Absence-action. [72]

Someone asked: "If that's true, what about all those Buddhas throughout the ten distances of time and space—is there a dharma they all teach when they appear in this world?"

The master answered: "When they appear in this world, those Buddhas all teach the same dharma of primal-unity mind. That's what Shakyamuni Buddha silently entrusted to the great Kasyapa: this dharma-potency of primal-unity mind all emptiness empty clear through to the far boundaries of dharma. It's called *the inner-pattern of all Buddhas.*

"If you try to talk about this one dharma, what kind of realization will all your words get you? And seeing through the loom-of-origins unfurling this world or even this world itself—what kind of realization will that get you? The only realization comes in darkness shared. That's the single gate, and it's called *the dharma gate of Absence-action*. If you want to master it, just understand the sudden awakening of Absence no-mind itself.

"If you use mind to study mind, you're soon turned around and gone far away. And if you don't have a cragged mind of mountain paths, you've given up mind completely. Make your mind a chunk of wood or rock, then you can begin to study the Way in all its intricacy." [79–80]

If your mind is unborn and thoughts arise—it's *tzu-jan*, not illusion. That's why they say, "When mind is born, all sorts of dharmas are born. When mind is extinguished, all sorts of dharmas are extinguished." [80]

The dharma of all things is not fundamentally Presence, and it's also not Absence. What has arisen from the origin-tissue is not Presence, and what has vanished back into the origin-tissue is not Absence. Original source-tissue is surely not Presence, for *original source-tissue* is not the fact of original source-tissue. Mind is surely not mind, for *mind* is not the fact of mind. Form and appearance are surely not form and appearance, for *form and appearance* are not the fact of form and appearance. Anything said is not dharma and is not original source-tissue mind. In this, you begin to understand dharma transmission mind-to-mind. Dharma is not-dharma, not-dharma is dharma, Absence dharma and Absence not-dharma. That's why dharma transmission is mind-to-mind.

. . .

Right now, thought following thought after thought: just don't dwell in it. [106]

To penetrate the depths of Ch'an's Way, you must inhabit the full expanse of unborn mind. [127]

I have only one thing to teach you: unborn mind. When mind is unborn, *tzu-jan* itself becomes the great wisdom. [130]

臨濟義玄

Purport Dark-Enigma (Lin Chi, d. 866)

PURPORT DARK-ENIGMA WAS THE DHARMA-HEIR OF Yellow-Bitterroot Mountain, and was therefore in the direct line of transmission from Sudden-Horse Way-Entire. Purport Dark-Enigma (義玄) is commonly known as Lin Chi (臨濟) because he was abbot of a small monastery at Lin Chi, which means "River-Crossing Overlook." And so, his full name means "Purport Dark-Enigma of River-Crossing Overlook," and his collected teachings is entitled *River-Crossing Overlook Record*.

Purport Dark-Enigma's stature is hard to overstate. In modern times, there are two major schools of Zen: Rinzai and Soto. *Rinzai* is the Japanese pronunciation of 臨濟 (Lin Chi), adapted as the school's name because Purport is the founder of Rinzai Zen. Rinzai is considered the more spontaneous and action-oriented of the two schools (Soto the more gradual and contemplative), and Purport Dark-Enigma is perhaps *the* archetypal master of Sudden-Horse Way-Entire's "wild words and woolly actions" Ch'an (p. 176). He set the standard for passing on Ch'an's wordless "transmission outside all teaching" by means of spontaneous and outrageous action—shouts perhaps most famously, but also blows and incoherent utterances—a teaching method that he learned from Yellow-Bitterroot Mountain (see the enlightenment story below, pp. 211–13) and that eventually came to define sangha-case practice (see part VI, p. 257ff.).

At the same time, this quintessentially wordless teaching and practice still operates within the Taoist conceptual framework. Purport not only adopted Dark-Enigma as his Ch'an name, but dark-enigma and the other foundational Taoist concepts also subtly shape the framework of Purport's teaching in his *River-Crossing Overlook Record*: Absence, Tao/Way, loom-of-origins, etc. Indeed, Purport Dark-Enigma's own enlightenment is described as seeing the "inner-pattern Way" (p. 212), a description we also find in chapter 28 of *No-Gate Gateway* (p. 294) and elsewhere in the Ch'an literature.

As was often the case for influential Ch'an masters, Purport began studying conventional Buddhism with its scriptural truth, otherworldly abstraction, and subservience to teachers and tradition. But he soon turned to Ch'an, eventually mastering it's anti-Buddhist posture (one among countless examples is his "*bodhi*-awakening and nirvana are just hitching-posts for donkeys"). The intent of Purport's teaching is to demonstrate the liberation that results when you dismantle all concepts and certainties. Without those outside authorities, you are left to your own original-nature. Quite the contrary of his seemingly demeaning teaching methods (shouts, blows, insults), this is perhaps Purport's most insistent teaching: that we are each always already enlightened, that we only need to trust ourselves. This is emphasized in the noble ways he so often addresses his students as already enlightened ones: "You who soar the Way-flood," "You masters of Way dependent on nothing," "You great heart-sight clarity masters."

The radical nature of Purport Dark-Enigma's demolition strategy was revealed at his death, the ultimate moment of personal deconstruction. When he asks how his dharma-heir will continue his teaching, the dharma-heir gives a resounding Dark-Enigma shout, echoing Purport's teaching exactly. This dharma-heir is named, with typical Ch'an irony, Thrice-Sage. Purport declares the shout mere "sophistry," and declares that his teaching is doomed (p. 219). In this, he demolishes even his own teaching. And at the same time, he insists for a last time that realization requires a radical self-reliance, a liberation from all external dependence, including dependence on the teaching of Purport himself. This point is emphasized with no small amount of comic irony in the Ch'an legend, with its profound distrust of teaching and texts—for there, the compilation of Purport Dark-Enigma's teaching into the *River-Crossing Overlook Record* is attributed to this very Thrice-Sage, whose echo of Purport's teaching signaled the end of Purport's teaching!

For examples of Purport Dark-Enigma's appearances in sangha-case collections, see pp. 267, 270.

NOTE

For translation comparison: Bracketed numbers refer to page numbers in Ruth Sasaki's *The Record of Linji* (2009, Thomas Kirchner ed.; original Sasaki translation, 1975) and Burton Watson's *The Zen Teachings of Master Lin-chi* (1993).

River-Crossing Overlook Record

When he was a beginning student in Yellow-Bitterroot Mountain's sangha, Master Purport Dark-Enigma was simple and single-minded in his practice. Admiring this, the head monk said, "He's still young, but he's different from the others." Then he asked, "How long have you been here?"

"Three years," answered Purport Dark-Enigma.

"And have you asked the abbot for instruction?"

"No. I don't know what to ask."

"Why don't you go ask what the Buddha-dharma's great *ch'i*-weave insight is?"

Purport went to ask. But before he finished his question, Yellow-Bitterroot struck him a blow. Purport left.

The head monk asked, "What happened?"

"Before I even finished asking my question, the abbot struck me. I don't understand it."

"Okay, go ask again."

So, Purport went again to ask, and Yellow-Bitterroot again struck him a blow. The master asked three times, and three times received a blow.

Finally, Purport returned to the head monk and explained: "You were kind, sending me to inquire of the abbot. But three times I asked, and three times I received a blow. There must be some awful delusion blinding me to the depths of his wordless teaching. So, I've come to say goodbye. I'm leaving."

"Well, if you're leaving, you'd better say goodbye to the abbot," responded the head monk.

The master bowed reverently and left.

The head monk went directly to the abbot and said: "That young man who was asking for instruction, he's truly of the dharma. If he comes to say goodbye, show him warmth and kindness. Someday, he'll bore right through and sprout up into a vast tree spreading cool shade for people throughout all beneath heaven."

Purport Dark-Enigma went to bid Yellow-Bitterroot farewell, and Bitterroot said, "You don't need to go somewhere else for realization.

But if you're going, go to Dolt-Vast's place along the banks of Lofty-Serene Stream. He'll explain things."

When Purport arrived at Dolt-Vast's temple, Dolt-Vast asked: "Where have you come from?"

"From Yellow-Bitterroot's place," replied Purport.

"How did Yellow-Bitterroot teach you?"

"Three times I asked about the Buddha-dharma's great *ch'i*-weave insight, and three times I was struck. I don't know if I was at fault or not."

"Yellow-Bitterroot's such a kind old grandmother! He cleared away your troubles just like that. And you come asking if you're at fault!?"

Hearing these words, Purport Dark-Enigma had a great awakening. "Yellow-Bitterroot's Buddha-dharma straight out of origins: how simple it is!"

Dolt-Vast grabbed hold of Purport and shouted, "You bed-pissing demon! A minute ago you asked if you're at fault, and now you say Yellow-Bitterroot's Buddha-dharma is simple! What inner-pattern Way did you just see? Speak! Speak!"

Purport hit Dolt-Vast three times in the ribs.

Dolt-Vast shoved him away and said, "Yellow-Bitterroot's your teacher. It's not my affair."

So, Purport left Dolt-Vast and returned to Yellow-Bitterroot. When Yellow-Bitterroot saw him coming, he asked: "All this coming and going, coming and going. When will it ever end?"

"It's all because you were such a kind old grandmother," replied Purport, "the way you cut clean through to the intimate essence of mind." And after giving Bitterroot the messages people had entrusted to him, he stood waiting.

"Where did you go?" asked Yellow-Bitterroot.

"The other day, after the kindness of your wordless teaching, you said I should go to Dolt-Vast for instruction, so I did."

"And what did Dolt-Vast have to say?"

Purport Dark-Enigma told him what had happened.

"I wish that guy would come here. I'd love to whack him a good one," said Yellow-Bitterroot.

"Why wait?" responded Purport. "You can have it right now!" At that, the master suddenly slapped Yellow-Bitterroot!

"You crazy maniac!" cried Bitterroot. "You come back here and tug at this tiger's whiskers!?"

"*KHO-AAAA!!*" shouted Purport Dark-Enigma.

"Someone get this crazy maniac out of here," called Bitterroot. "Take him to the Meditation Hall."

Later, River-Act Mountain told the story to Reliance Mountain[26] and asked, "So, did Purport Dark-Enigma here rely on Dolt-Vast's strength or Yellow-Bitterroot's?"

"He not only rode on the tiger's head," answered Reliance Mountain, "he lashed its tail around too!" [312–17; 104–7]

. . .

Purport Dark-Enigma ascended to his seat in the Dharma Hall, and said: "In your body's lump of red flesh there is a nowhere person all thusness-clarity. For every one of you, that person is forever leaving and entering your eyes and mouths. If you haven't yet found direct evidence of this—Look! Look!"

A monk stepped forward from the assembled sangha and asked, "What is this nowhere person all thusness-clarity?"

The master leapt from his meditation seat, seized the monk, and cried: "Speak! Speak!"

The monk paused to consider. The master shoved him away and said, "Hey, you nowhere person all thusness-clarity—what kind of dry shit-wipe stick are you?" Then he went back to his rooms.[27] [129–31; 4–5]

Purport Dark-Enigma ascended to his seat in the Dharma Hall. A monk asked, "What is the Buddha-dharma's great *ch'i*-weave insight?"

The master raised his whisk straight up.

The monk shouted: "*KHO-AAAA!!*"

The master struck him a blow.

Another monk asked: "What is the Buddha-dharma's great *ch'i*-weave insight?"

Again, the master raised his whisk straight up.

The monk shouted: "*KHO-AAAA!!*"

The master shouted: "*KHO-AAAA!!*"

When the monk paused to consider, the master struck him a blow.

Then Master Purport Dark-Enigma spoke: "Great friends, listen. Those who practice dharma don't hesitate to ditch selfhood and abandon the inevitable unfolding of things. Twenty years ago, at my old teacher Yellow-Bitterroot Mountain's place, three times I asked what the Buddha-dharma's great *ch'i*-weave insight is, and three times I was blessed with a blow of his walking stick. It felt like he was fanning me with the fresh leaves of a mugwort charm. How I long for another blow of that stick. But who could do that for me now?"

A monk stepped forward from the assembled sangha and said, "I'll do it!"

The master offered his stick. When the monk paused to consider, the master struck him a blow. [135–36; 15–16]

"Students today never find realization. It's a sickness—and why? They don't trust themselves. So they bustle around this world of transformation, tumble through the surge of circumstance, chasing its ten thousand ever-arising appearances, never finding the realization that comes only from themselves. That mind galloping far and wide, searching, searching: if only you bring it to rest, you're no different than a patriarch or buddha.

"You want to know the patriarchs and Buddhas? They're precisely you here facing me and listening to the dharma. But you students don't trust yourselves. You gallop around searching outside yourselves. The only thing you'll find like that is fancy words and wondrous images. You'll never realize elsewhere the living *ch'i*-weave insight of the patriarchs." [155; 23]

"You who soar the Way-flood, listen. Dharma-mind is without form, is Absence-form. It opens clear through the ten distances of time and space. In the eye, it's called sight; and in the ear, it's called hearing. In the nose, it smells scents; and in the mouth, it talks philosophy. In the hand, it grabs hold; and in the foot, it hurries away.

"At source-tissue origins, it's a single pure illumination. And differentiated into the senses, it's harmonious and whole. This one primal-unity mind: it's without form, it's Absence—so everywhere you go is liberation!" [165–66; 25–26]

"You who soar the Way-flood, listen. When this mountain monk talks about dharma, what dharma am I talking about? I'm talking about mind-ground[28] dharma—mind-ground that can so easily awaken in commoners and in sages, in pure and in defiled, in thusness-clarity and in rapt confusion. And yet, it isn't *thusness-clarity* or *rapt confusion, commoner* or *sage.*

"We can use names to define thusness-clarity or rapt confusion, commoner or sage—but those defining names aren't the actual itself. You who soar the Way-flood, listen. Just grasp the actual and act! Don't bother with names. We call this *the wordless depths of dark-enigma.*" [181–83; 30]

Instructing the assembled sangha, the master said: "You who soar the Way-flood, listen. Buddha-dharma isn't about hard work. It's just ordinary life: Absence itself moving at ease, no purpose, nothing to do. Shit and piss, dress and eat. And when you're tired, sleep.

> Simpletons laugh at me,
> but the wise understand. [185; 31]

You here listening to this dharma, you masters of Way dependent on nothing—you alone are the mother of all Buddhas. Buddhas are therefore birthed from this dependence on nothing. So if you're awakened and truly dependent on nothing, there's no Buddhahood to attain. And if you see this, this realization—it's liberation, it's seeing the wild thusness of things all clarity-absolute. [197; 36]

"If you want to move through the wandering and dwelling of life and death with the easy freedom of donning and shedding clothes, just recognize this person here right now listening to this dharma: no form and no appearance, no root and no source, and no dwelling-place. For your form is Absence and your appearance is Absence, your root is Absence and your source is Absence, and your dwelling-place, too, is Absence. It's the you alive throughout everything everywhere, for the place to plant the ten thousand seeds of our teaching and practice is no place.

"The more you chase it, the further away it is. The more you seek it, the more it turns away. And so, people call it *mystery profound*. But you who soar the Way-flood, listen. Don't just imagine this companion is some dream-mirage. Before long, it's gone home to perennial Absence." [198–99; 36]

"The moment people arrive here, I understand them through and through. Whatever teacher they've come from, it's all a yammering dream-mirage of names and scriptures. But if someone appears simply riding the surge of circumstance—that is the wordless dark-enigma all Buddhas teach. On that surge of circumstance, such Buddhas cannot praise themselves, saying, "I am Buddha riding the surge of circumstance." No, they're just masters of Way dependent upon nothing and always setting out on the surge of circumstance." [206; 40]

Buddhas and patriarchs live at ease, nothing to do. A life full of this world's confusion and action, or a life of Absence-action free of all that: for them, it's pure clarity either way. And all these monks bald and blind: they eat their fill, then sit in *ch'an* stillness, practicing great Bodhidharma's wall-gaze meditation. They pin down the confusion of thought to stop its arising; they detest noise and seek tranquility. But all this has nothing to do with Way's dharma. Some old patriarch said: "Whether you turn mind inward to gaze at tranquility or turn mind outward to illuminate things, whether you nurture mind's own clarity or freeze mind into *samadhi*-stillness—it's all your own spellbound conjuring." [212–14; 43]

"You who soar the Way-flood, listen. If you want to understand existence-tissue dharma, if you want to understand it completely, it's simple: just don't buy into the delusions people cook up. Looking within, looking without: whatever you meet, kill it. If you meet Buddha, kill Buddha. If you meet patriarchs, kill patriarchs. If you meet *lohans*, kill *lohans*.[29] If you meet parents, kill parents. If you meet kith and kin, kill kith and kin. That's how liberation opens. Just don't hold things so close, and you'll leap free into the composure where you are wholly what you are.

"It seems students who soar the Way-flood come here from every corner of the world, but none arrive dependent on nothing. As soon as I see them, this mountain monk starts dealing out blows. If they come with a raised hand, I strike the hand raised. If they come with mouth talking, I strike the talking mouth. If they come with eyes gazing, I strike the gazing eye. Never has one come in solitary freedom. They all arrive clamoring after something outside themselves: that idleness of old masters, this surge of circumstance woven out by the loom-of-origins.

"This mountain monk doesn't have the least dharma to teach anyone. All I can do is heal sickness and unravel knots. You who soar the Way-flood have come from every corner of the world—now, if you could just stand here before me dependent on nothing, then we could really talk things over. But in fifteen years, there's been no one. It's always ghostly spirits clinging to grass and leaves among bamboo and trees, wild-fox demons mountains breathe out. Every time they find some lump of shit, it's a feeding frenzy. . . .

"Facing you right here and now, I say this clearly: There is no Buddha: Buddha is Absence. There is no dharma: dharma is Absence.[30] There is no practice: practice is Absence. And there is no direct enlightenment: direct enlightenment is Absence." [236–38; 52–53]

"You who soar the Way-flood, you great sages and elders, what doubts can remain? Who is it that uses what is there before our eyes, who acts on it? Just grasp the actual and act! Don't bother with names. We call this the *wordless depths of dark-enigma*. So what kind of realization is this? It's the dharma that has no aversion to anything. And so, an ancient sage spoke of

mind following this surge of circumstance, its
ten thousand changes wholly origin-dark quiet.

And following its flow reveals original-nature:
no more cause for joy, no more cause for grief. [244; 55]

"You who soar the Way-flood, listen. To feel this seen world belonging
as part of you, that's enormously difficult. And Buddha-dharma is dark-
enigma at quiet origins. But you can, you really can see through it all . . .

"You great heart-sight clarity masters, listen. When this mountain
monk says there is no dharma outside yourselves, students can't fathom
it. They immediately turn inside, and there try to see through it all. They
sit facing a wall, tongues tight against their palates, and keep profoundly
still. They imagine that's Buddha-dharma, gate of the patriarchs. It's
complete nonsense!

"If you think stillness is the loom-of-origin's surge of circumstance
given crystalline clarity, you've made blackness your slave-master. That's
why the ancient sage said, *It's terrifying how deep, how profoundly deep
it is: that black hole of inky dark!* But if you understand movement
the way grasses and trees understand it, then you've found Way. For
them, it's vast wind that brings movement, and vast earth that brings
stillness.

"Neither movement nor stillness possesses its own original-nature.
Absence is their original-nature. If in movement you try to grasp Way,
it's somewhere in stillness. If in stillness you try to grasp Way, it's somewhere in movement. This is like a fish hidden in spring-water: it drums
the waves, then suddenly leaps clear. You great heart-sight clarity adepts,
listen. Movement and stillness are both forms the surge of circumstance
takes. The master of Way dependent on nothing wields movement, and
wields stillness too. [247–50; 56–58]

The master was nearing his return to the Great Transformation of
things, so he sat with firm dignity and said: "After I vanish, don't let my
perfect dharma of the eye's treasure-house[31] vanish too."

Thrice-Sage rose and said, "How could I ever let your perfect dharma of the eye's treasure-house vanish?"

"When people ask you about it, what will you say?"

"*KHO-AAAA!!*" shouted Thrice-Sage.

"Who could have known my perfect dharma of the eye's treasure-house would vanish in this blind donkey's sophistry?"

Done with talk, the master sat in regal meditation and soon manifested complete nirvana-tranquility. [340; 126]

趙州

Visitation-Land (Chao Chou, 778–897)

VISITATION-LAND WAS A FRIEND OF PURPORT DARK-Enigma, and he too taught in an obscure and impoverished mountain temple far from the institutional centers in the capital cities. He was a master less of "woolly actions" than of "wild words," and this mastery made him one of the most influential of T'ang masters. Because of his "wild words," he appears more often in the Sung sangha-case collections (part VI, p. 257ff.) than any other figure, with the exception of Cloud-Gate Mountain (p. 234). And he is especially associated with Taoist cosmology/ontology in the effortless spontaneity of his "wild words" Ch'an, the way responses to questions just seemed to pour out of him: and so, the consummate master enacting Absence-action (*wu-wei*).

This is emphasized in the structure of Visitation-Land's *Teaching Record*. Normally in Ch'an texts, interchanges with students each appear more or less independently. But in the *Teaching Record*, they usually appear in long teaching sessions, each beginning with the announcement that Visitation-Land "ascended to his seat in the Dharma Hall, and began instructing the assembled sangha." And so, we see him responding effortlessly to sometimes dozens of students one after another, in a steady stream of Ch'an insight. This is an especially clear illustration of how exchanges with a master were originally public. These exchanges came to be called "sangha-cases" for exactly this reason: they were exchanges that happened when the sangha was gathered for teaching. Only later, when formal sangha-case training developed, did they become private.

Not surprisingly, given Visitation-Land's preference for "wild words," the Taoist cosmological/ontological framework is especially apparent in his *Teaching Record*. Indeed, the *Teaching Record* describes his enlightenment in terms of that framework, saying he was "suddenly awakened to the wordless depths of dark-enigma" (p. 224). And perhaps the most important sangha-case, the one generally considered the foundation of sangha-case training and the first normally assigned to students, retells an exchange between a student and Visitation-Land that turns on Absence, that foundational concept in Taoist cosmology/ontology:

> A monk asked: "A dog too has Buddha-nature, no [無]?"
> "No/Absence [無]," Visitation-Land replied.
> "Things lofty as buddhas and low as ants—they all have Buddha-nature. How could a dog not?"
> "Because now you've made its nature into a bundle of karma-curse idea-mongering."

Here, the student fails to recognize the deeper meaning of 無 as "wordless Absence," and Visitation-Land scolds him for resorting to concepts as a way of understanding.

When this encounter is reconfigured as the first sangha-case in *No-Gate Gateway* (p. 290), it appears in the context of *No-Gate Gateway*'s central motif of 無 as "Absence" (see pp. 286–87 for a full discussion). Hence, the encounter is reduced to the first question-and-answer exchange to focus all attention on 無, and the commentary makes explicit the "Absence" that Visitation-Land defends in his scolding of the student who only heard 無 as "no." Because this exchange comes first in sangha-case training, it might be said that Visitation-Land and the most fundamental levels of Taoist cosmology/ontology came to preside as Ch'an's "first teacher."

For examples of Visitation-Land's appearances in sangha-case collections, see pp. 269, 272, 290, 296.

NOTE

For translation comparison: Bracketed numbers refer to section numbers in James Green's *The Recorded Sayings of Zen Master Joshu* (1998).

Teaching Record of Ch'an Master Frontier Thusness-Clarity from Visitation-Land

When he was a student, Visitation-Land asked Wellspring-South Mountain:[32] "When you're done understanding, where have you gone?"

"You've gone to be a water-buffalo facing mountains at some rich Buddhist's house," answered Wellspring.

"Thank you for such precise instruction."

"Last night," continued Wellspring, "in the third watch, moonlight entered the window." [3]

Visitation-Land was the firekeeper at Wellspring-South Mountain. Everyone was out thinning vegetables in the garden, but Land was working inside. Suddenly he cried, "Fire! Fire!" The monks all ran to the Sangha Hall—but Visitation-Land had bolted the door, so they couldn't get in. Wellspring-South tossed a key in through the window. Land opened the door. [4]

The east and west Sangha Halls at Wellspring-South Mountain were arguing over a kitten. Wellspring-South arrived at the courtyard between the halls, and said: "Say it, and I won't chop this kitten in half. Don't say it, and I will." The sangha fell silent, no idea what Wellspring could be thinking. So, Wellspring chopped the kitten in half.

That night, when Visitation-Land returned from a journey, he asked if there was any news. Wellspring-South told him what happened, and said: "What would you have done to save the kitten?"

Land took off a sandal and balanced it on his head, then stomped out of the room and walked away.

"If you'd been here," Wellspring called after him, "you would have saved that kitten!" [6]

Visitation-Land asked Wellspring-South Mountain: "What is Way?"

"Ordinary mind is Way," answered Master Wellspring.

"Still, it's something I can set out toward, isn't it?"

"To set out is to be distant from."

"But if I don't set out," objected Land, "how will I arrive at an understanding of Way?"

"Way isn't something you can understand, and it isn't something you can not-understand. Understanding is delusion, and not-understanding is pure forgetfulness. If you truly comprehend this Way that never sets out for somewhere else, if you enter into it absolutely, you realize it's exactly like the vast expanses of this universe, all generative emptiness you can see through into boundless clarity. And how can you understand that by insisting *yes it's like this, no it's not like that?*"[33]

Hearing those words, Visitation-Land was suddenly awakened to the wordless depths of dark-enigma, his mind bright and clear as the moon. [1]

· · ·

Master Visitation-Land ascended to his seat in the Dharma Hall, and began instructing the assembled sangha: "The grand and wondrous affair is evident and clear. And it's limitless. But unless they're deep in the midst of it, even great talents can never fathom it.

"When I was at River-Act Mountain's monastery, a monk asked: 'What is the *ch'i*-weave mind Bodhidharma brought from the West?' And River-Act said: 'Could you bring that chair over here for me?'

"If you're a true master in our ancestral Ch'an household, you use source-tissue roots to explain the grand and wondrous affair. That's how you help people fathom it."

At that, a monk asked: "What is the *ch'i*-weave mind Bodhidharma brought from the West?"

"That cypress in the courtyard," replied Visitation-Land.

"You can't just use blatant facts to teach people."

"I'm not."

"Then what is the *ch'i*-weave mind Bodhidharma brought from the West?"

"That cypress in the courtyard." [12]

A monk asked: "Where is it you were born of origin-tissue?"

Visitation-Land pointed away and said: "At the western frontier, you face still more west." [16]

A monk asked: "What is the one precept that says primal-unity whole and complete?"

"Fuss over precepts like that," replied Visitation-Land, "and you'll be an old fool in no time." [25]

A monk asked: "What is dark-enigma within dark-enigma?"³⁴

"How long ago did this dark-enigma begin?" replied Visitation-Land.

"Ages ago."

"It's a good thing you found me," said Land. "That dark-enigma could have killed you!" [46]

A monk asked: "What is this person I am?"

"You see that cypress in the courtyard, right?" [47]

A monk asked: "What is the *ch'i*-weave mind Bodhidharma brought from the West?"

"How long has that free-spirit gourd been blooming there on the east wall?" [274]

A monk asked: "The majestic Way all rootless Absence: how do you teach that?"

"You just taught it," replied Visitation-Land.

"There must be something more."

"It's rootless Absence. Period. What's got you tangled in such knots?" [72]

A monk asked: "What is Visitation-Land?"

"East gate. West gate. South gate. North gate." [99]

A monk asked: "What is meditation?"

"Not meditation," replied the master.

"Why *not meditation*?"

"It's a creature alive!" shouted the master. "A creature alive!" [100]

A monk asked: "What is dark-enigma deep within dark-enigma?"

"Which dark-enigma within dark-enigma should we talk about?" replied Visitation-Land. "Seven within seven? Eight within eight?" [38]

. . .

Master Visitation-Land ascended to his seat in the Dharma Hall, and began instructing the assembled sangha: *"Dharma is originally unborn, and even now undying.*[35] There's nothing more to say. Talk is birth, and no talk death. So how will you reveal the unborn and undying inner-pattern Way?"[36]

A monk asked: "Just now, you talking: Was that unborn and undying?"

"This guy only understands lifeless words." [104]

A monk asked: "What is your own *ch'i*-weave mind?"[37]

"Absence: no teaching, no practice." [60]

A monk asked: "A dog too has Buddha-nature, no [無]?"

"No/Absence [無]," Visitation-Land replied.[38]

"Things lofty as buddhas and low as ants—they all have Buddha-nature. How could a dog not?"

"Because now you've made its nature into a bundle of karma-curse idea-mongering." [132]

A monk asked: "A dog too has Buddha-nature, no [無]?"

"Everyone's house has a gate that leads to Peace-Perpetua."³⁹ [363]

A monk asked: "What is it when the moon floats radiant and clear in the emptiness of sky?"

"What's your name, *acharya*?" replied Visitation-Land.

"Unbegun."

"That moon floating radiant and clear in the emptiness of sky—where is it?" [134]

A monk asked: "What is ordinary mind?"

"It's fox, wolf, coyote." [147]

A monk asked: "What is *returned to root*?"⁴⁰

"To set out toward it," replied Visitation-Land, "that's the mistake." [165]

A monk asked: "What is the *clear and evident*?"

"A time before first thoughts arise." [173]

A monk asked: "I can't figure it out: here in this land, who is the patriarchal master?"

"Ever since Bodhidharma came, we all are," replied Visitation-Land.

"What number in the patriarchal lineage are you?"

"I'm not part of it," declared Land.

"Then, where is it you are?"

"Inside your ears." [177]

A monk asked: "When I'm trying to become Buddha, what am I doing?"

"Squandering a lot of energy," replied Visitation-Land.

"And when I don't squander my energy like that, what then?"

"Isn't that when you are yourself Buddha?" [190]

A monk asked: "What is the Buddha-Way Terrace of enlightenment?"⁴¹

"From the Buddha-Way Terrace you come, and from the Buddha-Way Terrace you depart," replied Visitation-Land. "This very world itself: across the length and breadth of its sheer actuality, is there anywhere that is not the Buddha-Way Terrace of enlightenment?" [214]

. . .

Master Visitation-Land ascended to his seat in the Dharma Hall, and began instructing the assembled sangha: "A dame dragon offering up kindred mind: that is occurrence-appearing-of-itself."

"If that's occurrence-appearing-of-itself," asked a monk, "what is it when we offer up mind?"

"Without offering up mind, how can we know occurrence-appearing-of-itself?" [121]

A monk asked: "What is a sage face-to-face with Buddha?"

"Someone ploughing fields with an ox." [225]

A monk asked: "What is it when four mountains crowd together?"

"No roads through: that's Visitation-Land." [227]

A monk asked: "What is Buddha?"

"You're Buddha, aren't you?" [232]

A monk asked: "Once you master Absence-action and tranquil silence, aren't you deep in profound emptiness?"

"Yes, deep in profound emptiness," replied Visitation-Land.

"And where does that lead?"

"You become a donkey. Or a horse." [237]

A monk asked: "What is dark-enigma within dark-enigma?"

"Dwelling there," replied the master, "you live like you're seventy-four or five." [41]

A monk asked: "What is the *ch'i*-weave mind Bodhidharma brought from the West?"

"That chair's legs," replied Visitation-Land.

"There's more to it than that, isn't there?

"If there is," said Land, "break them off and take them away with you." [238]

A monk asked: "What is it when there's no dust on the sheer actuality of this inner-pattern earth?"

"Right here inside it all, and more." [241]

A monk asked: "What is my teacher?"

Visitation-Land replied:

> "Clouds rising out of mountains seething,
> streams cascading into valleys soundless."[42]

"That's not what I'm asking about," objected the monk.

"But that *is* your teacher," said Land. "You just don't know it." [270]

A monk asked: "I'm going to the south. I'd like to take a little Buddha-dharma understanding along. What should I do?"

"In the south," replied Visitation-Land, "if you get somewhere there's a Buddha, pass by quickly. And if you get somewhere there isn't a Buddha, don't linger."

"Is there nothing I can rely on?"

"Willow catkins! Willow catkins!" [282]

A monk asked: "What is this person I am?"

"Have you eaten your mush?" Visitation-Land asked.

"Yes."

"Then go wash your bowl."[43] [291]

. . .

Master Visitation-Land ascended to his seat in the Dharma Hall, and began instructing the assembled sangha: "*Buddha*, that one word they call whole and complete: I can't bear to hear it."

"And you still teach us?" asked a monk.

"Apparently."

"How do you teach us?"

"*It hides wordless dark-enigma depths*," recited Land, "*turns tranquil thought into toil*."[44]

"That *dark-enigma*," said the monk, "how do you reveal its *wordless depths*?"

"I'm not so fond of source-tissue roots and origins."

"What are the wordless depths of dark-enigma?" pressed the monk.

"My answering you here is itself wordless depths." [126]

A monk asked: "In day, there's sunlight. In night, there's firelight. But what is the light of awareness infusing things with wonder?"

"Sunlight. Firelight." [298]

A monk asked: "What is selfless Absence-action?"

"That was hardly selfless!" [301]

A monk asked: "What is the *ch'i*-weave mind Bodhidharma brought from the West?"

"Those wooden old-timer's teeth of yours are growing fur." [307]

A monk asked: "What is the changeless inner-pattern Way?"

"You explain it: Did those wild ducks fly here from the east or from the west?" [323]

A monk asked: What is it to polish dust away and see Buddha?"

"There's no dust to polish," replied Visitation-Land, "and no Buddha to see." [336]

A monk asked: "What is the teacher of Buddha and the six Buddhas before him?"[45]

"Sleeping when you're sleepy, rising when you're not." [349]

A monk asked: "What is the realm of no-thought?"

"Say it! Quickly, quickly!" [358]

A monk asked: "What is the precept right here before my eyes?"

"I'm not you." [365]

A monk asked: "Two mirrors face each other. Which is illumination most radiant?"

"Acharya," replied Visitation-Land, "Sumeru Mountain at the very center of Thirty-Three-Peak Heaven: close your eyes, and you've hidden it away!" [370]

A monk asked: "What is a monk's practice?"
"Keeping free of practice." [398]

A monk asked: "What is Buddha?"
"Who are you?" [430]

A monk asked: "What is perpetual dark-enigma within dark-enigma?"
"You asking me is itself perpetual dark-enigma." [431]

A monk asked: "When the flower of Buddhahood hasn't yet opened, how can I see into the wild thusness of things all clarity-absolute?"
"It's already opened," replied Visitation-Land.
"But I still can't distinguish wild thusness and clarity-absolute."
"Wild thusness is clarity-absolute, and clarity-absolute is wild thusness." [432]

Master Visitation-Land went to Lucid-Kingdom Monastery in the Heaven-Terrace Mountains to see Cold Mountain[46] and Fathom-Gather.[47] When he found them, he said: "I've long heard of you two—but now, I see you're just a couple of water-buffalo!"
Cold Mountain and Fathom-Gather stomped around like water-buffalo.
"Whoa! Whoa!" shouted Land.
They bared their teeth, grunted, and glared at him.
Land fled back into the Dharma Hall.

Cold Mountain and Fathom-Gather came in after him, and asked: "Just then, out there: what kind of game was origin-tissue playing?"

At that, Visitation-Land roared with glorious laughter. [491]

To take flight on the majestic Way, to soar
clear: that's the nirvana gate. And it's easy:

just sit, mind wide-open beyond all bounds.
Then, next year, spring is yet again spring. [518]

雲門

Cloud-Gate Mountain (Yün Men, 864–949)

CLOUD-GATE MOUNTAIN IS PERHAPS THE MOST INTENSE exemplar of the "wild words and woolly actions" Ch'an invented by Sudden-Horse Way-Entire and perfected by Purport Dark-Enigma. As we have seen, this approach often takes the form of startling and violent antics, but Cloud-Gate is especially renowned for his concise examples of wild-and-woolly Ch'an known as "one-word gateways" (一字關)—instructional responses to student questions that are concise and piercing and profound: all of Ch'an distilled into a single word or brief utterance.

The term *gateway* (關) is especially telling. It refers first to gateways in mountain passes at the frontier, which can be either locked to block passage or opened to allow passage. Hence, the idea that it is a gateway one must open and pass through into realization. This reveals the primacy of wild landscape in Ch'an, for to pass through a 關 is to enter into a wild landscape beyond the civilized world. One of Cloud-Gate's most insistent themes is that we are always already realized, that we are ourselves the "gateway" and therefore have no need for ideas and answers and teachings. This appears in his full name: Culture-Sutra Desist of Cloud-Gate Mountain. It appears even more tellingly in the pictographic structure of the "gateway" ideogram (關), for its basic element is a gate (門: pictograph of a gate with two doors). Culture-Sutra Desist's "gateway" is therefore he himself: Cloud-Gate Mountain. We will see a variation on this in the great sangha-case collection *No-Gate Gateway* (p. 285), where the teacher's name is No-Gate—but here it is especially remarkable in that Cloud-Gate himself, sole locus of awakening, is identified with mountain landscape.

Because he is such a quintessential master of the piercing illogic of "wild words and woolly actions," Cloud-Gate appears more often than any other figure in the great sangha-case collections that we will encounter in the following part as the preeminent literary form in Sung Dynasty Ch'an (see part VI, pp. 257–298). Indeed, the Cloud-Gate *Record* contains a series of teachings structured exactly like sangha-case collections: the teacher cites a concise statement or anecdote from Ch'an history, and then comments on it in revealing ways (pp. 242–43). And so, again, Cloud-Gate as the primary antecedent of sangha-case collections, the great innovation to come in Ch'an.

For examples of Cloud-Gate Mountain's appearances in sangha-case collections, see p. 282.

NOTE

For translation comparison: Bracketed numbers refer to section numbers in Urs App's *Master Yunmen: From the Record of the Ch'an Master "Gate of the Clouds"* (1994). Sections without numbers are not translated in App's book.

Extensive Record of Ch'an Master Thusness-Clarity Aid-and-Abet of Cloud-Gate Mountain

Master Cloud-Gate Mountain ascended to his seat in the Dharma Hall and sat silently for a long time. Then he said: "There's no talking through Way's loom-of-origins unfurling moment-by-moment. You can't just dissect it with explanation, lay it out to view. Even if everything you say is perfectly clear and accurate, it always leads to countless other paths. The more words slice and probe, the worse it gets. And now that we're here in the midst of this teaching, it's hopeless." [1]

Someone asked: "What are the teachings of Buddha's entire lifetime?"

Cloud-Gate replied: "Face primal-unity entire, and it's all spoken." [13]

Someone asked: "What is the *ch'i*-weave mind Bodhidharma brought from the West?"

Cloud-Gate Mountain replied: "Gazing at a mountain in broad daylight." [9]

One day, Cloud-Gate Mountain said: "Buddha-dharma can never be explained in words. If you try, it's nothing but shit-scatter and pissspray." [175]

Someone asked: "What is this self I am?"

The master replied: "Wanders among mountains, delights along rivers." [11]

Someone asked: "What is the eye's perfect dharma?"

"All-encompassing!" [14]

Someone asked: "What is sitting regal in meditation and contemplating the actual itself, all this form and appearance?"

"A coin lost in the river goes tumbling downriver." [15]

Cloud-Gate ascended to his seat in the Dharma Hall and said: "All you pilgrims wandering here and there for no reason—what have you come looking for? This old monk understands nothing but eating and drinking and shitting. You think I've mastered any more understanding than that?

"But you pilgrims keep tramping around asking about the nature of Ch'an and Way. So okay, I'm asking you here directly: What has come of all your searching, and what realization has it brought you? Come on, right now, show me!"

Then he continued: "And all the while, you're just scaring that old sage in your own house away. You chase after, watching that old guy's ass, and when you find a little spit there, you snarf it down. You take it for your own and say: *I understand Ch'an! I understand Way!*

"Even if you can chant every teaching in the vast treasure-house of sutras, what good do you think it is? Those ancient masters—they're utter failures. When they see you scurrying around in confusion, they talk about *bodhi*-awakening and nirvana. That's like burying you in a grave, like lashing you to a stake driven deep. And when they see you don't understand, they talk about no *bodhi*-awakening and no nirvana. But even if you see this kind of teaching is a ruse, you just set out looking for more teaching, more explanation. You Buddha-killers, you've always been like this. And where's it gotten you?

"When I was a young pilgrim wandering from teacher to teacher, there were plenty of wise-guys happy to teach me and explain things to me. They weren't bad at heart, but one day I realized what a joke they were. If I make it another few years without dying, I'll take an axe to those Buddha-killers and smash their legs.

"These days, hermit monks everywhere are faking it. Why don't you go see them? What kind of dry shit-wipe stick are you looking for here?"

Suddenly seizing his travel-staff, Cloud-Gate leapt down from his seat unleashing blows and drove the monks away. [144]

Cloud-Gate ascended to his seat in the Dharma Hall and said: "There's radiant illumination within each and every one of us. Once you recognize it, you're done looking into the shadows of dark confusion."

Then Cloud-Gate descended from his seat. [143]

Someone asked: "Where does the selfhood of all Buddhas originate?"

"East Mountain walking on the river." [20]

A monk asked: "What is the darkness in talk?"

Cloud-Gate replied: "The entire crystal-clear loom-of-origins just slipped through your fingers!"

"Well, what is the talk in darkness?" asked the monk.

"ARGHH!"

"How about no talk and no darkness—what is that?"

Cloud-Gate grabbed his staff and drove the monk away. [23]

Someone asked: "What is the eye's perfect dharma?"

"Mush-rice steam!" [18]

Someone asked: "What is Cloud-Gate Mountain's sword?"

"Patriarchs!" [24]

Someone asked: "What is dark-enigma's single existence-tissue potency?"

Cloud-Gate replied: "You have one more question."

"What is brightly evident within dark-enigma?"

"Crap!"

"What's crap?"

"Get out! Get out of here! You're blocking people's questions!"

Someone asked: "What is the original source-tissue mind?"

"You just revealed its every illumination." [35]

Someone asked: "What is Ch'an?"

"Is!"

"Alright then, what is Way?"

"Realized!" [44]

Cloud-Gate ascended to his seat in the Dharma Hall and said: "Embrace all the buffet and flutter of your own thinking and calculating and looking. As your days lengthen into years, that's your only path into the depths of occurrence-appearing-of-itself. No one else can travel that path for you. After all, we're each on our own among the lofty insights people offer, aren't we? Old masters appeared here to teach you direct illumination, but your path into occurrence cannot begin somewhere outside you. That *outside* only obscures things and forecloses realization—so what good is all their teaching, their *expedient means*?" [46]

Someone asked: "The crush of life and death has come. How do I drive it away?"

"Come where?" [51]

Someone asked: "What is the source-ancestral teaching at origins?"[48]

"No question. No answer." [30]

A monk asked: "What is the small-talk that surpasses Buddhas and transcends patriarchs?"

"Gruel-cake."

"Where's the connection?" asked the monk.

"Exactly! Where's the connection!?" exclaimed Cloud-Gate.

Then he continued: "Listen. You haven't understood anything. The moment you hear someone mention the *ch'i*-weave mind of patriarchs, you start asking about small-talk that surpasses Buddhas and transcends patriarchs! You're already inner-pattern Way itself, so why ask how to be a Buddha or patriarch?" [58]

Someone asked: "What is Ch'an?"

"Can't we just ditch that word?" [72]

A monk asked: "What is mind?"

"Mind."

"I don't get it," said the monk.

"I don't get it."

"Alright. Fine." persisted the monk. "But what is it?

"*AI-OO!*" cried Cloud-Gate. "Just find a quiet place and walk around a little." [76]

"Someone asked: "Please show me the path leading inside."

"Mush-eating! Rice-eating!" [21]

Someone asked: "What is it like at the Absence-gate, the no-gate into this wild thusness of things all clarity-absolute, its wondrous and deep silences?"

"Loom-of-origins weaving out the turning seasons—luminous, radiant."

"And to be right there in the midst of it?"

"No error. No confusion."

Someone asked: "What is Buddha's very self?"

"Dry shit-wipe stick." [85]

Someone asked: "The dark-enigma loom-of-origins, its entire primal-unity path: How do I simply live it?"

"After thirty years of practice, when you give it all up." [88]

Someone asked: "What is a child of the ancestral patriarchs?"

"Among words, there's a sound." [97]

Someone asked: "What is Way?"

"Set out beyond the last word," replied Cloud-Gate.

"And once you've set out beyond—what's it like?"

"A thousand miles, the same wind." [103]

Cloud-Gate ascended to his seat in the Dharma Hall and said: "Buddha Existence-Tissue Arrival realized Way utterly when he saw the morning star appear, radiance shimmering."

"What is it to realize Way utterly when you see the morning star appear, radiance shimmering?" asked a monk.

"Come. Come stand right here facing me."

The monk came and stood facing Cloud-Gate. Suddenly seizing his travel-staff and unleashing blows, Cloud-Gate drove the monk away. [106]

Instructing the assembled sangha, Cloud-Gate said: "All ten distances of time and space, heaven-and-earth and this vast land: a single blow of my staff shatters it all into a hundred pieces!

"If you give up the library of Buddhist teachings—the twelve divisions of the Three Vehicles—and everything Bodhidharma brought from the West: if you give all that up, you'll fail. And if you don't give it all up, you'll never understand my shout: *KHO-AAAA!!*" [145]

Someone asked: "If it isn't the dark-enigma loom-of-origins, and it's not this world that enters the eye—what is it?"

"Turn either idea inside out and upside down." [89]

Presenting a topic for consideration, Cloud-Gate Mountain cited the Third Patriarch:

> *For primal-unity mind is unborn.*
> *It keeps all ten thousand dharmas.*[49]

Then Cloud-Gate commented: "That's all his awakening amounted to?" And raising his travel-staff, he continued: "Throughout all heaven-and-earth and this vast land, is there anything less than perfect?" [157]

Presenting a topic for consideration, Cloud-Gate cited: "*Presence-action never encompasses time's three realms of past, present, and future. But Absence-action always encompasses those three realms.*"

Then he commented: "Presence-action may be the dharma leading to nirvana, but where will you ever find those three realms? Absence-action always encompasses those three realms, and so has nothing to do with the dharma of coddling some nirvana-tranquility."

Presenting a topic for consideration, Cloud-Gate cited: "*I give medicine appropriate to the illness. Throughout the vast expanses of this earth: everything is medicine. And isn't all of that your very self?*"

Then he commented: "Meet the worthless as if priceless."

A monk asked: "Could you explain a little more?"

Cloud-Gate clapped his hands together once. Then raising his travel-staff, he said: "Here, take this travel-staff."

The monk took the staff and broke it in two.

"Oh, perfect! Now you've done it! Now I can give you your thirty blows!" [185]

Presenting a topic for consideration, Cloud-Gate cited: "*This existence-tissue all thusness-clarity absolute: the whole of it exhausts wholeness.*"

Then he commented: "So what do you call rivers-and-mountains and this vast earth?"

"It's all the forms and appearances of dharma's emptiness," he continued. "No birth and no death, nothing stained and nothing pure." [196]

Presenting a topic for consideration, Cloud-Gate cited: "*Sages and awakened ones live the dharma of Absence-action. And so, they're always setting out unburdened.*"

Then he commented: "This travel-staff isn't the dharma of Absence-action. Nothing anywhere is the dharma of Absence-action." [209]

One day, Cloud-Gate Mountain said: "Bodhidharma sat in meditation facing a wall, and Buddha sat inside closed courtyard gates. So how could they fathom this here right now?"

Answering for the assembled sangha, he said: "This here right now: what kind of shit-wipe stick is that?"

Then he exclaimed: "Primal-unity entire!"[50] [226]

Instructing the assembled sangha, Cloud-Gate said: "I'm not asking you about the days before a full moon. But the days after a full moon: say something about that. Quick!"

Answering for the assembled sangha, he said: "One day after another, and they're all marvelous days!" [243]

Sun's *ch'i*-bright solar-blaze brims eyes full, and it's dark-enigma's
shadowed-emergence. People all say so clearly everything I cannot,

for the path is there in every utterance, and we're voicing it always.
How can it be so hard to meet the original loom-of-origins head-on?

Gathered peaks provision crowded mountains
one by one, realizing this tawdry-dust world.

Still, you talk about dark-enigma mystery, as if
roof tiles can melt away like ice into liberation.

唐詩

T'ang Dynasty Poetry

IN THE CHINESE POETIC TRADITION, A DISTINCTION is made between Ch'an/Buddhist poetry and mainstream poetry. However, mainstream poets belonged to the same artist-intellectual class as Ch'an monks and teachers. They often visited monasteries to see friends, practice, and consult Ch'an masters. In addition, when traveling far from home, they often stopped at monasteries, which functioned as inns. These artist-intellectuals saw Ch'an not as a religion, but as a philosophical practice that cultivates profound insight into the empirical nature of consciousness and Cosmos, and their poetry was deeply influenced by Ch'an.

The difference between mainstream and Ch'an poetry is that mainstream poetry is rarely explicitly doctrinal. It attends, instead, to immediate experience amid the everyday struggles of the world outside the cloistered realm of monasteries. That is, it simply assumes Ch'an insight as it addresses immediate experience. This, of course, is Ch'an's ultimate goal: not to limit itself to the monastic realm, but to transform people's ordinary lives. So, in a sense, mainstream poetry is more Ch'an than doctrinal Ch'an poetry. Or put another way: it enacts Ch'an insight, much like sangha-cases (see part VI, pp. 257–298), rather than simply talking about it. And so, even if it isn't usually considered part of the Ch'an literary tradition, it is an especially direct form of practice/teaching.

It was during the T'ang Dynasty that this mainstream poetry came to its full flowering. This renaissance was catalyzed by the rediscovery of proto-Ch'an landscape poets Hsieh Ling-yün (p. 92) and T'ao Ch'ien (p. 107), but it was driven more fundamentally by the rise of Ch'an. Ch'an's empty mirror-mind was perhaps the primary transformative element, grounding poetry in the clarity of landscape (literally, "rivers-and-mountains") images. In empty mirror-mind, the ten thousand things (landscape) become the very content of consciousness, of identity. But that mirror-mind is the immediate experience of Ch'an no-mind, and always there in an imagistic landscape poem is no-mind's integration of self and Cosmos: for without mind/self, there is no separation between mind/self and the ten thousand things.

This imagistic clarity became the fabric from which mainstream poetry was made, a primary reason it was widely considered a form of Ch'an practice and teaching. And this makes sense. The term generally translated "mind" (心) also means "heart"—there is no distinction between the two. So, perception clarified by meditation until it is empty-mind mirroring the ten thousand things, mirroring rivers-and-mountains landscape: it isn't just an intellectual or spiritual experience; it is also an emotional experience, an experience of the *heart*. That experience of the heart is presumably the purview of poetry, and it is the very nature of ancient China's rivers-and-mountains poetry.

This rivers-and-mountains poetry of images weaves the identity-center into landscape as accurately as language can. It thereby renders a larger identity, an identity that is made of landscape. This is the heart of Ch'an as landscape-practice: in mirror-deep perception, earth's vast rivers-and-mountains landscape replaces thought and even identity itself, revealing the unity of consciousness and landscape/Cosmos that was sage dwelling for Ch'an practitioners, and indeed for all artist-intellectuals in ancient China. It returns us to our most primal nature, that inner wilds where we are indeed the awakened landscape gazing out at itself.

Further, Ch'an emphasized the idea that deep understanding lies beyond words. In poetry, this gave rise to a much more distilled language—minimal grammar, concise imagism (mirroring *tzu-jan*), surprising and spacious juxtapositions between ideas and images—all of which opened new inner depths, nonverbal insights, and even out-right enigma. In this way, too, poems can work very much like sangha-cases (see part VI, pp. 257–298). And because that enigma and imagistic concision opens poems to silence, they also function as a form of meditation. So taken altogether, this new Ch'an poetics weaves consciousness into landscape and Cosmos, making that weave the very texture of poetic experience.

Virtually all T'ang and later classical poetry is built on these Ch'an principles, and there is no end to the variations this poetic practice takes.[51] So nearly any T'ang poem could be used to illustrate poetry as Ch'an practice/teaching. The small sampling below includes a number of exemplars representing the distilled and imagistic Ch'an poem. And it also includes a number of poems revealing these mainstream poets explicitly engaged with Ch'an.

Autumn Begins

Autumn begins unnoticed. Nights slowly lengthen,
and little by little, clear winds turn colder and colder,

summer's blaze giving way. My thatch hut grows still.
At the bottom stair, in bunchgrass, lit dew shimmers.

Anchored Beside Shore-Seek Brights in
Evening Light, I Gaze at Thatch-Hut
Mountain's[52] *Incense-Burner Peak*

Our sail up full, a thousand miles pass
without meeting mountains of renown,

then anchored here beside Shore-Seek,
I'm suddenly gazing at Incense-Burner.

I've read Prajna-Distance's teachings,[53]
traced his pure path beyond the dust,

and now his East-Forest home is close.
It is dusk. A bell sounds, and it's empty.

On a Journey to Thought-Essence Monastery, Written on the Wall of the Abbot's Mountain Hut

Happening into realms peach-blossom pure,
I begin to feel the depths of a bamboo path,

and soon come to know a master's timeless
dwelling. It's far beyond things people seek.

Cranes dancing over steps all stone idleness,
gibbons in flight howling amid thick forests,

I slowly fathom dark-enigma's inner-pattern,
and sitting at such depths, forget mind itself.

WANG WEI, 701–761

Deer Park

No one seen. Among empty mountains,
hints of drifting voice, faint, no more.

Entering these deep woods, late sunlight
flares on green moss again, and rises.

Golden-Rain Rapids

Wind buffets and blows autumn rain.
Water cascading thin across rocks,

waves lash at each other. An egret
startles up, white, then settles back.

In the Mountains, Sent to Ch'an Brothers and Sisters

Dharma companions filling mountains,
a sangha forms of itself: chanting, sitting

ch'an stillness.[54] Looking out from distant
city walls, people see only white clouds.

In Reply to Vice-Magistrate Chang

In these twilight years, I love tranquility
alone. Mind free of our ten thousand affairs,

self-regard free of all those grand schemes,
I return to my old forest, knowing empty.

Soon mountain moonlight plays my *ch'in*.[55]
Pine winds loosen my robes. Explain this

inner-pattern behind failure and success?
Fishing song carries into shoreline depths.

LI PO, 701–762

Night Thoughts at East-Forest Monastery
on Thatch-Hut Mountain

Alone, searching for blue-lotus roofs,
I set out from city gates. Soon, frost

clear, East-Forest temple bells call out,
Tiger Creek's moon bright in pale water.

Heaven's fragrance everywhere pure
emptiness, heaven's music endless,

I sit silent. It's still, the entire Buddha-
realm in a hair's-breadth, mind-depths

all bottomless clarity, in which vast
kalpas begin and end out of nowhere.

Reverence-Pavilion Mountain, Sitting Alone

The birds have vanished into deep skies.
A last cloud drifts away, all idleness.

Inexhaustible, this mountain and I
gaze at each other, it alone remaining.

TU FU, 712–760

Overnight at Master Illumine's House

How did your abbot-staff ever get you here?
Autumn winds already a desolate moan, rain

tangles depths of courtyard chrysanthemums,
and in the pond, frost topples lotus blossoms.

Cast into exile, you never abandon original-
nature. Emptiness empty, you keep close to[56]

ch'an-stillness. All night long, we share this
ridge-dragon moon facing us round and full.

Gazing at Ox-Head Mountain Monastery

It's Buddha's White-Crane death-grove:[56]
Steps wind into depths quiet in mystery

here, spring colors float beyond peaks,
Star River fills meditation-hall shadow.

Sun-bright Absence transmits the lamp;[57]
yellow-gold Presence reveals the earth.

No more this song-wild old man, I turn
and look away into mind nowhere it is.

Night

A sliver of moon lulls through clear night.
Half abandoned to sleep, lampwicks char.

Deer wander, uneasy among howling peaks,
and forests of falling leaves startle cicadas.

I remember mince treats east of the river,
think of our boat adrift in falling snow . . .

Tribal songs rise, rifling the stars. Here,
at the edge of heaven, I inhabit my absence.

WEI YING-WU, CA. 737–792

Evening View

Already at South Tower: evening stillness.
In the darkness, a few forest birds astir.

The bustling city-wall sinks out of sight—
deeper, deeper. Just four mountain peaks.

PO CHÜ-I, 772–846

Li the Mountain Recluse Stays the
Night on Our Boat

It's dusk, my boat such tranquil silence,
mist rising over waters deep and still,

and to welcome a guest for the night,
there's evening wine, an autumn *ch'in*.

A master at the gate of Way, my visitor
arrives from exalted mountain peaks,

lofty cloud-swept face raised all delight,
heart all sage-clarity spacious and free.

Our thoughts begin where words end.
Refining dark-enigma depths, we gaze

origin dark into each other and smile,
sharing the mind that's forgotten mind.

At Home Giving Up Home[58]

There's plenty of food and clothes. My children are married.
Now that I'm free and clear of all those duties to the family,

I fall asleep at night with the body of a bird reaching forests
and eat at dawn with the mind of a monk who begs for meals.

A scatter of crystalline voices calls: cranes beneath pines.
A single fleck of cold light burns: a lamp in among bamboo.

On a sitting cushion, I'm all *ch'an* stillness deep in the night.
A daughter calls, a wife hoots: no answer, no answer at all.

CHIA TAO, 779–843

Evening Landscape, Clearing Snow

Walking-stick in hand, I watch snow clear.
Ten thousand clouds and streams banked up,

woodcutters return to their simple homes,
and soon a cold sun sets among risky peaks.

A wildfire burns among ridgeline grasses.
Scraps of mist rise, born of rock and pine.

On the road back to a mountain monastery,
to hear it struck: that bell of evening skies!

Sitting at Night

Crickets ever more plentiful, autumn's far from shallow,
and now that the moon has sunk away, night grows deep.

It's the third watch, and branches of snow streak my hair.
Two peaks in a single thought: mind of the four patriarchs.

TU MU, 803–853

Egrets

Robes of snow, crests of snow, and beaks of azure jade,
they fish in shadowy streams. Then startling up into

flight, they leave emerald mountains for lit distances.
Pear blossoms, a tree-full, tumble in the evening wind.

PART VI

Complete Ch'an: Sung Dynasty Sangha-Case Collections

(11th-13th centuries C.E.)

DURING THE SUNG DYNASTY, CH'AN'S BASIC ELEMENTS as defined by the T'ang Dynasty masters continued and evolved: countless Ch'an masters in a more extensive and formalized monastic system; and the second great age of Chinese poetry, its poets even more closely associated with the Ch'an community. To this was added the Sung's great artistic innovation: majestic landscape painting (p. 299ff.). And like poetry, it too was shaped by Taoist/Ch'an principles. It too was considered a form of Ch'an practice and teaching, or even a breathtaking embodiment of enlightenment. And it was a further adventure in Ch'an's ongoing engagement with rivers-and-mountains as the topography of enlightenment.

During the Sung, Ch'an became aware of itself in a new way—as a vast and coherent tradition. This tradition was codified in a number of large histories that collect the stories and teachings of sage-masters in the tradition. These histories represent one of the two great innovations in Sung Dynasty Ch'an. The most important such history is the *Lamp-Transmission Record* (傳燈錄)—full title, *Lamp-Transmission Record of the Heart-Sight Lumen-Clarity Reign*—a voluminous history chronicling the "separate transmission outside all teaching." That transmission is the "lamp" of radiant empty-mind handed down through upward of two thousand teachers. Especially important for us, the *Lamp-Transmission Record* reveals how the Taoist/Ch'an conceptual framework continues to orient Ch'an thought and practice, for the key concepts defining that framework appear there thousands of times.[1] As its accounts of the figures presented in this selection are so similar to the individual *Records*, the *Lamp-Transmission Record* is not included here.

The other great innovation in Sung Dynasty Ch'an is the sangha-case collection. As we have seen, the Ch'an written tradition is composed primarily of prose works by and about Ch'an masters, records of their lives and teachings. These records contain a great deal of conventional explanatory teaching, which is necessary to prepare students for Ch'an's wordless insight. That direct insight is conveyed in the more literary dimension of those records: poetry, which was perfectly suited to the quick, deep insights of Ch'an; and storytelling typified by poetic distillation— enigmatic sayings and wild antics intended to upend reason and tease mind past the limitations of logical thought. These are performative, rather than explanatory—enacting insight rather than talking about it. As such, they operate with poetic wildness and immediacy, rather than the usual explanatory or utilitarian discourse. In this, they come as close as language can to Ch'an's transmission outside of words and teaching.

Ch'an teachers began drawing especially revealing moments from the records of earlier teachers, moments that distill the essential insights of Ch'an, and assigning them as puzzles for students to ponder.[2] These scraps of story came to be known as *kung-an* (公案, now widely known in its Japanese pronunciation *koan*), a term that had come into use prior to the Sung, no later than the eighth century. *Kung-an* means a "court case," and more literally a "public case." The term was adopted to the Ch'an situation for a number of reasons. First, a *kung-an* is a factual situation that needs to be understood accurately, like a court case (although understanding here demands responding within the enigma, at a level that precedes thought and analysis). Second, each *kung-an* represents a kind of precedent to which practitioners can refer. And finally, masters originally conducted *kung-an* training in "public," when the entire monastic community was gathered together (cf. pp. 220–21). Hence the translation adopted here: "sangha-case" (*sangha* meaning "a Buddhist community").

Eventually, in tenth-century Sung China, teachers began gathering these sangha-cases into collections used for training students. Three of these collections established themselves as the enduring classics, perennially employed over the centuries in China, then Japan, and on into Zen practice around the world today: *Blue-Cliff Record, Carefree-Ease Record, No-Gate Gateway*. Such sangha-case collections are now generally considered mere collections of stories that provide an occasion for teaching. But in fact they are carefully constructed literary/philosophical texts designed to create—in and of themselves and without further explanation—a direct and immediate experience in the reader: the experience of enlightenment. Indeed, they are perhaps the pinnacle of Ch'an literary creation: a new and unique and profound literary form that combines zany storytelling with poetry and philosophical prose. Although an oversimplification, it almost seems as if the history of Ch'an leads us through the path of practice: centuries of teaching preparing for the direct non-verbal realization induced by sangha-case practice. Hence, sangha-case practice represents the culmination of Ch'an's "separate transmission outside all teaching."

In the Great Transformation of things, however, fruition is always the beginning of decline. And that is true here in a certain sense. Early Ch'an teaching was spontaneous and idiosyncratic, each teacher finding a unique method of transmission. But in sangha-case practice, an established set of teachings became the standardized curriculum used by virtually all Ch'an teachers. And this reliance on standardized sangha-case training has continued to the present. So, some say sangha-case practice might be seen as a diminution of the spontaneous energy of Ch'an teaching, a routinization and standardization—and therefore a contradiction of the very spirit of Ch'an.

Perhaps, but sangha-case practice places Ch'an's wrecking-crew center stage, for the demolition of analysis and thought is itself the matter immediately at hand. As such, sangha-cases are a primary means of resolving what is the most fundamental question for Ch'an practice, and perhaps for human consciousness in general: how to move past the seeming separation between thought and silence, subjective and objective, mind and landscape, self and Cosmos. And in this, they find their ultimate philosophical source in the profound paradox of Lao Tzu's *Tao Te Ching* and Chuang Tzu's zany sages and perplexing pronouncements, such as this:

When Lao Tzu died, Modest-Ease went in to mourn for him.
He shouted three times, then left.

Sangha-case training reinforces meditation, which remained the heart of Ch'an practice. Solutions to sangha-cases always involve responding with a spontaneous immediacy that lies outside any logical analysis; and sangha-case training pushes the student toward that goal with enigmatic utterances and outbursts and antics. The correct answer to a sangha-case is whatever emerges spontaneously from that silent emptiness cultivated in meditation practice, where the logical construction of thoughts has not yet begun—the generative emptiness of *wu*-mind: no-mind or Absence-mind. It is *wu-wei* at the most profound level: "Absence-action," improvisational action in which one moves as the generative source, as the Cosmos unfurling its possibilities. And in this, it is a cultivation of the sage dwelling that defines Ch'an enlightenment, dwelling heart and mind as an organic part of the Great Transformation of things.

碧巖錄

Blue-Cliff Record (ca. 1040)

THE *BLUE-CLIFF RECORD* IS THE EARLIEST OF CH'AN'S classic sangha-case collections. It established the form employed by collections that followed: the sangha-cases themselves supplemented with poems and explanatory commentary. In the *Blue-Cliff Record*, this structure divides neatly into two levels written by two different Ch'an masters. The primary text was written by Snow-Chute Mountain (Hsüeh Tou, 980–1052) sometime around 1040. Each chapter of this collection contains a sangha-case, which Snow-Chute selected and retold, and a poetic response to the sangha-case (a *gatha*, meaning a Buddhist "sutra-poem"). These function as direct experience itself, as close to wordless insight as we can get in language. This collection containing one hundred sangha-cases and gathas was known simply as *Snow-Chute's Gathas on the Ancients*, and it was widely influential.

The secondary text came nearly a century later, when a Ch'an master named Awake-Entire (Yüan Wu, 1062–1135) used Snow-Chute's collection as a teaching text, giving lectures on each of the chapters. Awake-Entire's students took careful notes, which were eventually compiled and shaped into an extensive commentary on Snow-Chute's primary text. Although there is some direct teaching here, shocking and illogical utterances, it mostly operates as secondary explication. The compilation of these two texts became the *Blue-Cliff Record* (1125), named after the site where Awake-Entire taught.

As we have seen (p. 50), original text combined with commentary as a literary/philosophical form grew out of early Taoist and Dark-Enigma Learning texts. But it presents a clear example of the conflict between Ch'an as direct mind-transmission outside of teaching and the natural belief that understanding comes through words, through ideas and explanations. This latter view serves the needs of institutional Ch'an, which is based on explanatory teaching. And it is enticing, because it's easier and more tangible than the hard work of direct understanding, which always remains beyond measure or quantification. There is a strong temptation to rely on words and explanations in an attempt to understand conceptually. And it is certainly necessary preparation for the real work—but in Ch'an, that real work requires us to move beyond ideas and explanations.

The conflict between direct transmission and explanatory teaching is a problematic running all through the Ch'an tradition—not only because explanation precludes direct insight, but also because some explanation is inevitably necessary as preparation for that wordless awakening. This conflict was famously enacted when Awake-Entire's successor, Prajna-Vast (Ta Hui, 1089–1163), violently insisted that Ch'an awakening only comes through direct non-verbal insight, and that eloquent explanation is a hindrance because it encourages students to rely on conceptual understanding. In a grand act of direct Ch'an teaching, he destroyed the original edition of the full *Blue-Cliff Record* and burned the wooden printing-blocks—thereby forcing students to encounter the direct teaching of sangha-cases and poems, rather than explanation that defies the wordless spirit of wild Ch'an. Awake-Entire's commentary only survives because a century and a half later (ca. 1300), an imprecise version was reconstructed from fragmentary manuscripts that had survived.

Consistent with this principle of direct teaching, there are few explicit references to Ch'an's foundational cosmological/ontological framework in Snow-Chute's primary text. Those key concepts are taken for granted by Snow-Chute. After the intellectual preparation of Ch'an history, they are here simply the framework within which the direct teaching of sangha-case practice operates. However, as one might expect, those key terms and concepts pepper Awaken-Entire's commentaries, the explanatory level of the *Blue-Cliff Record*: *tzu-jan*, inner-pattern, and dark-enigma, to take three examples, occur about a hundred times each, and the loom-of-origins appears no less than three hundred times!

At this point in the history of Ch'an, after centuries of explanation, we should be prepared to encounter the direct teaching of sangha-cases. And so, the selection that follows includes only the direct literary level of the *Blue-Cliff Record*, Snow-Chute's original sangha-case storytelling and poetry.

NOTE

For translation comparison: Chapter numbers correspond to those in J. C. Cleary and Thomas Cleary's *The Blue Cliff Record* (1977) and Katsuki Sekida's *Two Zen Classics* (1977; part two, "Hekiganroku").

7

Prajna-Leap Asks about Buddha

A monk named Prajna-Leap asked Dharma-Eye: "I wonder if the master would explain what Buddha is?"

"You are yourself Prajna-Leap," answered Dharma-Eye.

GATHA

In river country, spring wind still, a mountain partridge deep among wildflowers cries out. Three-Cascade Gorge: it's there

amid towering waves that fish are transformed into dragons, but dullards just keep dipping out buckets of pondwater night.

20

Dragon-Fang Mountain's
Ch'i-Weave Mind from the West

Dragon-Fang Mountain asked Kingfisher Shadowed-Emergence: "What is the *ch'i*-weave mind Bodhidharma brought from the West?"

"Hand me that meditation plank," said Shadowed-Emergence.

Fang handed the plank to Shadowed-Emergence, who swung it and struck Fang a blow.

"You can strike me all you want," hissed Dragon-Fang. "But there's still no *ch'i*-mind for Bodhidharma to bring from the West."

Later he asked Purport Dark-Enigma: "What is the *ch'i*-weave mind Bodhidharma brought from the West?"

"Hand me that meditation cushion," replied Dark-Enigma.

Dragon-Fang handed the cushion to Dark-Enigma, who swung it and struck Fang a blow.

"You can strike me all you want," cackled Dragon-Fang. "But there's still no *ch'i*-mind for Bodhidharma to bring from the West."

FIRST GATHA

Dragon-Fang Mountain's blind dragon haunts dead
water. How can ancient wind ripple that back to life?

Meditation plank and cushion: if you can't use them,
just pass them over to Master Thatch-Hut Mountain.[3]

SECOND GATHA

Pass them to old Thatch-Hut, and you're free: no more
meditation promising you the lamp patriarchs transmit.

Just face evening clouds drifting uneasily home, distant
ridgeline rising above blue ridgeline boundlessly away.

29

Tumble-Vast Mountain's *Kalpa*-Fires

A monk asked Tumble-Vast Mountain: "When the perfect understanding of *kalpa*-fire burns down this thousand Buddha-realm Cosmos into ruins, will this unthought here right now also be burned down into ruins?"

"Down into ruins," replied Tumble-Vast.

"Will thusness itself vanish away with it?"

"Away with it."

GATHA

There in the midst of blazing *kalpa*-fires, the moment he asks,
that patchrobe monk swings the grave gateway to awakening

closed. *Away with it*: how wondrous that precept. And yet, he
searched on here and there alone, ten thousand hell-bent miles.

30

Visitation-Land's Huge Radishes

A monk asked Visitation-Land: "They say you met Wellspring-South Mountain face-to-face. Is that true?"[4]

"They grow huge radishes in Wellspring-South country."

GATHA

They grow huge radishes in Wellspring-South country:
you patchrobe monks everywhere think it's an answer,

insight whole all the way from ancient to future times.
How can you even tell white egrets from black crows?

Thief! Thief!
Old Visitation-Land has snatched your original-face clean away![5]

Purport Dark-Enigma's Great *Ch'i*-Weave Meaning of Buddha-Dharma

Head monk Samadhi-Still asked Purport Dark-Enigma: "What is the great *ch'i*-weave meaning of Buddha-dharma?"

Dark-Enigma leapt from his meditation seat, grabbed hold of Samadhi-Still and gave him a single slap, then pushed him away.

Samadhi-Still froze and just stood there.

"Head monk Samadhi-Still," called out another monk, "Why don't you bow?"

Samadhi-Still thereupon bowed reverently, and suddenly had a great awakening.

GATHA

Yellow-Bitteroot taught Purport the decisive slice exhausting each loom-of-origins moment. Who needs carefree ease then?

Opening a way through, the Yellow River god raised his hand and simply split ten million Flourish Mountain ridges asunder.

40

Wellspring-South Mountain's Very Blossom

Once, when he was talking with Wellspring-South Mountain, high minister Solar-Extent Continual said: "Dharma-master Sangha-Fundament[6] claimed *This heaven-and-earth Cosmos and I share the same root. The ten thousand things and I share the same original potency.* How absolutely wondrous that is!"

Walking out and pointing to a blossom in the courtyard, Wellspring-South called to Solar-Extent: "These days, people see this very blossom as if it were some kind of dream-mirage."

GATHA

In awakened perception, there's no longer this me and that other,
no longer a mirror holding rivers-and-mountains in its deep gaze.

Frost-laden skies, moon sinking low—now, midway into night,
who shares reflections shimmering cold in crystalline lakewater?

41

Visitation-Land's Great Death

Visitation-Land asked Dice-Thrown Mountain: "After dying utterly to this world, mind exquisitely vacant, the Great Death—how is it when a person comes back to life?"

"You needn't travel by night," replied Dice-Thrown, "to arrive in the thrown enlightenment of morning."

GATHA

Eyes wide-open here in this life: that too is the Great Death.
If you want healing medicine, why examine revered masters:

even sage Buddha said he himself never arrived. Occurrence
numberless as the sands: who can scatter it like garden seed?

Clarity-Mirror Mountain's
Clatter of Falling Rain

Clarity-Mirror Mountain asked a monk: "What's that sound outside?"

"The clatter of falling rain," answered the monk.

"People have turned themselves upside-down," mused Clarity-Mirror. "Following after things, they've lost themselves."

"What about you, master?"

"I never lose myself anymore," replied Clarity.

"What does it really mean, to never lose yourself?" asked the monk.

"When you've just begun, it seems easy. But once you get free, it's impossible to talk about."

GATHA

Empty Dharma Hall, the clatter of falling rain,
sage-master facing a monk, answer impossible:

if you call that entering the stream of everyday
life, it's the same as ever: you don't understand

anything, not anything. In all that
torrential rain, North Mountain and South Mountain switch places!

從容錄

Carefree-Ease Record (ca. 1145)

THE SECOND GREAT SANGHA-CASE COLLECTION,
Carefree-Ease Record, replicates precisely the structure of the *Blue-Cliff
Record*. The sangha-cases were selected and retold by the illustrious
Wisdom-Expanse (Hung Chih, 1091–1157), who also added the gathas.
Then perhaps seventy-five years later, Ten-Thousand Pines (Wan Sung,
1166–1246) added an extensive commentary to Wisdom-Expanse's text.
This combined text was published in 1224 as the *Carefree-Ease Record*.

But the star here is Wisdom-Expanse. He survives outside of the
Carefree-Ease Record in an especially large and influential collection of
teachings and poems, though none so celebrated as his primary text in
the *Carefree-Ease Record*. Like Prajna-Vast (destroyer of the *Blue-Cliff
Record* commentary), Wisdom-Expanse studied under Awake-Entire
(author of the *Blue-Cliff Record* commentary). And in creating a sangha-
case collection including only the immediate teaching of sangha-case
and gatha, and no discursive commentary, he effectively corroborated
Prajna-Vast's extreme critique of Awake-Entire's explanatory approach
to teaching (an illustrious instance of "killing" your Buddha-teacher).

Indeed, Wisdom-Expanse famously advocated "silent illumination"
(默照) Ch'an: Ch'an that focuses on empty-mind meditation, which
he described as silently wandering the radiance of mind's boundless and
formless emptiness, and there gazing into the origin of things. This ex-
cludes all verbal teaching, of course, and it therefore follows naturally

that he would advocate teaching that is as direct and penetrating as possible in words. This is the very nature of sangha-cases and poetry—both in terms of literary strategy and their relentless insistence on the immediacy of empty-mind mirroring as the condition of awakening. Consistent with this direct non-verbal method, and again following the model of *Blue-Cliff Record*, the great cosmological/ontological concepts rarely (but tellingly) appear in Wisdom-Expanse's primary text, but they positively litter the secondary commentary: *tzu-jan* appears 21 times, for instance, *inner-pattern* 92 times, *dark-enigma* 101 times, and *loom-of-origins* 168. So in the end, Wisdom-Expanse's "silent-illumination" is not simply the quietism of Dhyana Buddhism; it is dynamic with the generative energy of Absence, and sangha-case training cultivates that dimension of "silent-illumination."

This is registered from the beginning in the collection's title. *Carefree-Ease* is usually translated "Serenity" or "Equanimity." This is yet another instance of how the assumption that Ch'an is an extension of conventional/Dhyana Buddhism infects modern translation and understanding of Ch'an texts—and so, how they are mistakenly perceived in contemporary Zen. Indeed, the *Carefree-Ease Record* begins in chapter 1 with Ch'an's anti-Buddhist clarity brilliantly dismantling the vast mythological realms of conventional Buddhism and any reverence for the teachings even of Buddha himself. Although *carefree ease* does involve a state of profound tranquility, the term has nothing to do with the "serenity" or "equanimity" of conventional Buddhism's aspiration for nirvana-peace.

Instead, it is borrowed from the *Chuang Tzu*, where it describes *wu-wei* movement in accord with the ongoing unfolding of Tao/Way, living integral to the spontaneous energy of the Cosmos seen as a single generative tissue—a definition of sagehood later emphasized in the very influential *Chuang Tzu* commentary by the Dark-Enigma Learning philosopher Kuo Hsiang (p. 65). Chuang Tzu famously uses the term to describe fish joyfully drifting here and there in a pond. Elsewhere, Chuang Tzu says a sage who moves with "carefree ease" is "like a dragon, like a tiger," and is "a dragon seething in the stillness of death, thunder booming in the dark abyss of silence." And the term's full philosophical depth becomes clear when he explains that when you "move with the carefree-ease of Absence-action (*wu-wei*), you're stitched through the ten thousand woven things." Carefree ease is, therefore, to move through life with the "profound tranquility" of the Cosmos itself as it unfurls through its perennial transformations.

NOTE

For translation comparison: Chapter numbers correspond to those in Thomas Cleary's *Book of Serenity* (1990) and Gerry Wick's *The Book of Equanimity* (2005).

World-Honored-One Ascended and Sat

One day, the World-Honored-One[7] ascended to the teaching platform and sat. Manjusri[8] sounded the announcement mallet and called out: "Behold the Dharma Emperor's dharma! Look closely! The Dharma Emperor's dharma is exactly this here before you!"

The World-Honored-One thereupon rose and descended from the teaching platform.

GATHA

Can you see each wind-gust of thusness-clarity? Gossamer
mother of change, a busy shuttle working the inner-pattern's

loom-of-origins weaves out the aboriginal tapestry of spring:
all those secrets Lord Sun simply won't stop rising to reveal.

Twofold Mountain's Dharma Body

Twofold Mountain asked the venerable monk Heart-Sight Clarity: "Buddha's thusness-clarity dharma-nature: it's exactly like the emptiness of empty sky. It reflects the shimmering appearance of each particular thing—like a moon in water. How would you explain the inner-pattern Way of such reflecting?"

"Donkey peering into a well," replied Heart-Sight Clarity.

"Your words have spread Way out nicely in the sun," said Mountain, "but that's only 80 percent."

"And you, master, how would you say more?"

"Well peering into a donkey," answered Mountain.

GATHA

Donkey peering into well,
well peering into donkey:

this wisdom enfolds Absence and beyond,
its clarity suffusing the bounty of Presence.

Decipher Buddha-nature talismans hidden under robes?
You won't find any books in our household—just that

threadless loom-of-origins. There, shuttle weaving out the spangled
grain of things far and wide, *ch'i*-weave mind reveals its every possibility.

68

Stealth Mountain Swings Sword

A monk asked Stealth Mountain: "What's it like when you cut through the dust of this world and see Buddha?"

"You just have to swing the sword," replied Mountain. "And if you don't, you're like a fisherman perched high in a nest."

The monk went and asked Stone-Frost: "What's it like when you cut through the dust of this world and see Buddha?"

Stone-Frost answered: "There are some without a homeland, nowhere they belong: Where will you meet them?"

When the monk returned, he asked Stealth Mountain about Stone-Frost's answer. Stealth Mountain ascended to his seat in the Dharma Hall and said: "For our Ch'an household's teaching and practice, Stone-Frost can't compare to this old monk. But for profound words that lead deep into the inner-pattern, he's a hundred steps beyond me."

GATHA

Awesome *ch'i*-sword sweeping stars and rinsing armies clean,
stilling confusion, bringing realization home: Isn't it you, you

clearing dawn haze, leaving skies crystalline to the four seas?
Lord Change, too, all Absence-action trailing out regal robes.

77

Reliance Mountain's Well Enough

A monk asked Reliance Mountain: "Can you still decipher written words, master?"

"Well enough," replied Mountain.

The monk then walked a single circle to the right around Reliance Mountain and said: "What word is this?"

Mountain etched the word *ten* onto the ground: 十.

The monk walked a single circle to the left around Reliance Mountain and said: "Then what word is this?"

Mountain changed 十 into the sacred word *ten thousand*: 卍.

The monk thereupon drew a circle and raised it over his head with both hands like a demon colossus revealing and embracing sun or moon wild with *ch'i*-origins. Then he said: "And this? What word is this?"

Mountain drew a circle at full arm's length around the 卍 graph.

At this, the monk struck the pose of a thunderbolt Buddha—wild, too, with *ch'i*-origins.

"That's it!" cried Mountain. "That's it exactly! You've taken such good care of it all!"

GATHA

The gaping ring of Way's empty sky is never filled.
Words carved into the emptiness seal have no form.

On earth's pivot, heaven wheels wondrous mystery.
Threads of war and culture weave fabric of silence.

Cleave it all apart or knead it whole,
stand alone or set out together where

loom-of-origins reveals dark-enigma
                    hinge, ah, lightning amid clear blue skies,
where eyesight harbors tranquil-deep
                    radiance, ah, stars seen in broad daylight.

78

Cloud-Gate's Gruel-Cake

A monk asked Cloud-Gate Mountain: "What is small-talk that surpasses buddhas and transcends patriarchs?"

"Gruel-cake," replied Cloud-Gate.[9]

GATHA

Gruel-cake as the small-talk surpassing buddhas and patriarchs:
understood clear through, that counsel is altogether flavorless.

You patchrobe monks: one day, you'll realize your belly's full
and see old Cloud-Gate's original-face no other than your own.

88

Hewn-Beam's Not Seeing

The *Hewn-Beam Sutra* says: *When I'm not seeing original-nature,*[10] *why don't you look at the place I am when I'm not seeing original-nature? If you see that terrain clearly, you'll see occurrence-appearing-of-itself is nothing other than the very form of that not-seeing. If you don't see clearly, occurrence-appearing-of-itself seems to be something else. But how could it not be you yourself?*

GATHA

In this vast ocean of things gone bone-dry,
this limitless Cosmos of emptiness brimful,

a patchrobe monk's far nose senses every distance,
but ancient Buddha's whispering tongue falls short.

Strung-Pearls twisting stars through nine meanders[11]
and the jade loom-of-origins hardly begun its weave,

we meet in such absolute clarity there's no one at all to recognize.
That's when you begin to see you have no companions anywhere.

Jewel-Fang's Rivers-and-Mountains

A monk asked Master Jewel-Fang Awake: "It was all Buddha's crystalline source-tissue clarity in the beginning. But how could it suddenly give birth to rivers-and-mountains and this vast earth?"

"It was all Buddha's crystalline source-tissue clarity in the beginning," said Awake. "But how could it suddenly give birth to rivers-and-mountains and this vast earth?"

GATHA

To see Presence and not Presence: it's like
turning your hand palm-down and palm-up.

That guy wandering around Jewel-Fang Mountain
keeps right up with Wary-Cloud Buddha himself![12]

無門關

No-Gate Gateway (1228)

ASIDE FROM THE FACT THAT IT IS HALF AS LONG, containing forty-eight sangha-cases instead of a hundred, *No-Gate Gateway* continues the basic structure of the two earlier sangha-case collections. But there is one important difference. Here, almost as if scolding earlier commentators for their lengthy explanations swamping the primary texts, the commentaries are concise and part of the original primary text: direct teaching made of the same philosophical depths as the sangha-cases and poems themselves. And further, *No-Gate Gateway* is constructed even more as a literary text: written entirely by a single very distinctive author, and with the additional shaping of a foreword and afterword.

That author is No-Gate Prajna-Clear (Wu-men Hui-kai; 無門慧開), a particularly philosophical Ch'an master who lived from 1183 to 1260. Philosophical, but also full of profound mischief, his poems and commentaries inevitably ridiculing and undermining the teachings of Ch'an. This mischief begins in his Buddhist name: Ch'an masters had long described the essence of their teaching as their "gate"—but in true wrecking-crew style, the name this Ch'an master took was No-Gate. And in another quite different example of his mischief, No-Gate chooses four different sangha-cases that begin with the question "What is Buddha?" and then gives very different answers—answers that are not just paradoxical in themselves, but taken together are contradictory and meant to dismantle all reverence for Buddha and his teachings:

Flax. Three pounds.

Dry shit-wipe stick!

Mind itself is Buddha.

Not mind, not Buddha.

No-Gate's philosophical bent appears at the outset in both his name and in the title of his great book, where the double-meaning of 無 (no/Absence) is again at work: hence, No-Gate and *No-Gate Gateway* mean simultaneously Absence-Gate and *Absence-Gate Gateway*. This is perhaps not surprising, because No-Gate himself struggled for six years with 無 as a student, and that struggle led to his enlightenment. On the day after his awakening, he wrote this poem in the traditional quatrain form, quite remarkable poetically for its audacity in making an entire poem with a single word, *Absence* (無):

無 無 無 無 無
無 無 無 無 無
無 無 無 無 無
無 無 無 無 無

No-Gate struggled with 無 by means of the ancient sangha-case—by then 350 years old—that he placed first in his collection (see p. 226 for the original). Because of this prominence, it subsequently became the foundation of sangha-case practice—and so, perhaps the most important sangha-case in the Ch'an tradition, because it forces a direct encounter with Absence and Buddha-nature. And here, too, the double-meaning of 無 is crucial:

A monk asked Master Visitation-Land: "A dog too has Buddha-nature, no [無]?"
"No/Absence [無]," Visitation-Land replied.

Rendered here in a translation that mimics the original's grammatical structure, this might seem a simple exchange. But No-Gate's comment to this sangha-case claims that Visitation-Land's 無 is nothing less than the "no-gate gateway" to Ch'an's source-ancestral essence. In the American tradition of Zen, Visitation-Land's "not" is taken as a blank denial of meaning-making, which is registered by letting the word remain untranslated, an inexplicable nothing: *mu* (the Japanese pronunciation of 無, pronounced *wu* in Chinese). Hence, something like:

> A monk asked Master Visitation-Land: "Does a dog have Buddha-nature?"
> "*Mu*," Visitation-Land replied.

This leaves the sangha-case at a generic level of "Zen perplexity." But when this word is seen in its native conceptual context, No-Gate's claim begins to reveal itself in its full richness, for here the meaning of 無 is not just utter negation, but also "Absence," that pregnant emptiness from which all things arise.

In the sangha-case, a monk is asking about Buddha-nature, the essence of consciousness, our original nature, and Visitation-Land mysteriously replies: "Absence." The master's response is multifaceted. It is an expression of his mind at that moment, implying the monk should emulate his empty-mind rather than struggle for understanding. It is an enigmatic response to the question, a reflection/enactment of Buddha-nature. And all the while, it is simply Absence, that empty and generative cosmological/ontological tissue. Hence, it is a challenge directed at the monk, insisting that giving up thought and explanation is the only way to fathom Absence in a number of different ways—empty-mind in its most profound sense. So the sangha-case asks us to ponder Absence, the realization that our original-nature is that generative emptiness at the heart of the Cosmos. Not simply the tranquil silence we encounter in meditation, but something much deeper: that dark vastness beyond words and thought, origin of all creation and all destruction. And so, the sangha-case points the way to profound dwelling, integral to Way's generative cosmological/ontological process. This is what No-Gate means when he calls 無 *the gateway to Ch'an's source-ancestral essence.* And when he takes Absence-Gate as his name, he makes a magisterial assertion of our inherent nobility, saying that we are each in our very nature awakening itself.

NOTE

For a complete translation, see my *No-Gate Gateway: The Original Wu-Men Kuan* (2018). For translation comparison: Chapter numbers correspond to those in R. H. Blyth's *Zen and Zen Classics*, volume 4, *Mumonkan* (1966); Katsuki Sekida's *Two Zen Classics* (1977; part 1, "Mumonkan"); Robert Aitken's *The Gateless Barrier* (1990); Thomas Cleary's *No Barrier: Unlocking the Zen Koan* (1993); Zenkai Shibayama's *The Gateless Barrier* (2000); Koun Yamada's *The Gateless Gate* (2004); Guo Gu's *Passing Through the Gateless Barrier* (2016).

No-Gate's Foreword

Buddhism calls mind its *source-ancestral*, its *household*, and no-gate its *dharma-gate*. If it's an absent gate, no gate at all, how could anyone pass through it? We've all heard that whatever enters through a court-yard gate can't be the household treasure, and whatever arises from the origin-tissue must be limited to beginning and end, fruition and ruin. But that kind of talk—it's like waves churned up without any wind, like wounds cut deep into healthy flesh. In the search for understanding, what's worse than using a tangle of words? You're just swinging a stick as if you could hit the moon, scratching a boot as if you could itch a foot! How could that ever work?

In the Bestowal-Accord reign, *wu* year of the rat, I, Prajna-Clear, led the sangha at Dragon-Soar Monastery in East-Revered. It was the summer ses-sion, and monks were hungry for insight. So I taught in accord with what-ever moment the loom-of-origins unfurled, using sangha-cases from ancient masters like clubs to batter down that gate and scatter the roof-tiles.

I copied them down without a goal. I just started, not thinking about structure, the befores and afters, a finished book. Now there are forty-eight, and together I call them the *No-Gate Gateway*.

If you're like the long edge of the Star River, wielding your lone blade fearlessly, no care for danger and death, you'll enter through the gate with a single slash. Not even the eight-armed demon-king could stop you. Heaven's twenty-eight Indian patriarchs and earth's six Chinese patriarchs: you'll leave them all gazing at wind and begging for their lives. But if you hesi-tate, it's like looking through a window across the room and glimpsing a horse gallop past outside: scarcely seen and already gone vanishing away.

GATHA

The great Way is a single Absence-gate
here on a thousand roads of Presence.

Once through this gateway, you wander
all heaven-and-earth in a single stride.

Visitation-Land Dog Nature

A monk asked Master Visitation-Land: "A dog too has Buddha-nature, no?"

"Absence," Land replied.[13]

NO-GATE'S COMMENT

To penetrate the depths of Ch'an, you must pass through the gateway of our ancestral patriarchs. And to fathom the mysteries of enlightenment, you must cut off the mind-road completely. If you don't pass through the ancestral gateway, if you don't cut off the mind-road, you live a ghost's life, clinging to weeds and trees.

What is this gateway of our ancestral patriarchs? It's the simplest of things, a single word: *Absence*. Absence is the sole gateway of our ancestral source-gate household. And so, it's called the *No-Gate Gateway* into Ch'an's source-ancestral.

Pass all the way through it, and you meet Master Visitation-Land eye to eye! Visitation-Land, and the whole lineage of ancestral patriarchs too! You wander hand in hand with them, eyebrows tangled with theirs, looking with the same eyes, hearing with the same ears. How is that not great good fortune and wild joy? Don't you, too, long to pass through this gateway?

To penetrate the depths of this single word, *Absence*, summon all three-hundred-sixty bones and joints, all eighty-four-thousand sacred apertures of your intelligence, summon your whole being into a single mass of doubt. Devote yourself day and night. Absence: don't think it's emptiness, and don't think it's Presence.

You'll feel like you've swallowed a red-hot iron ball: wretching and wretching at something that won't vomit out. But let all the delusions of a lifetime go, all the understanding and insight; and slowly, little by little, nurture the simplicity of occurrence-appearing-of-itself.

Soon, inner and outer are a single tissue. A single tissue, and you're like a mute in the midst of dream: all that understanding for yourself alone. Then suddenly, the whole thing breaks wide-open, and all heaven-and-earth shudder in astonishment.

It's as if you've snatched General Gateway's vast sword away, as if you carry it wherever you go. If you meet Buddha, you kill Buddha. If you meet ancestral patriarchs, you kill ancestral patriarchs.

Out there walking the cliff-edge between life and death, you're per-fectly self-possessed, vast and wide-open in such wild freedom. Through all four transformations in the six forms of existence, you wander the playfulness of *samadhi*'s three-shadowed earth.[14]

Can you do it: devote a life, delve with all your lifelong *ch'i*-strength into this single word, *Absence*? Don't give up, and it will soon seem so easy: a mere spark setting the whole dharma-candle afire!

GATHA

A dog, Buddha-nature—the whole
kit and caboodle revealed in a flash.

Think about Presence and Absence,
and you're long lost without a clue.

6

World-Honored Held Flower

Long ago on Spirit-Vulture Peak, Shakyamuni Buddha, the World-Honored-One, held a flower up and revealed it to the sangha. Everyone sat in shadowy silence. Then Mahakasyapa's face broke into a faintly emergent[15] smile.

The World-Honored-One said: "I possess the perfect dharma of the eye's treasure-house,[16] the nirvana of mind's mysterious depths, the true form of formlessness, the subtle mystery of the dharma-gate. Not relying on words and texts, outside teaching and beyond doctrine—I here entrust all that to Mahakasyapa."

NO-GATE'S COMMENT

His face yellow, color of earth, Shakyamuni treated those people like they were nothing. He made the wondrous appear worthless, hung dog meat out for sale as fine lamb. He might have thought it the most marvelous of things, but what if the whole sangha had smiled? How could he have handed down that perfect dharma of the eye's treasure-house? And supposing Mahakasyapa hadn't smiled? How could he have handed it down then?

If you claim that perfect dharma of the eye's treasure-house can be handed down using the ten thousand things of Presence, that yellow-faced Lao Tzu's just a hawker swindling people at the gates of a market village. And if you claim it can only be handed down using Absence, how could he acknowledge its transmission to Mahakasyapa alone?

GATHA

Holding a flower out, raising it up:
it's the final insight fully revealed,

Mahakasyapa's smile-creased face
baffling all heaven-and-earth alike.

8

What-Next Invented Cartwheel

Master Moon-Shrine Mountain asked the monks: "When What-Next invented the cartwheel, it had a hundred spokes. But what if hub and rim are broken off, spokes scattered away—do you understand the bright clarity of what it could do then?

NO-GATE'S COMMENT

See straight through to the bright clarity in this, and your Buddha-deep eye's like a shooting-star, the loom-of-origins playing out its cycles sudden as a lightning-flash.

GATHA

There where the loom-of-origins wheels
around, a sage too is bewildered, sets out

wandering above and below through all
four directions—south, north, east, west.

28

Dragon-Lake Long Renowned

Mirror-Sight Mountain hungrily questioned Dragon-Lake into the night. Finally, Lake said: "The night is deep. You should have left by now."

Mountain bowed in homage, raised the blinds, and left. But seeing it was dark out, he stepped back in and exclaimed: "It's pitch-black out there!"

Lake lit a paper-lantern candle and offered it to him. Then, just as Mountain reached out to take it, Lake blew it out. At this, Mountain was suddenly awakened. He bowed reverently, and Lake asked: "You just saw the inner-pattern Way. Tell me, what is it?"

"That from this day on, here amid all beneath heaven, I'll never doubt the tongue of an old master."

The next morning, Dragon-Lake took his place before the sangha and said: "Here among you worthy monks is someone with fangs like a forest of swords and mouth like a bowl of blood. Attack him with a stick, and he won't even turn his head. The day will come when he'll journey to a lone mountaintop and establish our Buddha-Way there."

Mountain thereupon gathered all of his writings, his notes and commentaries, carried them to the front of the Dharma Hall and piled them there. Holding a torch, he explained: "Even if you understand all the intricacies of dark-enigma itself, it's barely a hair's-breadth adrift in the vast emptiness of this Cosmos. And even if you comprehend through and through that loom-of-origins at the heart of things, it's barely a drop tossed into endless seas." Having said this, he lit the pile of papers, bowed reverently, and then walked out.

NO-GATE'S COMMENT

Until he'd gone through the gateway and left his homeland, Mirror-Sight Mountain was a mind seething with zeal, a mouth aching to speak out. Full of grand ambitions, he came to these southlands on a mission to eradicate our doctrine of transmission outside teaching. When he reached Revere-Land Road, he ordered a mind-kindle bun from an old woman at a shop.

"Great Mirror-Sight, what's all that stuff there in your cart, all those books and papers?" asked the shop-woman.

"My writings on the *Diamond Sutra*, notes and commentaries," replied Mountain.

"Like it says in your sutra," the old shop-woman continued: *"Mind done and gone cannot be realized. Mind now aglimmer cannot be realized. Mind yet to come cannot be realized.* Great Mirror-Sight, which mind is it you want kindled and set ablaze?"

With that single question, Mirror-Sight Mountain was dumbfounded. He stood there like a puppet with its mouth hanging open. Even so, he was too proud to find death in an old shop-woman's words, so he asked her: "Who is it teaches source-ancestral Ch'an around here?"

"Master Dragon-Lake—just two miles from here."

Mountain set out for Dragon-Lake's monastery, and when he arrived his blunders completely ruined him. All that he had once said, he now contradicted. And it seems Dragon-Lake was so full of fatherly love for a son that he felt no shame. Seeing a little spark of flame smoldering in Mountain, he grabbed a bucket of rancid water in a wild frenzy and drowned him with it! Destroyed him absolutely!

Find a place of quiet solitude: from there you'll see it's all a grand ruse and farce!

GATHA

Hearing the name is nothing like seeing the face.
Seeing the face is nothing like hearing the name.

No one lops off your nose for crimes committed,
but why all this struggle? It'll blind you for sure.

37

Cypress in the Courtyard

A monk asked Master Visitation-Land: "What is the *ch'i*-weave mind Bodhidharma brought from the West?"

Land replied: "That cypress in the courtyard."¹⁷

NO-GATE'S COMMENT

If you can face that place where Visitation-Land's answer emerged and see through answers to kindred intimacy whole, cut clean through to the intimate essence of all this, then you're free of teachers: no Shakyamuni Buddha in times gone by, no Maitreya Buddha in *kalpas* to come.

GATHA

Words can't say the life of things;
nor talk render the loom-of-origins.

Depend on words and you're lost;
refuse them and you live delusion.

47

Buddha-Land's Three Gateways

Master Buddha-Land Mountain established three gateways to test his students:

"Open wild origins and penetrate depths of dark-enigma: that's the only way to see your original-nature.

"So tell me, you monks here now today: Your original-nature, where is it?"

   . . .

"Know your original-nature in and of itself, know it perfectly, and you're free of life and death.

"So tell me: At death, when the radiance of your eyes is falling away, how can you get free of life?

   . . .

"If you're free of life and death, perfectly free, you know where you dwell in the end.

"So tell me: The four elements you are—earth, air, fire, water—when they scatter away, where is it you're going?"

NO-GATE'S COMMENT

If you conjure hinge-phrases for these three gateways, you'll be in accord with wherever you are, empty and facing there Ch'an's source-ancestral, its origin-tissue. If you're free from doubt, coarse food fills you easily. Just chew it well, and you won't go hungry.

GATHA

A single thought sees everything across measureless *kalpas*, everything happening across measureless *kalpas* alive today,

alive here now looking through that single thought, looking clear through here now today into the very bottom of things.

NO-GATE GATEWAY · 297

No-Gate's Afterword

In their instruction, our ancestral patriarchs reveal the loom-of-origins and origin-tissue itself. Following them and trusting sincerely to the depths these sangha-cases open, I begin without the least trace of words. Turning my skull inside out and laying my eyeballs bug-eye bare, I show everyone here in this sangha how to see for yourselves with absolute and immediate clarity, how to make that source-ancestral teaching your own and carry it forward. There's no need ever to search outside yourself.

If you've mastered this, really mastered it, you understand my explanations before I say a word. There's absolutely no gate to enter, and no staircase to climb. You just stand proud and walk right through the gateway, no thought of asking permission from some guardian. Then you'll see right through Dark-Enigma-Sand Mountain, that great master, when he says: "No gate is the liberation gate, and no *ch'i*-weave mind the Buddha-Way *ch'i*-weave mind." And Cloud-Lucent Mountain, when he says: "If you illuminate Way itself with understanding's radiant clarity, you see that it's simply this, this, this here right now. Then how could you pass through and not continue on beyond?"

All this talk of mine: it's like dirt smeared into ox milk. If you pass through the No-Gate Gateway wholly, you understand No-Gate's a useless dimwit. And if you don't pass through the No-Gate Gateway wholly, you betray what you yourself are.

宋山水畫

Sung Dynasty Landscape Painting

SUNG DYNASTY POETRY RIVALS T'ANG POETRY, AND it is perhaps even more deeply infused with Ch'an principles. But it clearly continues the tradition developed in the T'ang. The great artistic innovation during the Sung was the ascendence of breathtaking rivers-and-mountains (landscape) painting. Like poets, painters belonged to the same artist-intellectual class as Ch'an monks and teachers, and they often associated with one another. And like poetry, painting too embodied Ch'an principles and was considered a form of Ch'an practice and teaching.

Ancient artist-intellectuals saw in the wild forms of rivers-and-mountains landscape the very workings of the Taoist/Ch'an Cosmos: not as abstraction, but at the intimate level of immediate experience. Because it is where existence reveals its most dramatically cosmological dimensions, immediate mirror-deep experience of rivers-and-mountains landscape opens consciousness most fully to the depths of those dimensions. And rivers-and-mountains painting renders visible this most dramatic incarnation of Tao's living existence-tissue, for its deep subject matter is nothing other than Taoist/Ch'an cosmology/ontology.[18]

The most immediately apparent feature of such paintings is emptiness. Chinese landscape paintings are full of it. Mist and cloud, sky, lakewater, even elements of the landscape itself are all rendered as space where the paper/silk is left untouched or only faintly colored with a thin wash:

emptiness. This emptiness portrays Absence, the generative emptiness from which the landscape elements (Presence) are seemingly just emerging, or into which they are just vanishing. Whatever the compositional particulars of a painting may be, this is always the underlying structure.

Chinese landscape paintings render that dynamic Cosmos in yet another way. Painting was an extension of calligraphy, images built from calligraphy's dynamic brushstrokes (pp. 307–08). Calligraphers aspired to create with the selfless spontaneity of a natural force, evident most dramatically in the dynamic energy of their brushstrokes. And so, the calligraphic line enacts Ch'an empty-mind moving with the selfless spontaneity of Way or *tzu-jan*. It was a practice in moving there at origins in that generative moment where the Cosmos perennially creates itself—for when a calligrapher first touches inked brush to a blank sheet of silk, it enacts that originary moment where Presence emerges from Absence. As the brushstroke traces through its arcs and twists, it is always there at that originary moment, just like awakened mind. It is *wu-wei* (Absence-action) become visible: an awakened mind moving with the unbridled energy of the Cosmos itself, Presence tumbling through its myriad transformations. And using this calligraphic brushstroke, painting infuses rivers-and-mountains landscape and awakened mind with that wild energy. It is the essence of Ch'an practice.

These are landscapes that seem to subsume the viewer, rendered in a way that lets us enter into them and wander trails; explore canyons and valleys, streams and mountain peaks. And viewing such paintings is also a kind of Ch'an practice: one gazes into a painting with the mirror-deep penetration of Ch'an empty-mind, allowing the painting's space to become the space of consciousness, of identity itself. It is a breathtaking integration of human consciousness and landscape/Cosmos, which makes belonging to rivers-and-mountains not just an idea, but a wondrous and beautiful emotional experience. And again, it reveals rivers-and-mountains landscape as the topography of Ch'an awakening, even as the very body of Buddha—as in this enlightenment poem written by Su Tung-p'o, the great poet and calligrapher (p. 307), written at East-Forest Monastery, birthplace of Ch'an (p. 76):

Presented to Abbot Perpetua All-Gathering at
East-Forest Monastery

A murmuring stream is Buddha's tongue broad, unending,
and what is mountain color if not his body pure and clear?

Eighty-four thousand gathas fill a passing night. But still,
once day has come, how could I explain them to anyone?

Li T'ang (late 12th century), attributed. *Rivers-and-Mountains,
Autumn Color.* Boston Museum of Fine Art, New York.

Mi Yu-jen (1074–1151). *Cloudy Mountains* (ca. 1145).
Metropolitan Museum of Art, New York.

Chiang Shen (12th century), attributed. *Mist and Cloud, Valley Stream in Mountains*. Detail. Museum of Fine Art, Boston.

Hsia Kuei (12th–13th centuries). *Streams and Mountains, Pure and Remote*. Detail. National Palace Museum, Taipei.

Anonymous (early 13th century). *Waiting for the Ferry,
Landscape Snow-Lit.* Detail. Metropolitan Museum of Art,
New York.

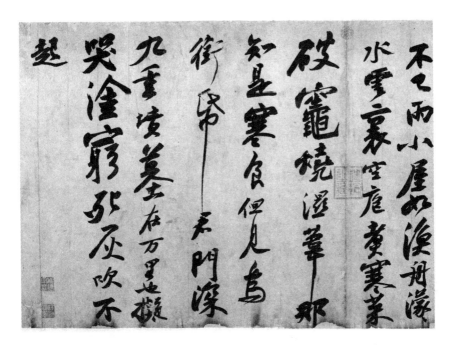

Su Tung-p'o (1037–1101). *Cold Food Observence*. Detail.
National Palace Museum, Taipei.

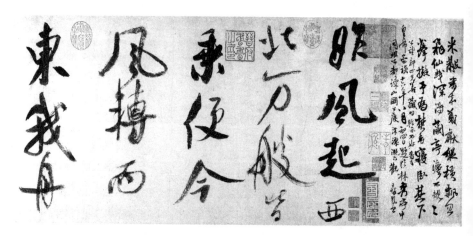

Mi Fu (1052–1107). *Clamor River, Poem Written in a Boat* (1095).
Detail. Metropolitan Museum of Art, New York.

Ongoing Ch'an

With Sung sangha-case collections and sangha-case practice, the Ch'an house was complete. Ch'an had generated and explored all of its fundamental dimensions—and yet, Ch'an remained *ongoing* in China. Histories generally say Ch'an withered there, its dynamic life transferred to Japan and eventually on to the West. But the essential dimensions of Ch'an remained vital in China throughout the centuries, even up to the present. There were no further developments and innovations in Ch'an's fundamental nature—but then, there weren't in Japan or the West either. On the contrary, elements were simply lost. Even while Ch'an flourished in Japan as Zen, developing a new constellation of distinctive characteristics, its fundamental orientation seems to have faded. It was no longer built around that deep-earth generative cosmology/ontology we have seen as the foundation of Ch'an practice and liberation. And this abstract and earthless Zen is the form of Ch'an that passed eventually on to America and the West in the twentieth century.

As for China, Ch'an simply settled in as the conventional operating assumption among artist-intellectuals. To take only one among countless examples, a particularly illustrious one: Stone-Waves (Shih T'ao) and Eight-Mountain Vast (Pa Ta Shan Jen), who were working around 1700, a full five centuries after the supposed atrophy of Ch'an following the Sung. They were among the most singular and innovative painters in the Chinese tradition, and both were Ch'an masters who considered their work very much a form of Ch'an practice and teaching. It was a typical assumption. And this Ch'an is miraculously *ongoing* in the texts translated here, wholly available to us as a body of assumptions about the nature of consciousness and Cosmos. So we are today in much the same position as the later Chinese. The house is complete and wide-open to us—all we need do is walk around enjoying the rooms and terraces, the sumptuous meals and incomparable views.

NOTES

INTRODUCTION

1. See his two seminal essays on Ch'an: "Development of Zen Buddhism in China" (1934) and "Ch'an (Zen) Buddhism in China: Its History and Method" (1953).

PART I

1. For this *heaven* and the *earth* of hexagram 2, see Key Terms, *Heaven*, p. 327.
2. Lieh Tzu: Reputed author of the *Lieh Tzu*, the third classic of ancient Taoism.
3. *yes this* and *no that*: This phrase/idea is a motif in the *Chuang Tzu* (see also section 5.6), and it echoes through the Ch'an tradition. It describes judgment/choice as a prime example of conceptualization alienating consciousness from the generative movement of Way or from its larger nature as the whole of Way.
4. Antecedent for the famous poetic dispute over the nature of mirror-mind in *The Platform Sutra of the Sixth Patriarch* (pp. 161–63, 165–67).
5. *ch'in*: Ancient stringed instrument much revered by Chinese intellectuals as a means for attaining enlightenment, often appearing in poems (pp. 251 and 254) and used as accompaniment when Chinese poets chanted their poems. In the hands of a master, a *ch'in* could voice with profound clarity the rivers-and-mountains realm, even the very source of all things.

PART II

1. Quotes are from *Tao Te Ching* 10, for which see p. 31.

2. Uncarved simplicity: Often translated "uncarved wood/block," this is Lao Tzu's famous metaphor for Way (Tao) or Absence, as well as for a fully realized sage mind:

   > Observe origin's weave, embrace uncarved simplicity,
   > self nearly forgotten, desires rare.

3. *yes this* and *no that*: A distinctive idea in the *Chuang Tzu* that echoes through the Ch'an tradition: see part I, note 3.

4. *seed time* and *breath-space-home*: 宇宙, which is generally translated "space and time." But that imposes a whole Western metaphysical scheme on the Chinese worldview. In fact, both ideograms contain the image for a roof at the top. Below that, 宇 has the image for breath spreading in the space beneath the roof, hence: "breath-space home," and 宙 has the image for a seed sprouting beneath the roof, hence: "seed-time home." All of this makes sense, of course, in the Taoist/Ch'an framework wherein reality is seen as a nurturing home and an organic and ever-emergent process of transformation.

PART III

1. For a more extensive discussion of the role rivers-and-mountains landscape plays in Ch'an practice, see the "Rivers-and-Mountains" chapter in *China Root*, pp. 72–81.

2. Three Vehicles: The three "conveyances" in traditional Buddhism that supposedly carry people across *samsara* to the shores of nirvana: disciple, sage-recluse, bodhisattva.

3. A play on *wu-wei*: Absence-action (see Key Terms, p. 328).

4. Bodhi Instant-Awakening: The Chinese name (須菩提) for Subhuti, who was one of Buddha's most prominent disciples. Among those disciples, he had the deepest understanding of emptiness. The *Diamond Sutra* is constructed as Buddha's discourse to Subhuti.

5. This is lines 6–10 of the *Wisdom-Beyond-Wisdom Mind Sutra*, for which see p. 153. Here, Sangha-Fundament is quoting the original translation, which was later expanded into the form translated on p. 153 and now widely used for chanting by Zen sanghas.

6. For a full presentation of Hsieh Ling-yün's poetry, see my book *The Mountain Poems of Hsieh Ling-yün*.

7. Sunset-Peak Return: Yen Hui, Confucius's most realized student. See *Chuang Tzu* 4.1 and 6.14 (pp. 41 and 44).

8. This draws on the Dark-Enigma Learning vision of Confucius that was initiated by Wang Pi and echoed down through the cultural tradition. In contrast to the conventional view, it sees Confucius as a Taoist sage who had mastered Taoist enlightenment so thoroughly that he had no need to talk about it. Instead, he simply put it into action through his social/political philosophy. This was seen as superior to Lao Tzu, who still felt the need to explain in his struggle to fully understand.

9. This and Hsieh's answer below reference a famous passage from the *Chuang Tzu*:

> The point of a fish-trap is the fish: once you've got the fish, you can forget the trap. The point of a rabbit-snare is the rabbit: once you've got the rabbit, you can forget the snare. And the point of a word is the idea: once you've got the idea, you can forget the word.
>
> How can I find someone who's forgotten words, so we can have a few words together?

10. Great Valley: A figure for Way that originates in chapter 12 of the *Chuang Tzu*:

> On his way to the Great Valley in the east, Diligent-Expanse happened to meet Whirl-Wind on the shores of the eastern sea.
> "Where are you going?" asked Whirl-Wind.
> "To the Great Valley."
> "Why?"
> "The Great Valley—it's something else. You could pour into it forever without filling it up, and ladle from it forever without emptying it out. So I'm going there to wander free."

PART IV

1. six paramitas: The virtuous practices in traditional Buddhism that can ferry one over into nirvana. *Paramita* also means "perfection" (cf. *prajnaparamita*, "perfection of wisdom," p. 149) as the result of those paramita practices. And in those "perfections," one is "gone beyond" or "gone to the other shore," the original literal meaning of *paramita*.

2. Also known as "The Two Entrances."

3. This place is described in the first chapter of the *Tao Te Ching*:

> In perennial Absence you see mystery,
> and in perennial Presence you see appearance.
> Though the two are one and the same,
> once they arise, they differ in name.

There's an alternate and complementary reading of this passage: "There without distinctions or explanations."

4. *ch'an*: 禪, meaning literally: "meditation." A transliteration of the Sanskrit *dhyana* (meditation), Ch'an was taken as the school's name because it focused so resolutely on meditation. The Japanese pronunciation of the ideogram is the well-known *Zen*.

5. Chuang Tzu's idea that recurs in the Ch'an tradition: see part I, note 3.

6. This echoes the beginning of the *Tao Te Ching*: "A Way you can say isn't the perennial Way." And there are two other complementary ways to read this line: "The Way of words ends here" and "This is where Tao's words fail."

7. For this understanding of the *Mind Sutra* as a native Chinese text rather than the translation of an original Sanskrit one, see Jan Nattier's "The Heart Sūtra: A Chinese Apocryphal Text?" *Journal of the International Association of Buddhist Studies* 15, no. 2 (December 1992): 153–223.

8. This line could also be read: "Absence not illumination and not illumination gone dark."

9. *Gaze* (觀) is the same word used for Bodhidharma's form of meditation: wall-gazing.

10. The five *skandhas*: World ("this beautiful world of things"), perception, thought, intention, awareness. These five skandhas appear in the poem below. Notice that here in these five "dimensions of consciousness" there is no subjective-objective divide—for "this world" is described as integral to "perception and thought, intention and awareness."

11. This line could also be read: "Absence not illumination and not illumination gone dark."

PART V

1. third watch: The nighttime hours between 11 p.m. and 1 a.m.

2. *seeing original-nature*: A reference to Bodhidharma's seminal definition of enlightenment: "Seeing original-nature, you become Buddha" (p. 123, 126).

3. *see original-nature*: Again referencing Bodhidharma's description of enlightenment, another dimension in Prajna-Able's knowledge of Ch'an's written tradition.

4. Prajna-Able's descriptions of mirror-mind in these two poems clearly echo *Chuang Tzu* 5.2: "If a mirror is bright, dust never settles on it. If dust can settle on it, the mirror isn't bright" (p. 42). Further evidence of the Sixth Patriarch's learnedness and connection to early Taoist thought.

5. no-thought Absence…no-form Absence…no-dwelling Absence: Three more instances of the philosophically productive double-meaning of 無 (no/Absence), for these terms mean simultaneously: no-thought/Absence-thought, no-form/Absence-form, no-dwelling/Absence-dwelling.

6. sitting *ch'an*: 禪, meaning literally "meditation." A transliteration of the Sanskrit *dhyana* (meditation), Ch'an was taken as the school's name because it focused so resolutely on meditation. The Japanese pronunciation of the ideogram is the well-known *Zen*.

7. ten thousand dharmas: A variation on the commonplace "the ten thousand things," "the ten thousand dharmas" refers to the entire Cosmos in all its particular variety and transformation.

8. mind-ground: "Ground" here is literally "earth" (地), as in "heaven-and-earth."

9. Spirit-Lightning Gather: Shen Hui, Prajna-Able's dharma-heir and the person credited with creating much of the Sixth Patriarch's myth and teaching. See the introduction, p. 160.

10. This is Nan-Yüeh Huai-Jang, the dharma-heir of Sixth Patriarch Prajna-Able, which establishes Way-Entire in a direct lineage from the Sixth Patriarch.

11. Chuang Tzu's idea that we've seen echoing through the Ch'an tradition; see part I, note 3.

12. mind-ground: "Ground" here is literally "earth" (地), as in "heaven-and-earth."

13. There's a more philosophical reading rustling below the surface here: "suddenly Presence and then vanishing into Absence again without a trace."

14. Or "like pure emptiness depending on nothing."

15. *seeing original-nature*: A reference to Bodhidharma's seminal definition of enlightenment: "Seeing original-nature, you become Buddha" (pp. 123, 126).

16. Hundred-Elder Mountain (Pai Chang) was Way-Entire's most illustrious dharma-heir. Through him, Way-Entire's lineage passed to Yellow-Bitterroot Mountain (p. 195).

17. Echoing the enlightenment story of Patriarch Sudden-Horse Way-Entire (pp. 178–79).

18. It almost sounds like Yellow-Bitterroot is describing that immortal soul familiar in the West. But there is no linear time in ancient China's generative cosmology/ontology. So when Yellow-Bitterroot describes mind as unborn and undying, he is talking about mind as Absence, source of all transformation and therefore "immortal." And at the same time, mind is empty because it is beyond all words and concepts.

19. emptiness empty: For the full implications of this recurring term (空虚) in Yellow-Bitterroot, see Key Terms, pp. 330–31.

20. six paramitas: The virtuous practices in traditional Buddhism that can ferry one over into nirvana. *Paramita* also means "perfection" (cf. *prajna-paramita*, "perfection of wisdom" p. 149) as the result of those paramita practices. And in those "perfections," one is "gone beyond" or "gone to the other shore," the original literal meaning of *paramita*.

21. Three Vehicles: The three "conveyances" in traditional Buddhism that supposedly carry people across *samsara* to the shores of nirvana: disciple, sage-recluse, bodhisattva.

22. Buddha-Way Terrace: Where Buddha attained enlightenment.

23. This little fable echoes *Tao Te Ching* 25 (p. 33), the ideas of which set the stage for what follows.

24. *Once you've got the fish, you can forget the trap*: from this famous parable from Chuang Tzu:

> The point of a fish-trap is the fish: once you've got the fish, you can forget the trap. The point of a rabbit-snare is the rabbit: once you've got the rabbit, you can forget the snare. And the point of a word is the idea: once you've got the idea, you can forget the word.
>
> How can I find someone who's forgotten words, so we can have a few words together?

25. *see original-nature*: A reference to Bodhidharma's seminal definition of enlightenment: "Seeing original-nature, you become Buddha" (pp. 123, 126).

26. River-Act Mountain (Kuei Shan) was Yellow-Bitterroot Mountain's dharma brother. They both studied under and received transmission from the same master. Reliance Mountain (Yang Shan) was River-Act's primary dharma-heir, which makes him Purport Dark-Enigma's dharma cousin.

27. Half a century later, Cloud-Gate Mountain would use this same answer when asked about Buddha (p. 241):

> Someone asked: " What is Buddha's very self?"
> "Dry shit-wipe stick!"

28. mind-ground: "Ground" here is literally "earth" (地), as in "heaven-and-earth."

29. *lohans*: In conventional Buddhism, lohans are "worthy ones" who have attained full realization and will enter nirvana upon death.

30. Here is another example of the philosophically productive double-meaning of 無 (not/Absence), for these phrases are literally "not/Absence dharma," "not/Absence practice," "not/Absence enlightenment."

31. perfect dharma of the eye's treasure-house: When Buddha held up the flower and Mahakasyapa smiled, revealing his understanding, Buddha described (in Chinese texts) that understanding "not relying on words and texts, outside teaching and beyond doctrine" as "my perfect dharma of the eye's treasure-house." As such, this idea continued through the Ch'an tradition as the essence of insight and awakening.

32. Wellspring-South Mountain (Nan-Ch'üan) was Visitation-Land's teacher. The first four episodes describe events that happened when Visitation-Land was still a student.

33. Chuang Tzu's idea: see part I, note 3.

34. This question, recurring in the *Teaching Record*, echoes the tenth line in the *Tao Te Ching*'s epochal first poem (p. 27): *Dark-enigma deep within dark-enigma.*

35. From the *Vimalikirti Sutra*.

36. Notice how the *Vimalikirti Sutra*'s "dharma" becomes equated with the Taoist "inner-pattern Way."

37. A telling variation on the classic question "What is the *ch'i*-weave mind Bodhidharma brought from the West?" which recurs here in the *Teaching Record* and throughout the Ch'an literature.

38. This question and answer were extracted to become the most preeminent of sangha-cases. See the introduction to this chapter (p. 221) and *No-Gate Gateway* (pp. 286–87, 290).

39. Peace-Perpetua is the name of the capital city (Ch'ang-an; present-day Xian). The usage here seems to refer to both the concept and city.

40. "Fact-Mind Inscription" (p. 140), line 33.

41. Referring originally to the open ground beneath the Bodhi tree where Buddha attained enlightenment, this term came to mean any place of practice and awakening, such as a monastery or meditation hall.

42. There is a second reading of these lines:

> Cloud Presence seething up from mountains,
> stream Absence burbling down into valleys.

43. A different version of this incident appears as chapter 7 in *No-Gate Gateway*. There, this exchange results in the monk's awakening.

44. "Fact-Mind Inscription" (p. 140), lines 10–12.

45. In Buddhist mythology, these are the seven Buddhas who lived in successive *kalpas* (world-cycles each lasting 4,300,000 years), one per *kalpa*: Vipasyin, Sikhin, Visvabhu, Krakucchanda, Kanakamuni, Kasyapa, and lastly: Shakyamuni Buddha.

46. See p. 187ff.

47. Cold Mountain's legendary sidekick (whose poems are included in the Cold Mountain collection).

48. This question might also be read: "What is the ancestral teaching at origins?"

49. "Fact-Mind Inscription" (p. 140), lines 47–48.

50. Primal-unity entire: The number one is in Chinese a simple line: 一. As here, it often means "entire" and, in its philosophical sense, "primal-unity." But even deeper, it was considered the aboriginal gesture that inscribes the first distinction imposed by mind on the undifferentiated whole of the Cosmos, a kind of horizon-line dividing heaven and earth.

51. This is also generally true of modern American poetry, as explored in my *The Wilds of Poetry*.

52. Thatch-Hut Mountain: Mountain that presided over the beginnings of Ch'an. See pp. 75–77.

53. Prajna-Distance: Founder of East-Forest Monastery, locus of Ch'an's origins. See p. 76.

54. sitting *ch'an*: 禪, meaning literally "meditation." A transliteration of the Sanskrit *dhyana* (meditation), Ch'an was taken as the school's name because it focused so resolutely on meditation. The Japanese pronunciation of the ideogram is the well-known *Zen*.

55. *ch'in*: Ancient stringed instrument much revered by Chinese intellectuals as a means for attaining enlightenment, often appearing in poems and used as accompaniment when Chinese poets chanted their poems. In the hands of a master, a *ch'in* could voice with profound clarity the rivers-and-mountains realm, even the very source of all things.

56. emptiness empty: For the full implications of this term (空虚), see Key Terms, pp. 330–31.

57. White-Crane: The orchard where Buddha died, so named because upon his death the trees burst into white blossoms and resembled white cranes.

58. transmits the lamp: In Ch'an Buddhism, this lamp is absolute insight, which is passed from teacher to student directly, outside of word and text, idea and institution. Hence: transmission of the lamp. One of the major texts in Ch'an literature is the *Lamp-Transmission Record*, which recounts enlightening stories from Ch'an's lineage of great teachers.

59. In Ch'an parlance, "giving up home" means to enter a monastery. Cf. Cold Mountain #247 (p. 192).

PART VI

1. Here are the precise numbers of occurrences for a few key concepts: Tao, 2,784; dark-enigma, 538; *tzu-jan*, 364; *wu-wei*, 52; loom-of-origins, 427; inner-pattern, 393.

2. For a full explanation of how sangha-cases functioned in Ch'an practice, see the "Sangha-Case" chapter in *China Root*, pp. 113–19.

3. Thatch-Hut Mountain: Mountain that presided over the beginnings of Ch'an. See pp. 75–77.

4. Wellspring-South Mountain was Visitation-Land's teacher for decades, and the teacher under whom he attained enlightenment. See pp. 223–24

5. original-face: Our inherently enlightened original-nature, also described as Buddha-mind or empty-mind.

6. Sangha-Fundament: see p. 78ff.

7. The World-Honored-One: Shakyamuni Buddha.

8. Manjusri: A mythological bodhisattva described as the father or teacher of the Seven Buddhas of mythic antiquity who lived in successive *kalpas* (world-cycles each lasting 4,300,000 years), one per *kalpa*, the last of which was Shakyamuni Buddha. Manjusri is also described as the embodiment of all the wisdom of all Buddhas. Perfectly suited to Ch'an, the Chinese transliteration (文殊) means something like "Culture-Sutra Kill."

9. For the source of this sangha-case, see p. 240.

10. *seeing original-nature*: A reference to Bodhidharma's seminal definition of enlightenment: "Seeing original-nature, you become Buddha" (pp. 123, 126).

11. Strung-Pearls: a constellation.

12. Wary-Cloud: Chinese transliteration for the Sanskrit *Gautama*.

13. For the source of this sangha-case, see pp. 221, 226.

14. This quintessential description of enlightenment hearkens back to very similar passages in the *Chuang Tzu* (1.10, 1.16, 6.6, 6.11) and numerous passages at key moments in the Ch'an literature playing on Chuang Tzu's "wandering boundless and free" (see Key Terms, p. 334).

15. faintly emergent: see entry for *shadowed-emergence* in Key Terms (p. 326) and the general introduction's discussion of this story (p. 6).

16. perfect dharma of the eye's treasure-house: see part V, note 31.

17. For the source of this sangha-case, see pp. 224, 225.

18. For an extensive account of how landscape paintings manifest Taoist/Ch'an understanding, see my book *Existence: A Story*.

KEY TERMS

An Outline of Ch'an's Conceptual World

CH'AN'S CONCEPTUAL WORLD IS DESCRIBED FULLY IN this book's companion volume: *China Root: Taoism, Ch'an, and Original Zen*. That book serves as the full philosophical introduction to this one. But Ch'an's conceptual world is easily outlined by defining a few foundational terms/concepts that recur often in the Ch'an literature. In fact, these concepts are inevitably crucial when Ch'an touches philosophical ground. But they have been lost, misconstrued, and mistranslated— a process that has largely erased original Ch'an from modern Zen. This Key Terms section functions as a glossary to those terms/concepts. It is also designed to be read straight through as an introductory essay describing Ch'an's conceptual framework.

Our understanding of Ch'an/Zen changes dramatically when we realize that these terms all come from early Taoist philosophy. By probing deeper into the native understanding of key terms/concepts, a new Ch'an is revealed. It is a Ch'an grounded in the rich earth of Taoist cosmology/ontology, reality experienced as a generative tissue—a Ch'an for which spiritual practice aspires to reintegrate consciousness with that tissue in perpetual transformation. Concepts at this foundational level blur, and Taoist terminology proliferates. So, what we find here in a survey of the key terms is a host of concepts, often nearly synonymous, each offering a different way into the fundamental nature of consciousness and Cosmos.

These terms/concepts occur so frequently that conventional notes would be onerous, especially as the book has so many independent sections that might be read independently, requiring every term to be noted anew in each section. So, this glossary of key terms also functions as the bulk of the textual notes for this book. These key concepts must be presented in a coherent order, for an understanding of one concept is often necessary for those that follow. Hence, the terms do not appear in alphabetical order. Here is an alphabetical index to the terms:

PRESENCE 有

The empirical universe, described in Taoist philosophy as the ten thousand things in their vast transformations.

ABSENCE 無

The generative source-tissue from which the ever-changing realm of Presence perpetually arises. This undifferentiated tissue is the ontological substrate infused mysteriously with a generative energy. We might almost describe it in scientific terms as matter itself: the formless material that is shaped into the ten thousand discrete forms of reality (Presence) and into which those forms dissolve at death. Because of its generative nature, it continuously shapes itself into the individual forms of the Cosmos, then reshapes itself into other forms: the ten thousand things in the constant process of change. So, a more literal translation of Absence might be "without form," in contrast to "within form" for Presence. Absence is known directly in meditation, where it is experienced as empty consciousness itself, known in Ch'an terminology as "empty-mind" or "no-mind" (see below): the formless generative source of thoughts. Hence, meditation as a spiritual practice reintegrating consciousness and Cosmos.

WAY (TAO) 道

The Tao of Taoism. *Tao* originally meant "way," as in "pathway" or "roadway," a meaning it has kept. But Lao Tzu reconceived it as a generative cosmological process, an ontological "path*Way*" by which things come into existence, evolve through their lives, and then go out of existence, only to be transformed and reemerge in a new form. As such, it might provisionally be divided into Presence and Absence. Here is a prime example of overlapping terminology struggling to name the fundamental nature of reality—for in practice, Tao/Way emphasizes the undifferentiated and generative nature of the existence-tissue, and is therefore nearly synonymous with Absence. Indeed, Lao Tzu describes it as "source" and "female" and "mother."

Tao represents one of the most dramatic indications that Ch'an is a refinement and extension of Taoism, because the term *Tao* is used extensively in Ch'an with the same meaning. It sometimes simply means "Ch'an's *way* of practice, its path*Way* to enlightenment," a usage that parallels its early use in Taoism and Confucianism. But more often, and more philosophically important, it is the Taoist Tao/Way, that generative ontological source-tissue. And sometimes it is both simultaneously, as in the quintessential Ch'an dictum: "Ordinary mind is Way" (pp. 177–79).

DARK-ENIGMA 玄

Perhaps the most foundational concept in this Taoist/Ch'an cosmology/ontology, dark-enigma is Way before it is named, before Absence and Presence give birth to one another—that region beyond name and ideation where consciousness and the empirical Cosmos share their source. Dark-enigma came to have a particular historic significance, for it became the name of a neo-Taoist school of philosophy in the third and fourth centuries C.E.: Dark-Enigma Learning (see part II, pp. 47–71), a school that gave Chinese thought a decidedly ontological turn and became central to the synthesis of Taoism and Dhyana Buddhism into Ch'an Buddhism. And indeed, the concept is at the very heart of Ch'an practice and enlightenment. It is there at the very beginning, concluding the first chapter of the *Tao Te Ching* (p. 27): "Dark-enigma deep within dark-enigma, / gateway of all mystery." And it recurs often at key moments throughout the Ch'an tradition. Among the countless examples is Fathom Mountain (Tung Shan, 807–869; founder of Soto Zen) saying that the most profound dimension of Ch'an's wordless teaching is dark-enigma within dark-enigma, which he evocatively describes as the "tongue of a corpse" (p. 157). And the very influential Stone-Head (Shih T'ou, 700–790) ends his still influential poem "Amalgam-Alike Compact" declaring dark-enigma to be the essential object of Ch'an inquiry:

> Please, you who try to fathom dark-enigma clear
> through, don't pass your days and nights in vain.

ORIGIN-TISSUE　緣
EXISTENCE-TISSUE　如

緣 and 如 are virtually synonymous with Absence, Tao/Way, and dark-enigma: reality as a single tissue, undifferentiated and generative. Birth, giving form to the ten thousand individual things, is described as 緣合: "origin-tissue coming together." And death, the unraveling of individuation, is described as 緣離: "origin-tissue scattering." So the vast and ongoing transformation of things is this *origin-tissue* coalescing into individual forms and then dispersing back into a single undifferentiated tissue. And it is important for Ch'an that this tissue is the "thusness" we encounter every moment in our everyday life, as emphasized in the recurring phrase 真如: "wild existence-tissue thusness," or "existence-tissue all thusness-clarity absolute."

CH'I　氣

氣 is often described as the universal life-force breathing through things. But this presumes a dualism that separates reality into matter and a breath-force (spirit) that infuses it with life. Like the Absence/Presence dichotomy, that dualism may be useful as an approach to understanding; but more fully understood, *ch'i* is both breath-force and matter simultaneously. It is a single tissue generative through and through, the matter and energy of the Cosmos seen together as a single breath-force surging through its perpetual transformations. And so, *ch'i* is nearly synonymous with Way and Absence-tissue, but emphasizing their generative dynamism.

INNER-PATTERN　理

The philosophical meaning of *inner-pattern*, which originally referred to the veins and markings in a precious piece of jade, is something akin to what we call natural law. It is the system of principles or patterns that governs the unfolding of Way (or Absence, or *ch'i*) into the various forms of the ten thousand things in their vast transformations. It is a pervasive concept in the Ch'an tradition, where moving integral to inner-pattern is one definition of awakening.

POTENCY 體
ACTUALIZATION 用

Together, these terms represent an important pair of foundational cosmological/ontological concepts in Chinese philosophy. *Potency* refers to the inherent potentiality or nature of things—a virtual synonym for *inner-pattern*. That potency gives shape to the particular *actualization*, the ongoing emergence (expression/manifestation) of things in the world.

ORIGIN-DARK QUIET 幽
SHADOWED-EMERGENCE 微

Appearing often in recluse poetry, 幽 always infuses the surface meaning "quiet solitude" with rich philosophical depths, beginning with the sense of "dark/secret/hidden/mystery." And that leads finally to the term's deepest level, "origin-dark quiet," which forms a terminological pair with 微. Here it means forms, the ten thousand things, just on the not-yet-emergent side of the origin-moment: just as they are about to emerge from the formless ground of Absence, or just after they vanish back into that ground.

The everyday meaning of 微 is "faint/sparse/hidden," but in poetic and philosophic contexts it takes on cosmological/ontological dimensions: things on the emergent side of the origin-moment in that cosmology of Tao's ongoing generative unfolding, just barely coming into existence as differentiated entities or not quite vanished back into the undifferentiated ground.

LOOM-OF-ORIGINS 機

A mythological description of Way's unfurling process—hence, the Cosmos in its perennial transformation seen as an ever-generative loom-of-origins. Chuang Tzu, the seminal Taoist sage (p. 38ff.), describes it like this: "The ten thousand things all emerge from a loom-of-origins, and they all vanish back into it."

DRAGON 龍

Another mythical incarnation of Way and its ten thousand things tumbling through their traceless transformations, dragon was feared and revered as the awesome force of change, as the embodiment of all creation and all destruction. Its form was therefore in constant transformation. To take one example: Small as a silkworm and vast as all heaven-and-earth, dragon descends into deep waters in autumn, where it hibernates until spring, when its reawakening means the return of life to earth. It rises and ascends into sky, where it billows into thunderclouds and falls as spring's life-bringing rains. Its claws flash as lightning in those thunderclouds, and its rippling scales glisten in the bark of rain-soaked pines.

HEAVEN 天

Heaven has a number of intertwined meanings that often function simultaneously. Originally a kind of impersonal divinity, heaven was reinvented by the seminal Taoist sages as an entirely empirical phenomenon—the generative cosmological force that drives the ongoing transformation of natural process—thereby secularizing the sacred while at the same time investing the secular with sacred dimensions. This transition moment was soon superseded by the entirely secular Way (*Tao*), which was essentially synonymous with "heaven," but without the metaphysical implications.

Heaven appears often in the phrase "heaven-and-earth," meaning the world of our everyday experience, for 天 means most simply "sky." But the phrase also means "the universe" in Taoism's cosmological sense, for heaven and earth were conceived as the grandest cosmological manifestations of *yang* and *yin*. Hence, the universe conceived as a living and dynamic interpenetration of *yang* and *yin*.

From this comes a second set of terms for heaven-and-earth: 乾 and 坤. These terms, the titles of the first two hexagrams of the *I Ching*, emphasize heaven as *yang* (the active generative force of the Cosmos) and earth as *yin* (the receptive generative force): the two forces whose ceaseless interaction generates the process of change. Accordingly, 乾 and 坤 might be read as "Creative" and "Receptive."

OCCURRENCE-APPEARING-OF-ITSELF 自然

A central concept in early Taoist cosmology/ontology, 自然 (*tzu-jan*) is a way of describing the process of Way that emphasizes individual entities rather than the process as a whole. Its literal meaning is "self-so" or "the of-itself," which as a philosophical concept becomes "being such of itself," hence "spontaneous" or "natural." But a more revealing translation of *tzu-jan* is "occurrence-appearing-of-itself," for the term is meant to describe the ten thousand things burgeoning forth spontaneously from the generative source (Presence from Absence), each according to its own nature, independent and self-sufficient, each dying and returning to the process of change, only to reappear in another self-generating form. As such, this inheritance from Taoism continued as a major element in Ch'an's conceptual framework.

ABSENCE-ACTION 無為

If there is a single term that describes the nature of Ch'an enlightenment, it is 無為 (*wu-wei*). Like *tzu-jan*, *wu-wei* dates to the earliest levels of Taoist thought, and means literally "not/Absence (*wu*)" + "acting (*wei*)." A spiritual practice broadly adopted by ancient artist-intellectuals, Absence-action became central to Ch'an practice: further indication of Ch'an's essentially Taoist nature. *Wu-wei* means "not acting" in the sense of acting without the metaphysics of self, or of being *absent* when you act. This selfless action is the movement of *tzu-jan*, so *wu-wei* means acting as an integral part of *tzu-jan*'s spontaneous process of Tao/Way: Absence burgeoning forth into Presence, and Presence dying back into Absence.

Wu-wei is perhaps the original exploitation of the double-meaning of 無 (not/Absence) that became crucial in Ch'an: examples include unborn/Absence-born and no-mind/Absence-mind (for which, see below), and a host of other variations: no/Absence-knowing, no/Absence-thought, no/Absence-form, no/Absence-dwelling, no/Absence-dharma, no/Absence-practice, no/Absence-enlightenment. This double-meaning opens to the deepest level of *wu-wei*'s philosophical complex, where the term's alternate sense of "Absence" + "acting" means *wu-wei* action is action directly from, or indeed *as* the ontological source. Ch'an masters dramatized this in their wild antics (behavior that likens them to

Chuang Tzu's zany Taoist sages): to practice *wu-wei* is to move with the wild energy of the Cosmos itself. But it also takes the form of unbridled mental processes: indeed, the *Lamp-Transmission Record* says: wu-wei *is meditation*. Taken altogether, *wu-wei* represents a return to Paleolithic consciousness—and is, again, the very definition of Ch'an enlightenment, enlightenment that is ideally the form of everyday life.

SOURCE-ANCESTRAL　宗

In the blur of concepts at deep cosmological/ontological levels, source-ancestral seems virtually indistinguishable from Way or Absence or inner-pattern, and it is at times described as equivalent to Absence-action (*wu-wei*). The full dimensions of this concept are revealed dramatically in the etymologies of its two pictographic elements: 宀 and 示. 宀 simply means "roof," and is a stylized version of 𠆢, the early form that portrays a side-view of the traditional Chinese roof with its prominent ridgeline and curved form. 示 derives from 川 and the more ancient oracle-bone form 示, showing heaven as the line above, with three streams of light emanating earthward from the three types of heavenly bodies: sun, moon, and stars. These three sources of light were considered bright distillations of, or embryonic origins of *ch'i*, the breath-force that pulses through the Cosmos as both matter and energy simultaneously. Hence, 宗 is the cosmological source of *ch'i* as a dwelling-place, a dwelling-place that is the very source of the Cosmos.

The common meaning of 示 was simply "altar," suggesting a spiritual space in which one can be in the presence of those celestial *ch'i*-sources. And indeed, enlightenment in Ch'an was to inhabit this dwelling-place altar, as it was for Chuang Tzu who described a sage as one who "holds fast to the source-ancestral." And indeed, the common meaning of 宗 is "ancestor," which suggests a remarkable sense of the source as ancestral to us, as kindred. And so, the source-ancestral as always already our very nature.

IDLENESS　閑, 閒

Way unfurls its process of transformation in an effortless and spontaneous movement that can be described as idleness. Recognizing this, ancient China's artist-intellectuals and Ch'an adepts took living in idleness as a spiritual ideal, a kind of meditative wandering in which you move with the improvisational movement of Absence-action. And so, it is Absence-action enacted in the context of everyday life.

Etymologically, the character for idleness connotes "profound serenity and quietness," its pictographic elements rendering a tree standing alone within the gates to a courtyard: 閑, combining two pictographic elements more clearly visible in their early forms as 門 (gate) and 木 (tree). Or in its alternate form, a moon shining through open gates: 閒, which replaces 木 with 月 (moon).

UNBORN (ABSENCE-BORN) 無生

無生 plays on the two meanings of 無 in much the same way as 無為 (*wu-wei*), to give: "not/Absence (*wu*) + born/alive (*sheng*)." 無生 means "not living" in the sense of living with the metaphysics of self *absent*, hence "selfless living." This opens to a deeper level in which the term means "Absence born" or "Absence alive," describing our most essential identity as Absence itself. And finally, 無生 also means "not born" or "unborn," describing the fact that we are each a fleeting form conjured in Way's process of perpetual transformation: not just born out of it and returned to it in death, a familiar concept that still assumes a center of identity detached from the Cosmos and its processes, but never *out of it*, totally unborn. Indeed, our fullest identity, being unborn, is Way itself, is therefore all and none of earth's fleeting forms simultaneously. And so, the double-meaning is beautifully complementary, for to be "unborn" is precisely to be "Absence-born/alive.

EMPTINESS 空, 虛

In its native Taoist and Dark-Enigma Learning context, *emptiness* is essentially synonymous with *Absence*: emptiness in the sense of undifferentiated reality *empty* of individual forms, reality as a single formless and generative tissue to which we belong. It was used to (mis-)translate the Sanskrit *sunyata* (for which, see the Glossary of Buddhist Terms, p. 341), a crucial moment in the creation of Ch'an. Free of the metaphysical dimensions of *sunyata*, 空 and 虛 are entirely this-worldly, notably in their common meaning "sky," archetypal form of emptiness in our everyday experience. Etymologically, the two elements of 空 portray *labor* (工, early form: 𠚑 suggesting something emerging from an absence, and labor is of course to make something where there was nothing) within a *cave* (穴, indicating the space beneath a roof 宀, stylized version of 𠆢, side view of the traditional Chinese roof with its prominent ridgeline). Hence, a generative emptiness in earth, a womb where the work of gestation happens. 虛 in its early forms contains a pair of mountain peaks (山) and, in the space above those peaks, the element for *tiger* (虍, deriving from early images like 𧇛). Together, these two elements form, literally: "mountain tiger-sky." This emphasizes the sense of emptiness as sky/heaven; however, rather than emptiness as mere stillness (as in conventional Buddhism), it is emptiness dynamic with the wild energy of a tiger. And so, the two complementary terms (which often appear together in Ch'an texts) at their origins suggest something like emptiness in its heavenly and earthly forms, and *heaven-and-earth* is a Chinese term for the Cosmos itself.

MIND 心
CH'I-WEAVE MIND 意

In Ch'an parlance, *mind* principally refers to consciousness emptied of all contents, a state revealed through deep meditation: hence, mind as "original-nature" or "Buddha-nature." This consciousness in its original-nature is nothing other than Absence, that generative cosmological tissue—for it is the empty source of thought and memory, and also an empty mirror open via perception to the ten thousand things of Presence. So once again: Ch'an's conceptual world as fundamentally Taoist in nature.

Ch'an sometimes also uses *mind* seemingly in the common English sense of the word, as the center of language and thought and memory, the mental apparatus of identity. It seems the same, but Taoist/Ch'an cosmology/ontology makes it radically different. Those processes of mind were described as 意, which has a range of meanings: "intentionality," "desire," "meaning," "insight," "thought," "intelligence," "mind" (the faculty of thought). The natural Western assumption would be that these meanings refer to human consciousness, but 意 is also often used philosophically in describing the non-human world, as the "intentionality/desire/intelligence" that shapes the ongoing cosmological process of change and transformation (here it is virtually synonymous with *inner-pattern*). Each particular thing, at its very origin, has its own 意, as does the Cosmos as a whole. 意 can therefore be described as the "intentionality/intelligence/desire" infusing Absence (or Tao/Way) and shaping its burgeoning forth into Presence, the ten thousand things of this Cosmos. It could also be described as the *intentionality*, the inherent ordering capacity, shaping the creative force of *ch'i*.

This range of meaning links human intention/thought to the originary movements of the Cosmos—for it operates in a cosmological context recognizing an "intelligence" that infuses all existence, and of which human thought is but one manifestation. So 意 is a capacity that human thought and emotion share with wild landscape and, indeed, the entire Cosmos, a reflection of the Chinese assumption that the human and non-human form a single tissue that "thinks" and "wants." Hence, thought/identity is not a transcendental spirit-realm separate from and looking out on reality, as we assume in the West. Instead, it is woven wholly into the ever-generative *ch'i*-tissue, which is to say they are woven wholly into a living "intelligent" Cosmos—and so, it seems best translated as "*ch'i*-weave mind," "*ch'i*-weave insight," "*ch'i*-weave thought," etc.

This concept appears perhaps most famously in the perennial Ch'an question: "What is the *ch'i*-weave mind Bodhidharma brought from the West?" This is said to be asking about the essence of Ch'an. Normal translations such as "purpose" or "meaning" cannot support such a claim. But once 意 is understood as "*ch'i*-weave mind," that claim makes sense, because then it's asking about mind woven into the generative tissue of the Cosmos. This is the heart of Ch'an understanding and enlightenment, and indeed one basis for the claim that we are always already enlightened.

EMPTY-MIND 空心, 虛心
NO-MIND 無心

The understanding of mind outlined above is the context within which we must understand one goal of Ch'an practice: to see through mind as the analytical faculty to mind as consciousness emptied of all contents. From this come the terms *empty-mind* or *no-mind*—which are, confusingly, virtually synonymous with *mind* in its primary Ch'an sense. And they are central to Ch'an awakening, but awakening as more than the simple emptiness and tranquility of conventional Buddhism as it arrived in China.

For empty-mind was recognized as Absence itself, that generative cosmological/ontological tissue—source in consciousness of thought, memory, emotion, etc. And so, empty-mind was now dynamic and alive, an understanding emphasized in the etymological dimensions of 虛: "mountain tiger-sky," a poetic description of dynamic emptiness if there ever was one. And rather than an ascetic pursuit for a mind of tranquility and stillness, a state that is always forced and temporary (illusory!), Ch'an's Taoist assumptions allow an embrace of emptiness as the generative tissue of Absence, Tao/Way, Cosmos. And so, an acceptance of ordinary mind as always already awakened, always already Buddha, Tao/ Way, *tzu-jan*, *wu-wei*.

And it is the same for *no-mind*. Because of the ever-productive double-meaning of 無 (no/Absence), 無心 (no-mind) describes mind both empty of content and made of the generative source-tissue (Absence-mind). It is accordingly here often translated "Absence no-mind." And so, again, an embrace of mind's processes as already awakened.

In ancient China, there was no fundamental distinction between heart and mind: 心 connotes all that we think of in the two concepts together. In fact, the ideogram is a stylized version of the earlier 𞣋, which is an image of the heart muscle, with its chambers at the locus of veins and arteries. This integration of mental and emotional realms means the experience of empty- or no/Absence-mind cultivated in Ch'an practice is not just a spiritual or intellectual experience, but also a rich emotional experience.

EYE/SIGHT 目, 眼, 見, 直, ETC.
MIRROR 鏡, 鑑

Once mind is emptied of all content (through meditation and sangha-case practice), the act of perception becomes a spiritual act: Absence no-mind mirror-deep, empty-mind mirroring the world, leaving its ten thousand things free of all thought and explanation—utterly simple, utterly themselves, and utterly sufficient. This image of the mirror is foundational in Taoism and Ch'an, recurring at key moments throughout the tradition. And it is the heart of Ch'an as a landscape practice. In such mirror-deep perception, earth's vast rivers-and-mountains landscape replaces thought and even identity itself, revealing the unity of consciousness/identity and landscape/Cosmos that is the heart of sage dwelling not only for Ch'an practitioners, but for all artist-intellectuals in ancient China. Indeed, when Buddha held up the flower and Mahakasyapa smiled (pp. 6, 292), the understanding he revealed was exactly that: the mirror-deep seeing of empty-mind. And in the Ch'an tradition, Buddha describes that understanding "not relying on words and texts, outside teaching and beyond doctrine" as "my perfect dharma of the eye's treasure-house." This idea continued through the tradition as the essence of insight and awakening (pp. 18–19, 292), for it encapsulates another way of meeting Buddha and all the patriarchs directly, but also of being indistinguishable from them, of being Buddha oneself.

Mirror refs: 31, 42, 45, 56, 67, 71, 80, 83, 88, 97–98, 100, 102, 136, 165–67, 169, 179, 182, 198, 231, 271, 273, 294 .

WANDERING BOUNDLESS AND FREE　逍遙
Originating in the *Chuang Tzu* (p. 38) and developed in Kuo Hsiang's commentary (p. 62), this wholly Taoist concept recurs at crucial moments where Ch'an literature dives directly into the nature of insight and enlightenment. It is an idea that invests consciousness with its full cosmological dimensions, describing enlightenment as the most magisterial realization of Absence-action (*wu-wei*) and our unborn nature, realization in which we inhabit the selfless *wandering* of our unborn "original-nature" through the selfless transformations of Way's vast and ongoing process.

Refs: 38, 40 (1.10, 1.16), 42 (6.6), 44 (6.11), 63, 65 (2 refs.), 66 (2 refs.), 68, 143, 192, 291.

AWAKENING/ENLIGHTENMENT　悟 / 見性
In Chinese, these two terms may seem quite different at the outset—but in the end, they describe the same awakening/enlightenment. 悟 (Japanese: *satori*) is composed etymologically of *mind* (心 appearing here in stylized form as 忄 on the left) and *me* (吾) on the right. This renders the term's common meaning of "waking" from sleep as a suddenly renewed

awareness of "my mind," or perhaps "me" returning to "mind" again. And that becomes in the Ch'an context something very close to a "sudden awakening" (that essential Ch'an principle) to empty-mind as "original-nature." 見性 (Japanese: *kensho*) means "see + original-nature," where the ideogram for "original-nature" is composed of *mind* again on the left and *birth* on the right, hence "mind at its origin." This realization, an observational clarity almost scientific in nature, becomes the definition of enlightenment in the last line of Bodhidharma's seminal poem (pp. 123, 126): "Seeing original-nature, you become Buddha."

In spite of their apparent differences, the two terms both describe enlightenment as an awakening to oneself, to one's inherent or original nature. And because that original-nature is whole and silent, prior to our mental machinery of words and concepts, awakening is instantaneous and outside of teaching and practice. That original-nature is unborn and empty is in fact Way or Absence itself. And so, awakening/enlightenment is, again, a selfless "wandering boundless and free" through the selfless transformations of Way's vast and ongoing process.

Ch'an also uses a third term for awakening/enlightenment: the Sanskrit *bodhi*, for which see *bodhi* in Glossary of Buddhist Terms, p. 338.

For a full account of Ch'an awakening/enlightenment, see the Awakening chapter in *China Root* (pp. 126–36).

GLOSSARY OF BUDDHIST TERMS

A NUMBER OF KEY BUDDHIST TERMS RECUR IN THE Ch'an tradition traced in this book. Inevitably, they have been transformed into Taoist concepts through two possible mechanisms. First, some are simply redefined as part of Ch'an's philosophical self-creation. This is sometimes intentional philosophical work. And sometimes it is misunderstanding the original by seeing it through the lens of Chinese thought, and thereby mistranslating it.

The second possible mechanism is more complicated. Sanskrit is alphabetic, and Chinese is not. So words were brought into Chinese through transliteration: Chinese ideograms would be chosen because their sounds corresponded to the Sanskrit sounds. Chinese ideograms all have a monosyllabic pronunciation, so multisyllabic Sanskrit words were typically transliterated using several Chinese ideograms. The complication here is that each Chinese word-sound is used for many different ideograms. So the scholars transliterating Sanskrit could choose between dozens, even hundreds of possible ideograms for each Sanskrit sound. And their choices often transformed original Buddhist concepts into native Taoist concepts. The new Chinese constructions were recognized as transliterations of Sanskrit words (and concepts), but the actual meanings of the words in Chinese described Taoist concepts. Hence, again, the original Buddhist concepts were transfigured into Taoist concepts.

In both of these mechanisms, the transformations generally grew out of a mistaken assumption among Chinese scholars that Indian Buddhism was simply a dramatically different expression of the same basic philosophical framework. By contrast, in the transmission of Ch'an to modern America, English translations have generally erred by presenting these terms as if their original Sanskrit meanings remained unchanged—as if, that is, Ch'an were a form of Buddhism. But Ch'an's embrace of these transformations in meaning from Sanskrit to Chinese represents one more example of how Ch'an is not at all Buddhist in its fundamental nature.

BODHI 覺, 菩提

Bodhi simply means "awakening," or "enlightenment." Hence the tree beneath which Buddha attained enlightenment was called the Bodhi tree. Conventional Buddhism taught that this awakening came as the result of complicated paths and practices, and that it was an awakening to *sunyata* (see below), to the fundamental emptiness of self and reality. And it involved liberation from the cycle of rebirth. In this, *bodhi* enlightenment was rife with transcendental implications.

Ch'an continues to use the term *bodhi* for enlightenment. But just as *sunyata* is transformed into a Taoist/Ch'an emptiness that is equivalent to Absence, so *bodhi* is transformed into the radically different Ch'an conception of awakening. In Ch'an usage, *bodhi* is transformed into a this-worldly awakening to Absence—to our unborn oneness with the cosmological/ontological process of Way (see "Awakening/ Enlightenment" in Key Terms, pp. 334–35).

BUDDHA 佛

Buddha refers most literally to Shakyamuni/Gautama, the historical Buddha, but also to a host of other Buddhas in Buddhist mythology. Ch'an invests no faith in those mythologies beyond their use as an element of storytelling. And it is primarily interested in Shakyamuni at the deep level of his essential nature, which is his empty-mind. So the meaning of the term *Buddha* expands to mean empty-mind, emphasized in the term *Buddha-nature*; and because empty-mind is the central concern of Ch'an, Buddha also comes to mean the essence of Ch'an.

Indeed, Ch'an's cultivation of empty-mind opens the possibility both of meeting the Buddha and the patriarchs directly, but also of being indistinguishable from them, of being Buddha oneself. And finally, as empty-mind is indistinguishable from Absence or dark-enigma, *Buddha* becomes synonymous with those terms too, and even the generative Way itself. Hence, *Buddha* is absorbed into the Taoist cosmology, becoming another term used to describe that generative tissue that remains always just beyond language. Further, as we saw in the introduction, the ideogram for *Buddha* is made up of the elements for "person" and "loom (-of-origins)." And from here, *Buddha* logically comes to mean reality itself—a usage we often find in the Ch'an tradition, and which has the effect of infusing our everyday world with a sense of the sacred. In particular, Buddha is identified with rivers-and-mountains landscape (the Chinese transliteration for *Gautama* means Wary-Cloud), as in Su Tung-p'o's enlightenment poem (p. 301):

> A murmuring stream is Buddha's tongue broad, unending,
> and what is mountain color if not his body pure and clear?

Buddha Existence-Tissue Arrival　如來

Tathagata is a name for Buddha, describing his nature as the "thus-come" or "thus perfected one." In its original Indian context, this suggests an enlightened sage who has entered nirvana. In the Chinese transliteration, it means "existence-tissue arrival." Hence, Buddha has been transformed into a virtual equivalent of Way (Tao) or Absence—the generative "existence-tissue" that is always, in its ongoing process of perennially sufficient transformation, a moment of "arrival." Or alternately, as an enlightened sage who has "arrived" by inhabiting his original-nature as integral to the "existence-tissue."

Dharma　法

Dharma in Ch'an is the teachings of the Ch'an tradition. But Ch'an's essential teaching is outside of words and ideas, and here is *dharma's* most fundamental meaning: the sheer thusness of things that is the true teaching. And this is actually the term's primary use in Ch'an—virtually synonymous with *tzu-jan*, *Tao/Way*, *Absence* (*emptiness*), *dark-enigma*, even *Buddha*. Another example of a Buddhist term being adapted to function at the deepest cosmological/ontological levels of the Taoist conceptual world.

KALPA 劫
A world-cycle of 4,300,000 years.

KARMA 業
In the Taoist/Ch'an framework, karma is very different than for Buddhism in general (though it is sometimes used in that conventional sense for literary effect). Rather than successive reincarnations of a "soul," karma in Ch'an involves the selfless unfurling of Way's Great Transformation according to inner-pattern. Another example of Buddhist concepts reconfigured in the Taoist/Ch'an framework.

PRAJNA 慧, 般若
In Indian Buddhism, *prajna* refers to a transcendental state of perfect wisdom in which one directly sees or even becomes the fundamental emptiness (*sunyata*: see below) of things. Reconceived in the entirely empirical terms of Taoist cosmology/ontology, it is defined in a host of related ways in the Ch'an tradition, but a good working definition is mind returned to its original-nature as "Absence," which is equated with empty-mind as a "dark-enigma mirror." And indeed, the Chinese ideograms used to transliterate *prajna* mean "accord-pleasure": hence, the pleasure of being in accord with Tao/Way. This reveals a profound shift from Sanskrit/Buddhism to Chinese/Ch'an, for *prajna* has been reconfigured into a Taoist concept. Again, metaphysics replaced by the Great Transformation itself: this wild earth we inhabit.

SAMADHI 三昧地
In the Dhyana Buddhism that migrated to China from India, *samadhi* simply meant "consciousness emptied of all subjective content," the goal of meditative practice. But its Chinese transliteration means "three-shadowed earth." And so, *dhyana*'s abstract and cerebral meditative state has been invested with the earthly dimensions of Taoism/Ch'an: empty-

mind free of all conceptual structures, self dismantled completely by the Ch'an wrecking-crew, leaving consciousness open to its "original-nature" as the Cosmos moving in perfect tranquility at that all-encompassing and perennial origin-place that Lao Tzu called *Absence*. In its consummate description of enlightenment, *No-Gate Gateway* declares that in awakening "you wander the playfulness of *samadhi*'s three-shadowed earth" (p. 291).

SAMSARA 輪迴

Samsara's traditional Buddhist meaning is "the universe we inhabit as we work out our karmic destiny," a meaning sometimes referenced in Ch'an. Generally though, *samsara* refers in Ch'an to the phenomenal universe of our everyday experience.

SUNYATA 空, 虛

In its original Indian Buddhist context, *sunyata* means "emptiness"— but "emptiness" in the sense that things have no intrinsic nature or self-existence, that they are illusory or delusions conjured by the mind. Here, it is closely associated with nirvana as a state of selfless and transcendental extinction or emptiness. This *sunyata* emptiness is essentially metaphysical, suggesting some kind of "ultimate reality" behind or beyond the physical world we inhabit. But this atmosphere of metaphysics is quite foreign to the Chinese sensibility and Ch'an. Indeed, there was no word in Chinese with the meaning of *sunyata*. 空 and 虛 (*emptiness*: see Key Terms, pp. 330–31), with their superficial similarities, were quite simply the only possibility. And in the Taoist context, *emptiness* is virtually synonymous with *Absence*, reality seen as a single formless and generative tissue that is the source of all things—a concept altogether different from the Buddhist *sunyata*. Translation and interpretation of Ch'an in modern America often treats 空 and 虛 as *sunyata*—but in the Chinese, the term has lost its Sanskrit meaning, replacing it with the native Chinese one. Indeed, this reinvention of *sunyata* as 空 and 虛 was a defining moment in the creation of Ch'an.

INDEX OF CH'AN FIGURES

2. Chinese Names with English Equivalents

Wade-Giles	Pinyin	English	Page
Chao Chou	Zhao Zhou	Visitation-Land	220
Han Shan	Han Shan	Cold Mountain	187
Hsüeh Tou	Xue Dou	Snow-Chute Mountain	263
Huang Po	Huang Bo	Yellow-Bitterroot Mountain	195
Hung Chih	Hong Zhi	Wisdom-Expanse	274
Lin Chi	Lin Ji	Purport Dark-Enigma	208
Ma Tsu	Ma Zu	Patriarch Sudden-Horse Way-Entire	176
Seng Chao	Seng Zhao	Sangha-Fundament	78
Seng Ts'an	Seng Can	Mirror-Wisdom Sangha-Jewel	136
Tao Sheng	Dao Sheng	Way-Born	92
Wu Men	Wu Men	No-Gate Prajna-Clear	285
Yün Men	Yun Men	Cloud-Gate Mountain	234